ECOLOGICAL GOVERNANCE

Ecological degradation has been an object of concern for the international community since the early 1970s, but legal approaches that have been employed to improve the protection of ecosystems have failed to halt this decline. *Ecological Governance* explores how the law should respond to this rapid global deterioration of ecosystems by examining the foundational scientific and ethical considerations for designing laws that are effective for ecological protection. Based on these analyses, it argues that developed states should prioritise the reduction of the ecological stresses for which they are responsible in decision-making on their future courses. The book also proposes structures for governance and associated legal frameworks that would enable the formulation and implementation of policies for ecological sustainability.

OLIVIA WOOLLEY is a lecturer in the School of Law at the University of Aberdeen. In her research, she explores how law can be used more effectively to protect ecosystem functionality, particularly by enhancing the sustainability of developed states.

ECOLOGICAL GOVERNANCE

Reappraising Law's Role in Protecting Ecosystem Functionality

OLIVIA WOOLLEY

CAMBRIDGE
UNIVERSITY PRESS

CAMBRIDGE
UNIVERSITY PRESS

University Printing House, Cambridge CB2 8BS, United Kingdom

Cambridge University Press is part of the University of Cambridge.

It furthers the University's mission by disseminating knowledge in the pursuit of education, learning and research at the highest international levels of excellence.

www.cambridge.org
Information on this title: www.cambridge.org/9781107060456

First published 2014

Printed in the United Kingdom by Clays, St Ives plc

A catalogue record for this publication is available from the British Library

Library of Congress Cataloguing in Publication data
Woolley, Olivia, author.
Ecological governance : reappraising law's role in protecting ecosystem functionality / Olivia Woolley.
pages cm
Based on author's thesis (doctoral – University College London), 2011), under title: Developing a system of ecological governance.
ISBN 978-1-107-06045-6 (Hardback)
1. Environmental law – Social aspects. 2. Environmental management. I. Title.
K3585.W66 2014
344.04′6–dc23
2014016704

ISBN 978-1-107-06045-6 Hardback

CONTENTS

Acknowledgements *page* ix

1 Introduction 1

1.1 Avoiding societal collapse 1

1.2 Ecosystems and ecological degradation 2

1.3 Overcoming epistemic challenges 6

1.4 Normative precaution 8

1.5 The state, non-governmental actors and collaborative governance 10

1.6 Adaptive governance 12

1.7 Structure 14

2 Scientific and ethical foundations 15

2.1 Introduction 15

2.2 Scientific foundations for ecological law 18

2.2.1 From stability to complexity 19

2.2.2 Ecosystems as complex adaptive systems 21

2.2.3 Interaction between ecosystems and the Earth System 23

2.2.4 Complexity, regime shifts and environmental decision-making 25

2.3 The meaning of resilience 27

2.3.1 Specified and general resilience 28

2.3.2 What makes an ecosystem generally resilient? 32

2.3.2.1 Biodiversity 34

2.3.2.2 Tightness of feedbacks 36

2.4 A legal framework for ecological protection 37

2.5 Ethical foundations for ecological law 40

2.5.1 The dominion perspective of nature 42

2.5.2 Revaluing nature 44

2.6 Duties and principles for ecologically oriented decision-making 47

3 Ecologically oriented policy-making 53

3.1 Introduction 53

3.1.1 Adapting to endemic uncertainty 54

3.1.2 Ecological policy-making 56

3.1.3 Political will 58

3.2 Decision-making in the face of uncertainty 59

3.2.1 Precaution under an ecological paradigm 61

3.2.2 Taking precautionary action 64

3.2.3 Normative precaution 65

3.3 A legal framework for ecologically oriented policy-making 67

3.3.1 Ecological protection as a strategic objective 70

3.3.2 Principles for ecological policy-making 71

3.3.2.1 Reducing consumption 71

3.3.2.2 Obviating development 73

3.3.2.3 Substitution 74

3.3.2.4 Sunsetting 76

3.3.3 Assessing alternative policy options 77

3.3.4 Forming strategic visions of desired futures 85

3.3.4.1 Picturing the future 87

3.3.4.2 Policy impact assessment 88

3.3.5 Public participation in policy-making 89

3.4 Reforming the policy-making process 93

3.4.1 A whole-of-government approach 96

3.4.2 Promoting change in the culture of governmental decision-making 98

3.4.2.1 The rolling review of policy 99

3.4.2.2 The independent review of policy proposals 101

4 Governing an ecological transition 104

4.1 Introduction 104

4.2 Designing a system of ecological governance 105

4.3 The limitations of devolution 107

4.4 The state's role in ecological governance 115

4.4.1 A guiding state 118

4.4.2 A communicative state 120

4.4.3 A coordinating state 121

4.4.4 An enforcing state 123

4.5 Expanding the state's range 126

4.5.1 Regional government 126

4.6 Local government 131

4.6.1 Legitimacy 132

4.6.2 Giving form to ecological sustainability 133

4.6.3 Promoting behavioural change 136

4.6.4 Constructing a sense of sustainable places 137

4.7 Marine governance 139

4.7.1 Bridging the land/sea divide 143

5 Ecological planning 146

5.1 Introduction 146

5.1.1 Reforming land use planning 150

5.2 Environmental limits and governance 153

5.2.1 Identifying environmental capacities 154

5.2.2 The limitations of limits-based regulation 158

5.2.3 Ecological and ethical difficulties 159

5.2.4 Ecological planning 162

5.3 A national framework for ecological planning 164

5.3.1 Comprehensive planning 165

5.3.2 Analytical planning 169

5.3.3 Strategic planning 172

5.3.4 Ecological land use planning 175

5.3.5 Decision rules 177

5.4 Environmental assessment 183

6 Public participation in ecological governance 187

6.1 Introduction 187

6.2 The promise of deliberation 190

6.2.1 Transforming preferences 190

6.2.2 Internalising environmental considerations 191

6.2.3 Catalysing value formation 193

6.2.4 Enhancing the acceptability of ecological governance 195

6.3 Putting deliberation into practice: challenges and responses 198

6.3.1 Unpredictability: problem or opportunity? 200

6.3.2 Levelling the playing field 202

6.3.3 Deliberation's reach 205

6.3.4 Consultation's inadequacy 208

6.4 Deliberative participation under ecological governance 210

7 Informing ecological governance 215

7.1 Introduction 215

7.1.1 Addressing the information deficit 216

7.1.2 Legal requirements for ecological information 218

7.2 Developing a capacity for institutional learning 219

7.2.1 Combining ecology and law: from problem-solving to permanence 220

7.3 Using law to maintain the flow of information 225

7.3.1 Increasing knowledge and understanding of ecosystems 226

7.3.2 Enabling reaction to change 227

7.3.3 Enabling responsiveness to systemic reactions 229

7.4 Using structures for decision-making to stimulate information flows 230

7.4.1 The adequacy of information for decision-making 230

7.4.2 Generating information through exploratory development 232

Bibliography 234

Index 257

ACKNOWLEDGEMENTS

I owe a debt of gratitude to several persons for their support and assistance during the time I spent both undertaking research at University College London for my doctoral thesis (on which the book is based) and working on this book whilst employed as a lecturer in Law at the University of Aberdeen. I am deeply indebted to Professor Jane Holder and Professor Maria Lee, both of the Faculty of Laws of University College London, for their excellent supervision of my research and for their astute comments on countless draft chapters of my thesis. I thank Professor Joanne Scott of University College London, Professor Catherine Redgwell (then of University College London, now of the University of Oxford) and Professor William Howarth of the University of Kent for their helpful feedback on my work at crucial points during my research.

I am most grateful to Professor Laurence Gormley of the Faculty of Law of the University of Groningen for introducing me to Cambridge University Press. Thank you also to Professor Gormley and to Professor Jeanne Mifsud Bonnici, also of the University of Groningen, for their helpful comments on my book proposal. In addition, I am obliged to Anne-Michelle Slater, Head of the School of Law at the University of Aberdeen, and to many of my colleagues at Aberdeen for lightening my workload during the second half of 2013 so that I could concentrate on writing the book.

I thank everyone with whom I worked at Cambridge University Press for their enthusiasm for the project, and for their help with preparing the book for publication. I am grateful to Sinéad Moloney for her interest in my book proposal and for commissioning reports on this. Thank you also to the two anonymous reviewers of the proposal for their positive reviews, constructive comments and helpful suggestions on further areas and literature that I should explore.

I owe much to the research student community at University College London for their friendship and support during the time I spent working on my thesis. Thanks in particular must go to Rebecca Smith, who spent many evenings listening patiently as I tested my ideas out on her. Finally, I thank my mother. This book would not have seen the light of day without her support, always unquestioningly given, for my endeavours.

1

Introduction

1.1 Avoiding societal collapse

Jared Diamond's case studies of failed civilisations provide several examples of societies whose collapse was due, in part, to a deterioration in the condition of the ecosystems that supported them.[1] Each case study follows a similar pattern.[2] The functioning of ecosystems on which the society depended was impaired through exploitation that exceeded their carrying capacities or through other disturbances (e.g., deforestation) that fundamentally altered the nature of the system. Resulting shortages of food, water and other essential materials brought famine, conflict and, ultimately, the breakdown of once-complex societal structures. The collapsed societies that Diamond describes operated only at local to regional scales, but all human societies are now faced with the threat of collapse in their support base due to a global deterioration in ecological conditions.[3] As with the historical instances of failure that Diamond studies, this is due to unsustainable levels of resource exploitation and disturbance. However, these are of such magnitude that all of the world's ecosystems are being damaged by them. The situation is exacerbated by anthropogenic climate change, another common contributory factor that Diamond identifies to the demise of societies (although past instances of this occurred naturally),[4] and one which is already affecting the structures and functioning of ecosystems everywhere.

As Diamond observes, an example can be found for every instance of societal collapse of a society that was able to overcome difficult environmental problems and survive.[5] He includes the ability of societies to respond to their problems effectively as one of five factors that can make the difference between their survival and demise when confronted by

[1] J. Diamond, *Collapse: How Societies Choose to Fail or Survive*, 2nd edn (London: Penguin Books, 2011).

[2] Ibid., p. 6. [3] Ibid., p. 7. [4] Ibid., pp. 12–13. [5] Ibid., pp. 10–11.

ecological problems.[6] The principal purpose of this book is to explore the role that law could play in enabling human societies (particularly those of developed states that bear the lion's share of responsibility for the present difficulties) to respond to the deterioration in the condition of ecosystems which imperils them. It presents proposals for a system of governance that seeks to lessen risks of ecosystem failure by securing reductions in the cumulative pressures that human living places on their functioning.

The following section of this chapter offers a brief explanation of the reasons why an urgent legal response is required to the mounting evidence of global ecological degradation. Sections 1.3 to 1.6 of the chapter summarise the proposals for a system of ecological governance that Chapters 2 to 7 set out in detail. The chapter concludes with an overview of the book's structure.

1.2 Ecosystems and ecological degradation

'Ecosystem' is a term used in ecology to refer to all of the organisms and the abiotic environment with which they interact in an area selected for study.[7] It also means the organisational patterns or systems that exchanges between organisms and their environments give rise to.[8] I have this second usage in mind when I refer to ecosystems and their protection, because the functioning of ecosystems, by which I mean the continuity of processes that sustain them,[9] has outcomes, collectively described as 'ecosystem services', which provide essential support for human living on the planet.[10] They include 'provisioning services' that yield food, clean water, fibre and other materials on which humans rely; 'regulating services' that help keep the Earth within liveable bounds by having a positive influence on global-scale processes such as climatic and hydrological cycles; and 'supporting services' such as soil formation, photosynthesis and primary production that enable ecosystems to deliver the other services that they render.

6 Ibid., pp.11, 14–15.

7 J. M. Blair et al., 'Ecosystems as Functional Units in Nature' (2000) 14 *Natural Resources and Environment*, 151–2.

8 Ibid., 152–3.

9 K. Jax, 'Function and "Functioning" in Ecology: What does it Mean?' (2005) 111 *Oikos*, 641.

10 Millennium Ecosystem Assessment, *Ecosystems and Human Well-Being: Synthesis* (Washington, DC: Island Press, 2005), pp. 103–22; F. S. Chapin III et al., *Principles of Terrestrial Ecosystem Ecology*, 2nd edn (New York: Springer, 2011), p. 21; K. Wallace, 'Classification of Ecosystem Services: Problems and Solutions' (2007) 139 *Biological Conservation*, 235–46.

Analyses of ecological conditions that have been conducted during the last decade emphasise the importance of ecosystem services, and therefore of the functioning of ecosystems from which they are derived, for humanity's well-being. The Millennium Ecosystem Assessment, a global survey of ecosystem health, describes humans as being 'fully dependent on Earth's ecosystems and the services that they provide'.[11] The World Wildlife Fund advises that humanity is 'wholly reliant on well functioning ecosystems' to supply services, many of which could not be replaced by technology if they were to be lost.[12] The UK's national ecosystem assessment stresses that the functioning of ecosystems underpins 'our very existence'.[13] This makes their consistent identification of significant deterioration in the ability of ecosystems to provide services all the more disturbing. The Millennium Ecosystem Assessment reports that 60 per cent of the ecosystem services that it examines are being degraded or used unsustainably, and that the condition of ecosystems is expected to worsen during the coming decades.[14] Its supporting studies also suggest that humanity's alteration and disturbance of ecosystems may be increasing the likelihood of non-linear changes in their states that can result not only in the deterioration of services, but also in the abrupt and irreversible withdrawal of their capacity to continue providing them.[15]

Direct human drivers such as the excessive exploitation of ecosystem services and changes to media (e.g., atmospheric composition) with which they interact are immediately responsible for ecological degradation. In turn, these are the product of indirect drivers including requirements for resources to support economic growth, unsustainable levels of consumption, population increases and technological change. It may be difficult to establish the proportional responsibility of indirect driving forces in particular instances of impaired ecosystem functionality because they are 'multiple and interactive'.[16] However, it can be said with confidence that unprecedented economic growth since the Second World War is the predominant cause of environmental decline, and therefore that the world's developed states, whose economies and high standards of living have driven this unbridled expansion, have been the major contributors to

[11] Millennium Ecosystem Assessment, 'Ecosystems and Human Well-Being', p. 49.

[12] World Wildlife Fund, 'Living Planet Report 2012: Biodiversity, biocapacity and better choices' (2012), p. 70, http://www.wwf.org.uk/what_we_do/about_us/living_planet_report_2012/.

[13] UK National Ecosystem Assessment, 'The UK National Ecosystem Assessment: Synthesis of Key Findings', UNEP-WCMC, Cambridge (2011), p. 5.

[14] Millennium Ecosystem Assessment, 'Ecosystems and Human Well-Being', p. 1.

[15] Ibid., p. 1, pp. 88–91. [16] Ibid., p. 64.

the deterioration of ecosystems during this period.[17] The ecological footprints of high-income states significantly exceed those of middle- and low-income states.[18] Together, they accounted for half of the global ecological footprint in 2006, although the states concerned house less than one sixth of the world's population.[19]

The international community of states has expressed strong concern over the deterioration of ecological conditions in each of the periodic meetings convened during the last 40 years to consider how development can be made sustainable.[20] Most of its members have also negotiated and ratified international treaties, such as the Biodiversity Convention,[21] that encourage participating states to improve their protection of ecosystems or to preserve specific types of systems (e.g., wetlands under the Ramsar Convention[22]).[23] However, the inescapable conclusion, to be drawn from

[17] J. G. Speth, *The Bridge at the Edge of the World: Capitalism, the Environment and Crossing from Crisis to Sustainability* (New Haven, CT: Yale University Press, 2008), pp. 1–9.

[18] World Wildlife Fund, 'Living Planet Report 2012', p. 140.

[19] World Wildlife Fund, 'Living Planet Report 2006' quoted in Speth, 'The Bridge at the Edge of the World', pp. 41–2.

[20] The declaration of the states that participated in the first of these meetings, the United Nations Conference on the Human Environment of 1972, notes in its preamble that '[w]e see around us growing evidence of man-made harm in many regions of the earth' including 'major and undesirable disturbances to the ecological balance of the biosphere'. See the 'Declaration of the United Nations Conference on the Human Environment', Stockholm, 16 June 1972, UN Doc-A/Conf.48/14/Rev. 1(1973); 11 ILM 1416 (1972). Principle 7 of the declaration made at the United Nations Conference on Environment and Development of 1992 requests states to 'co-operate in a spirit of global partnership to conserve, protect and restore the health and integrity of the Earth's ecosystem'. See the 'Rio Declaration on Environment and Development', Rio de Janeiro, 13 June 1992, UN Doc. A/CONF.151/26 (vol. I); 31 ILM 874 (1992). Finally, the many references to ecosystems and their protection in *The Future we Want*, the outcome document of the UN Conference on Sustainable Development of 2012, illustrates that significant concern over ecological conditions remains although many of them are couched in terms of sustainable use rather than outright protection. One of the stronger references recognises the 'severity of the global loss of biodiversity and the degradation of ecosystems', the threats that this presents for food security, access to water and health for 'the rural poor and of people worldwide', and the corresponding importance of 'the conservation of biodiversity, enhancing habitat connectivity and building ecosystem resilience'. See 'Report of the UN Conference on Sustainable Development', Rio de Janeiro, 20–22 June 2012, A/Conf.216/16.

[21] Convention on Biological Diversity, Rio de Janeiro, 5 June 1992, in force on 29 December 1993, 1760 UNTS 79, 31 ILM 818 (1992).

[22] Convention on Wetlands of International Importance Especially as Waterfowl Habitat, Ramsar, 2 February 1971, in force on 21 December 1975, 996 UNTS 246, 11 ILM 969.

[23] Accounts of the evolution of international and European law concerning the protection of ecosystems in this period can be found in: P. Birnie, A. Boyle and C. Redgwell, *International Law and the Environment*, 3rd edn (Oxford: Oxford University Press, 2009), pp. 583–649;

the negative picture that assessments of ecosystem health paint is that this political rhetoric and related legal responses have completely failed to stem the tide of ecological degradation. At best, they may have reduced the rate at which this is occurring.

The main premise of this book is that this perilous situation, and the evident inadequacy of measures taken to date to respond to it, demands something more than a critical analysis of, and tinkering with, the law for protecting ecosystems as it currently stands. Instead, a fundamental reappraisal is required of how we can use law to prevent our cumulative actions from undermining ecosystem functionality. I seek to provide this at the book's outset (Chapter 2) by examining the current understanding in ecology of how ecosystems behave, and considering how this affects long-standing beliefs on which our own behaviours are founded about the relations between humanity and nature. I conclude from this that human societies must show a much higher degree of restraint in their exploitation of the environment. I then go on, in the following chapters, to consider how a system of governance can be established (and law's role in its establishment) that would apply this restraint in public decision-making and encourage those subject to it to prefer ecologically sustainable ways of living in the personal choices they make.

My proposals for governance are intended for use in the developed states whose economies, standards of living and related demands on natural resources are the principal drivers of ecological degradation within, and beyond, their national borders. I recognise that the system would need to be tailored to particular situations and to reflect national circumstances. At the same time, it would be appropriate for any state that is a major contributor to the global deterioration of ecosystems to observe principles that I propose in Chapter 2 such as the under-utilisation of resources and the reduction in reliance on activities that are most likely to engender potentially unwelcome changes in ecosystem structure and functionality. It would also be appropriate for such states to employ the normative precautionary approach in decision-making that I call for in Chapter 3, given the difficulties that all states have in common with predicting the cumulative effects of human activities.

D. Tarlock, 'Ecosystems' in D. Bodansky, J. Brunnée and E. Hey (eds) *The Oxford Handbook of International Environmental Law* (Oxford: Oxford University Press, 2007), pp. 574–95; K. Baakman, *Testing Times: The Effectiveness of Five International Biodiversity-related Conventions* (Nijmegen: Wolf Legal Publishers, 2011), pp. 17–39; K. Mertens, A. Cliquet and B. Vanheusden, 'Ecosystem Services: What's in it for a Lawyer?' (2012) 21 *European Energy and Environmental Law Review*, 31–40.

The following sections provide summaries of the key conclusions that I drew from my reappraisal of law's role in protecting ecosystems about the form that a system of governance that is better equipped than those currently in place to preserve ecosystem functionality should take.

1.3 Overcoming epistemic challenges

The starting point for developing a system of ecological governance must be to identify what it is we wish to protect and how this can best be done. Whilst these questions are simply expressed, providing responses to them is anything but straightforward. The property of ecosystems that ecological scientists argue we should concentrate our efforts on preserving is their resilience.[24] This term is used to describe the ability of ecosystems to retain their structures and functionality in the face of external challenges both from human interventions and as a result of naturally occurring events. However, the resilience of an ecosystem is the product of myriad interactions between the biological components of ecosystems and their habitats. It is not, because of this complexity, amenable for use as a benchmark against which the ecological tolerability of activities can be judged. A related difficulty is that we cannot establish with any degree of confidence how activities affect the resilience of an ecosystem individually, and even less so when their cumulative effects are taken into account.

If this predicament were limited to inadequate knowledge of how ecosystems function, it would be conceivable (although perhaps not realistic in view of ecological complexity and the depths of our current ignorance) that we could move towards a point, through intensive research, where we are better able to predict how activities will affect resilience. However, two additional considerations call into question whether prediction-based decision-making could ever provide a reliable means of determining if proposed actions are compatible with the goal of preserving ecosystem functionality. The first is that ecosystems are constantly evolving due to internal dynamics and in response to external stimuli. As a result, resilience and the contributions that species make to this are not static. The second is that we do not know what challenges ecosystems will encounter or how this will affect their ability to withstand fundamental change in their structures and functionality. As a consequence, even if we could measure the resilience of an ecosystem at any particular point, this would not tell us

[24] See my discussion of resilience at Chapter 2, Section 2.3.

whether it is resilient *enough* to maintain its structure in the face of future disturbances.

Both of these considerations are significant for the design of a system of governance that aims to maintain resilience. The conclusion I draw is that, if we cannot advance this objective by identifying points at which the system is under threat, our aim should be to bolster resilience by progressively reducing the erosive effects of our actions on it.[25] This approach would at least ensure that ecosystems are as well placed as they can be to maintain their functionality. We should also reduce reliance on activities that are most likely to overwhelm resilience, and particularly those that would unbalance the natural systems (e.g., the climate) with which ecosystems interact.[26]

In amongst this realm of unknowns and unknowables, there are a number of certainties (or, at least, strong likelihoods) that are also highly relevant to the design of ecological governance. The first is that our activities clearly do combine to undermine ecosystem resilience and to trigger changes in their structures. This is readily apparent both from the assessments that I refer to in Section 1.2, and from studies of ecosystems that have undergone regime shifts.[27] In view of this, we must find some way of acting to reduce the pressures that our activities place on natural systems notwithstanding uncertainty over their effects. Secondly, the resilience of all ecosystems is likely to be confronted by changes in climate resulting from historic and current anthropogenic carbon emissions.[28] Whilst we do not know the extent to which the climate will change or with what consequences for ecosystem health, the risk is present and heightens the urgency with which we should act to reduce the stresses that human societies generate.

In view of these tangible concerns, the first main issue I address is how a system of governance could be developed with the objective of reducing the cumulative erosive effects of our actions on resilience. The principal complicating factor (amongst several resulting from the uncertain world in which ecological governance operates) is, as I discuss in the following section, how effective controls can be devised to reduce threats to

[25] Chapter 2, Section 2.4. [26] Chapter 2, Section 2.6.

[27] Chapter 1, Section 1.2. See also Chapter 2, Section 2.2.2.

[28] Intergovernmental Panel on Climate Change, *Climate Change 2007: Synthesis Report – Contribution of Working Groups I, II, and III to the Fourth Assessment Report of the Intergovernmental Panel on Climate Change*, Core writing team, A. K. Pachauri and A. Reisinger (eds) (Geneva: IPCC, 2008).

ecosystem health in circumstances where confidence in our ability to comprehend ecosystem behaviour is itself significantly eroded.

1.4 Normative precaution

Growing appreciation of our difficulty with predicting how proposed action may affect highly complex natural systems has been recognised in the evolution of the precautionary principle.[29] This provides a guide for decision-makers in circumstances where there is uncertainty about the effects of development. However, the principle in its current form and the direction that it gives fall far short of what is required to assist with addressing a situation that combines the certainty that human intervention has the potential to fundamentally alter ecosystem structures with our limited understanding of how anthropogenic stressors interact to undermine resilience. I argue in Chapter 3 that a new conception of precaution is required which is attuned to prevailing uncertainty both over the impacts that our actions have on ecosystem functionality and over whether ecosystems are at risk of failure.[30] A reconfigured precautionary principle would require that steps be taken as a matter of course to reduce levels of anthropogenic stress with a view to alleviating threats of harm to ecosystems. Normative precaution would institute stress reduction as the default position in decision-making over what goals we should pursue as a society, and on how their pursuit should be conducted.

Additionally, new legal and institutional structures are required that establish the maintenance of resilience as the core objective of policy-making, policy implementation and regulation. I propose a legal framework for policy-making in Chapter 3 that is built around this objective, and which uses two key mechanisms for exploring how ecological stresses can be reduced. The first is the assessment of different options for achieving policy objectives with a view to identifying those that would most likely be compatible with ecosystem functionality.[31] Principles of governance would require that the least ecologically consequential options be preferred and used where possible in policy formation (substitution[32]), and that options deemed to be too incompatible with the overarching objective of maintaining resilience for continued use should be phased out (sunsetting[33]).

[29] See my discussion of the precautionary principle at Chapter 3, Section 3.2.
[30] Chapter 3, Section 3.2.3. [31] Chapter 3, Section 3.3.3.
[32] Chapter 3, Section 3.3.2.3. [33] Chapter 3, Section 3.3.2.4.

The second is a process of strategy formation that examines how preferred options can be deployed, the policy measures that would support this deployment, the conflicts with economic and social policies and values that ecologically oriented policies would give rise to, and the additional measures that could be applied to address them, including staggering the timescales for policy implementation.[34] This strategic stage of policy-making reflects normative precaution's forward-looking nature in its use of backcasting techniques to analyse the feasibility of moving towards a desired endpoint (in this case scenarios in which progressive stress reduction is being achieved) and to identify the policy levers that could be used to promote its realisation.[35]

The policy-making framework is complemented by the legal structures for strategic planning that I present in Chapter 5. These lay down procedures for a corresponding investigation of how ecologically oriented policies can be implemented, and the extent to which this can be done in ways that are themselves compatible with the objectives of ecological governance. They also provide fora within which representatives of local and regional governmental authorities and members of the public can collaborate in exploring how patterns of living could be altered with a view to revising or, where necessary, replacing unsustainable practices. The legal framework for planning employs mechanisms for alternatives assessment to promote the use of preferred policy options in strategic planning and to prioritise land uses that would be least likely to have negative ecological impacts.[36] It also establishes decision rules that set firm limits on environmental exploitation by making clear the circumstances in which proposed development would or would not be regarded as being ecologically tolerable.[37]

The alternatives assessment stage of policy formation uses qualitative criteria to support the analysis and ranking of policy options.[38] Activities are assessed by reference to a range of considerations that explore whether they are likely to be compatible with, or pose a threat to, ecosystem health. This approach is necessary because of the problems noted above with predicting systemic reactions to disturbance. It is, in any event, well-suited to a system of governance that is founded on ecological values. The broader analysis of compatibility with the system's goals displays a due caution in our relationship with the environment that is not apparent in regulatory

[34] Chapter 3, Section 3.3.4. [35] Ibid. [36] Chapter 5, Sections 5.2.4 and 5.3.
[37] Chapter 5, Section 5.3.5. [38] Chapter 3, Section 3.3.3.

reliance on the accuracy of conclusions drawn through scientific research to determine whether proposals should or should not be authorised.

I envisage that policy-making and planning under ecological governance would, together, form part of an iterative process with the former guiding the latter, and with the information generated under the latter about what can be achieved on the ground feeding back into a rolling review of policy. I argue in Chapter 3 that the regular review of policy is essential for driving on-going reductions in threats of harm to ecosystems.[39] The ideal outcome would be the formation of policies that advance the system of governance's objectives effectively because they are rooted in knowledge of actual possibilities for ecologically progressive action once constraints on development and public views and concerns have been taken into account. An informed approach to policy-making would also allow the reappraisal of policy packages, of the balance struck between ecological, economic and social objectives, and of the adequacy of structures for governance as a whole if it (or, as I discuss at Section 1.6, evidence from monitoring of unabated ecological degradation) reveals that these, collectively, are not advancing the system's goals.

1.5 The state, non-governmental actors and collaborative governance

Reducing the stresses for which socioeconomic systems are responsible would involve much more than the reform of sectors individually or addressing obvious ecological black spots. Identifying how we can coexist with the healthy functioning of natural systems would require the active engagement of all governmental departments, all levels of government and all sections of society with exploration of the extent to which the negative effects of human activities can be addressed. It would necessitate analysis 'across the board' of how demands arise, examination of what scope exists for alleviating the stresses their satisfaction generates, and the agreement of comprehensive strategies for implementing ecological policies. A change in society's direction of such significance would also almost certainly flounder if public acceptance of, and support for, associated measures is not secured. Legal structures and institutions that orient collective decision-making towards the realisation of ecological objectives would be necessary to support an endeavour of this magnitude. In view of this, the next main question I address is what form a system of governance, whose

[39] Chapter 3, Section 3.4.2.1.

purpose is to secure a fundamental alteration in society's course, should take. In addition, I examine the related question of what law's role would be in promoting and, where necessary, driving the achievement of its ends.

I consider in Chapter 4 how a system of governance and relationships between different levels of government and between governmental institutions and non-governmental actors under it should be structured to secure progressive reductions in society's ecological footprint. Most notably, I argue that the state should take the lead in the establishment and operation of ecological governance as it alone possesses the authority to promote policies that would require radical societal change and the vantage point from which to determine how ecological objectives can best be advanced.[40] In making this argument, I am not suggesting that the role of regional and local governments would be limited to enacting central government's directives. To the contrary, I envisage that the different governmental levels would work together to explore how ecological policies could be applied.[41] The state's role would be to act as coordinator of local and regional planning both with a view to developing nationally optimal strategies for stress reduction and to ensure, as far as possible, that the burdens of an ecological transition are equitably distributed. The planning system that I propose in Chapter 5 creates a legal framework within which local, regional and national plans for ecological policy implementation can be formed.

The structures for governance I propose use three approaches to encourage popular support for ecological governance, the perception of governmental action as legitimate, and active public involvement with realising ecological goals. The first is by providing meaningful opportunities for public participation in the decision-making processes that the system employs. I consider in Chapter 4 the different respects in which public engagement is needed to support the operation of ecological governance.[42] The second is by structuring relations between the decision-making institutions at different governmental levels and using legal requirements for the conduct of decision-making to ensure that public views and values expressed primarily through participation at local levels are taken into account in decision-making at higher governmental levels.[43] The use of transparently 'bottom-up' arrangements for governance is, in part, intended to enhance the confidence in political processes that has been so eroded in recent years.

[40] Chapter 4, Section 4.4. [41] Chapter 4, Section 4.4.3. [42] Chapter 4, Section 4.6.
[43] Chapter 4, Section 4.6.3; Chapter 6, Section 6.3.3.

Third, participation is to be conducted primarily through deliberative fora in which members of the public would discuss and debate the reasons for the government's policies and explore different possibilities, if the need for improved ecological protection is accepted, for their advancement. In this regard, deliberation is preferable to forms of participation in which the public respond remotely to proposals. Reflection on positions held by others in a context where participants have been tasked with identifying what outcome(s) would advance the 'public good' may encourage people to question their own preferences and values, and to accept the need for ecologically responsible behaviour in both public and private decision-making. I consider in Chapter 6 the arguments made in favour of deliberative participation, and explain why I too have concluded that public involvement with decision-making through deliberative fora would provide a key element of an effective system of ecological governance.

1.6 Adaptive governance

The application of constraints under ecological governance is not triggered exclusively by the prediction of negative impacts on ecosystems if a development is authorised. Measures to reduce ecological stresses are applied as a matter of course because of difficulties with establishing when risks of harm are present. The greater emphasis on analysis of available alternatives at the outset of all decision-making processes also promotes a focus within governmental institutions and in their collaborations with developers on identifying options that are least likely to undermine ecosystem functionality before proposals for projects, plans and policies crystallise. Accordingly, ad hoc scientific analysis of likely effects would not have the decisive role that it currently occupies in environmental decision-making. However, the conduct of scientific research with a view to advancing understanding of ecosystem behaviour and of how anthropogenic stressors combine to erode resilience is important for its effective operation in other respects.

Improved knowledge of how different species are affected by human activities would clearly aid assessment of the compatibility with the goal of maintaining ecosystem functionality of proposed development. For example, the study of whether offshore wind turbine vibration and noise would disrupt the navigation of marine mammals would assist decision-making both on whether this technology is to be preferred over other possibilities for energy generation in policy formation, and whether it should be applied in specific contexts (i.e., in the vicinity of known migration routes).[44] Whilst resilience itself is not measurable, the constant study and monitoring of ecosystems would at least allow us to establish whether the condition of ecosystems appears to be improving as a result of governmental action for risk reduction. Evidence that degradation continues unabated would provide strong support for the application of additional restraints or for arguing that a more rapid deployment of less harmful options is required. Finally, whilst the system of governance would promote ecologically sound decisions in the first instance, the inevitable consequence of our ignorance and of ecosystem dynamism is that actions which are expected to be benign will turn out to have negative effects. Again, a capacity for monitoring coupled with legal requirements for the reassessment of prior judgments is needed to account for the likelihood that, despite a more conservative approach in decision-making, mistakes will still be made.

With these requirements in mind, I argue that the creation of capabilities for research and monitoring should be a central consideration in the design of ecological governance.[45] I explore in Chapter 7 how law could be used to maintain a flow of information to support the system's decision-making mechanisms. I argue that a permanent institution for research should be legally established to reflect the importance of improved knowledge and understanding of ecosystem behaviour for determining how reductions in ecological stresses can best be achieved.[46] In addition, I examine legal requirements that could be employed to ensure that on-going monitoring is conducted and to force information production by making consent for development conditional on its availability.[47]

These different legal mechanisms are not, as I note in the introduction to Chapter 7, intended to put us in a position where knowledge is sufficient for 'knife edge' choices to be made between economic growth and ecological protection. As I argue throughout, the fine balance that current approaches to environmental decision-making aspire to does not square with the dynamism and complexity of ecosystems or with the ethical desirability of caution in our relations with them. Rather, they are intended to facilitate a normative precautionary approach to governance by heightening awareness of the threats that different actions may pose for ecosystem health, and by providing sufficient information for ongoing assessment of the adequacy of policies and regulatory controls for risk reduction.

[44] K. N. Scott, 'Tilting at Offshore Windmills: Regulating Wind Farm Development within the Renewable Energy Zone' (2006) 18 *Journal of Environmental Law*, 92.

[45] Chapter 2, Section 2.6. [46] Chapter 7, Section 7.2. [47] Chapter 7, Sections 7.3 and 7.4.

1.7 Structure

The preceding sections provide a broad outline of the book's structure.[48] To recapitulate briefly, I consider in Chapter 2 what aspects of ecosystems we should concentrate on protecting, why economic growth should be constrained to further this end, and what methods and principles should be employed and adhered to in governance with a view to preserving ecosystem functionality. In the first part of Chapter 3, I argue that a normative precautionary approach to governance should be adopted to address the challenges that endemic uncertainty presents for our capacity to regulate activities effectively. This would involve a permanent effort to reduce the cumulative ecological stresses that socioeconomic systems generate. It would also replace the failed practice of attempting to balance economic and environmental concerns through the prediction of development's likely ecological effects.

I then go on to explore how a system of governance that embodies and gives practical form to normative precaution would be structured. In the second part of Chapter 3, I propose a legal framework for policy-making whose purpose is to produce packages of policies that collectively drive progressive reductions in risks of harm to ecosystems and strategies for their implementation. In Chapter 4, I consider how arrangements for governance would be structured to involve all levels of government and all sectors of society with collaborative decision-making over how ecological stresses can be reduced. The legal system for strategic planning that I present in Chapter 5 provides a framework for the collective decision-making structures and processes that I call for in the preceding chapter. I argue in Chapter 6 that public participation in decision-making should be conducted through deliberative fora. Involvement with deliberative discussion and debate is most likely to promote public understanding of and the formation of positive attitudes towards measures that would impinge significantly on peoples' lifestyles, and to engender change in their values and behaviours. I complete my proposals for ecological governance by examining, in Chapter 7, how law can be used to ensure that the requisite information is generated and research conducted to support the system's operation.

[48] Chapter 1, Sections 1.3–1.6.

2

Scientific and ethical foundations

2.1 Introduction

A reappraisal of law's role in protecting ecosystems should begin by examining two fundamental areas for the design of laws and institutions that seek to prevent human activities from undermining their functionality. The first is the scientific rationale for a new legislative approach. This requires exploration of the current understanding in ecology of how ecosystems behave, of what properties of systems are important for their healthy functioning and of how anthropogenic disturbance affects this. The second is the ethical platform for laws that prioritise the maintenance of ecological function over other 'goods' that might be yielded through the exploitation of natural resources for human benefit. Can a case be made for according supervening value to ecological processes over the pursuit of other objectives that are regarded as economically or socially desirable? If so, what ethical precepts and principles might be derived from this valuation, and how should they inform the development of new legal and institutional structures?

This chapter is concerned with these foundational issues and the scientific and ethical basis they provide for developing a system of governance that is equipped to tackle the causes of ecological degradation. In considering them, I advance the central argument of this book: that a paradigm shift is required in the way that we use law to lay down a framework for decision-making about whether human activities should be permitted, and, if so, how they might be conducted. That is a shift from an environmental perspective founded on assumptions that the world is ours to use unless scientific evidence indicates that this may be disadvantageous to us to an ecological perspective in which we see ourselves as components of ecosystems whose operation we do not understand fully, but on whose well-being our own is founded. The former perspective legitimates a continued instrumental valuation of nature constrained by ill-defined conceptions of what is, or is not, environmentally tolerable. The latter emphasises prudence in our relations with nature because our actions, if they are not made subject to appropriate restraint, will tend to weaken the ability of ecosystems to remain in states on which we and other members of biotic communities depend.

In Section 2.2 of this chapter, I consider how scientific understanding of ecosystems has moved away from a perception of them as relatively stable entities tending towards an optimal state if left undisturbed, and which could be understood through the study of ecological processes at different scales. They are now seen as dynamic, complex, adaptive systems whose behaviour, whilst not necessarily chaotic, does not follow a predictable path. Rather, they have a propensity to flip into alternative states when disturbed by natural or anthropogenic influences, which may result in the system assuming a fundamentally different structure and functions. As a consequence of both their inherent complexity and the complexity of influences acting on them, the response of these systems to disturbance is extremely difficult to predict. It is equally difficult to anticipate the effect that changes in ecosystem functionality may have on the global-scale processes, collectively referred to as the Earth System, that create the conditions necessary for life on the planet. However, it is recognised that there is a relationship between them and, therefore, that ecological degradation could trigger change in Earth System processes with potentially catastrophic consequences for the functioning of all of the planet's ecosystems.

I also consider the ramifications of the identification of resilience as the property of ecosystems that enables them to retain their structures and functions in the face of disturbance.[1] The developing understanding of the nature of this property, and of how human and natural impacts can combine to undermine and overwhelm it, has radical implications for the way that law is used to protect the environment. It is not possible to identify with precision the components of ecosystems in which resilience lies and therefore to use legal protection of them as a sole means of supporting ecosystem functionality. The complexity and dynamism of ecosystems preclude the use of this approach in isolation. The adequacy of resilience is also relative to the scale of the challenges that ecosystems encounter. This entails that the goal of ecological governance should be to reduce human pressures on resilience as far as possible in order to enhance the ability of ecosystems to withstand whatever future

[1] Chapter 2, Section 2.3.

disturbances confront them. These include the potentially serious consequences for ecosystem functionality of a changing climate.

This understanding of ecosystems as being complex, dynamic and vulnerable to external events, coupled with recognition that prediction cannot be relied on to inform decision-making on the likely effects of proposed actions, points to the need for a cautious approach to governing human activities. This should be adopted not just at the micro-level of environmental regulation, but, more importantly, at the macro-level of policy formation itself. This is not a caution based on an assessment of risk in particular circumstances, but one that entails broader notions of preferring options that favour non-use or under-exploitation of resources and, where acting is deemed to be appropriate, preparing developmental programmes that are least likely to increase stress on ecosystems (to the extent that we can assess what consequences our actions might have).

The radically altered conception of nature that stems from developments in ecological science invites reflection on how we see ourselves in relation to it, how we should value nature and the reasons for holding those values. It also makes necessary a reappraisal of ethical positions (and of laws whose contents reflect them) that are founded on a view of humanity as a species apart from the natural world, on confidence in our ability to know how ecosystems work and to address any environmental problems we encounter through technological fixes, and on a valuation of the environment primarily as a repository of resources for our use.

The debate on how we should value nature in ethical literature has considered whether intrinsic value can be found in non-human nature irrespective of its worth to humanity. I argue in Section 2.5 that this debate, with its reliance on patterns of reasoning that are far removed from the ways by which people determine what is important to them and why, has detracted from the contribution that environmental ethics might make to stimulating the development of effective structures for environmental protection. A better approach would be to look at the challenges that current ecological thinking presents to historically derived conceptions of humankind's place in the world, and to examine what values should flow from a new appreciation of our position as one component amongst many in biotic communities that owe their existence and ongoing viability to the maintenance of supportive natural systems. I suggest that this should lead to the formation of ethical positions that require that we seek not to undermine either the ecological processes from which we derive benefit or the diversity of biotic communities which is vital for the resilience of ecosystems. In addition, I argue that these positions are inseparable from an anthropocentric valuation of nature because they aspire to keep ecosystems in conditions that are supportive of human well-being.

In the final section of this chapter, I set out a range of duties and principles to guide decision-making on what activities are appropriate from an ecological perspective and how those that are approved should be conducted. These principles, which are drawn from the scientific and ethical considerations I explore in the preceding sections, are of general application to our relations with nature. Collectively they present an 'ethic of humility' in that they seek to capture a realistic conception of our place in nature, to reflect an appreciation of the enormous good fortune that has resulted in the development of ecological conditions that provide a support mechanism for human life, and to recognise that our ignorance of how natural systems work and our difficulty with predicting how they will behave or change demands a more humble approach to the way in which we use nature. It is an ethic which, in Aldo Leopold's words, represents an altered view of humanity in its relationship with nature as citizen rather than conqueror of the natural world.[2]

2.2 Scientific foundations for ecological law

If we are to design legal and institutional structures for the effective protection of ecosystems, we need, as a prerequisite, to have some comprehension of how the interaction between species and their environments results in the development of systemic structures and functions, of the nature of those systems and of the characteristics they possess that enable them to maintain functionality in a way that provides support for biotic communities. We also need to establish whether our knowledge of their behaviour is sufficient to predict how ecosystems may react to human disturbance. In this section, I examine how the understanding of ecosystems has changed over the last eighty years, and identify the aspects of this changed understanding that are most relevant for deciding how law might be used to reduce the contribution that our actions make to ecological degradation.

[2] A. Leopold, *A Sand County Almanac with Essays on Conservation from Round River*, reprint (New York: Oxford University Press, 1989) quoted in P. Curry, *Ecological Ethics: An Introduction* (Cambridge: Polity Press, 2011), p. 95.

2.2.1 *From stability to complexity*

For much of the twentieth century, ecosystems were understood to be entities that tend towards a single equilibrium state and whose patterns of development, in theory at least, could be predicted. Tansley, who in 1935 proposed the ecosystem concept to define biological assemblages interacting with their physical and climatic environments, viewed the components of ecosystems as being in a relatively stable dynamic equilibrium which would progress towards the formation of climax communities representing the nearest approach to perfect dynamic equilibrium that the system could attain.[3] His belief, and that of the ecologists who followed him, in ecological development as predictable, unidirectional and culminating in a maximal state engendered confidence that, through mathematical modelling, ecosystem behaviour could be understood, predicted and manipulated to humanity's benefit.[4]

Eugene Odum, in his work of the 1960s and 1970s, argued that the trajectory of ecosystems was less predictable than it had been assumed to be, and urged that the emergence of properties at a systemic level but that are not apparent at lower levels should be a focus of study.[5] However, he did not repudiate the notion that ecosystems tend towards order and harmony. Indeed, his view, that they have a strategy of development towards an optimally diverse state within the constraints of energy flows and prevailing physical conditions, is strikingly similar to that of his predecessors.[6] Although Odum concluded that ecosystems should, as far as possible, be left in a natural state if they are to fulfil their potential, his understanding of them bolstered the view that it would eventually be possible to comprehend their operation in entirety and to manage them so that production of the 'goods' they yield might be maximised.[7]

This confidence in our ability to understand ecosystem behaviour has been significantly challenged and, to a large extent, replaced by two

[3] S. K. Gaichas, 'A Context for Ecosystem-based Fishery Management: Developing Concepts of Ecosystems and Sustainability' (2008) 32 *Marine Policy*, 394; S. Bocking, 'Visions of Nature and Society: A History of the Ecosystem Concept' (1994) 20(3) *Alternatives*, 12.

[4] Gaichas, 'Ecosystem-based Fishery Management', 394.

[5] Gaichas, 'Ecosystem-based Fishery Management', 395; Bocking, 'Visions of Nature', 14–15.

[6] D. Worster, 'The Ecology of Order and Chaos' in C. Pierce and D. VanDeVeer (eds) *People, Penguins, and Plastic Trees: Basic Issues in Environmental Ethics* (Belmont, CA: Wadsworth Publishing Company, 1995), p. 282; Gaichas, 'Ecosystem-Based Fishery Management', 395; S. Esbjörn-Hargens and M. E. Zimmerman, *Integral Ecology: Uniting Multiple Perspectives on the Natural World* (Boston, MA: Integral Books, 2009), pp. 162–3.

[7] Worster, 'The Ecology of Order and Chaos', pp. 282–3.

strands of thought in ecological science during the last thirty years. The first strand of thought, which was initiated by Drury and Nisbet's work in the 1970s, and which represents a radical departure from the world-view of their predecessors, has been described as an ecology of chaos.[8] In complete contrast to prior assumptions of order and predictability in nature, Drury and Nisbet argued that they saw no evidence of a strategy or pattern of development in the behaviour of ecosystems.[9] Rather, they understood this to be without any determinable direction or progression towards stability, and, instead, to be the product of a constant impetus for change. Worster refers to their ideas and the views of theorists that followed them as having engendered a belief that nature 'is fundamentally erratic, discontinuous. . .unpredictable. . .[and] full of seemingly random events that elude our models of how things are supposed to work'.[10]

The second strand of thought views ecosystems not as indeterminate assemblages but as complex adaptive systems whose behaviour lies between past theoretical extremes of progression towards an optimal equilibrium state and complete unpredictability.[11] This outlook rejects the notion that our difficulties with plotting the trajectories of natural systems are due to their behaviour being essentially chaotic. Instead, it regards this as a product of the multiple developmental possibilities opened up by their complexity.[12] Complexity theory has been applied in a variety of contexts to aid understanding of how systems comprised of multiple components interacting at different levels operate to produce systemic properties, and of the factors which cause systemic change or, in cases of serious upheaval, collapse. For example, Ruhl refers to its use in connection with the analysis of economic and social structures to support his argument that it should also be employed in the design of legal systems for better ecological protection.[13] I consider below two aspects of its application for analysing the behaviour of ecosystems that are particularly relevant for considering how law might be used to control the effects of human activities on their functionality.

[8] Ibid., p. 283. [9] Ibid., pp. 283–4. [10] Ibid., p. 285.

[11] Gaichas, 'Ecosystem-based Fishery Management', 395–6; S. A. Levin, 'Ecosystems and the Biosphere as Complex Adaptive Systems' (1998) 1 *Ecosystems*, 431–2.

[12] Gaichas, 'Ecosystem-based Fishery Management', 396; Levin, 'Ecosystems and the Biosphere', 433.

[13] J. B. Ruhl, 'Thinking of Environmental Law as a Complex Adaptive System: How to Clean up the Environment by Making a Mess of Environmental Law' (1997) 34 *Houston Law Review*, 933–1002.

2.2.2 *Ecosystems as complex adaptive systems*

Ecosystem behaviour is the outcome of multiple interactions between the system's biotic and abiotic components. This interaction percolates upwards to produce and influence the development of macroscopic properties of the system.[14] In turn, the way in which systemic properties evolve feeds back to influence lower-level interactions.[15] For example, Levin notes that the aggregation of components into organisational structures as a result of interrelationships between them has a profound influence on the further development of an ecosystem as a whole.[16] The enormous complexity of these interactions, subject as they are to constant internal change as species evolve and to the effects of dynamic externalities such as the climate system and hydrologic cycles, results in non-linear behaviour at the systemic level.[17] Non-linearity refers to a situation in which the reactions of complex systems to disturbances are not strictly proportional to the event(s) that trigger them.[18] In an ecological context, it means that it is not possible to predict with certainty either what the exact responses of a system will be to any intervention or the emergent properties of a system that will arise through interaction between its components.[19] Gunderson describes the complexity of ecosystems as leading to 'inherent unpredictabilities' in their behaviour.[20]

A second product of their complexity is that ecosystems possess not one but multiple potential stable states.[21] Because of the dependency of the path they take on the interconnection between systemic levels and the effect that external influences have on their development, it is natural

[14] Levin, 'Ecosystems and the Biosphere', 431; G. Harris, *Seeking Sustainability in an Age of Complexity* (Cambridge: Cambridge University Press, 2007), pp. 25–6.

[15] Ibid. [16] Levin, 'Ecosystems and the Biosphere', 432–3.

[17] Gaichas, 'Ecosystem-based Fishery Management', 396; Levin, 'Ecosystems and the Biosphere', 433; Harris, 'Seeking Sustainability', p. 22; B. Walker and D. Salt, *Resilience Thinking: Sustaining Ecosystems and People in a Changing World* (Washington, DC: Island Press, 2006), pp. 34–6.

[18] W. Steffen et al., *Global Change and the Earth System: A Planet under Pressure* (Berlin: Springer-Verlag, 2004), p. 266.

[19] Walker and Salt, 'Resilience Thinking', pp. 34–5; Harris, 'Seeking Sustainability', p. 25.

[20] L. H. Gunderson, 'Ecological Resilience – In Theory and Application' (2000) 31 *Annual Review of Ecology and Systematics*, 433.

[21] M. Scheffer et al., 'Catastrophic Shifts in Ecosystems' (2001) 413 *Nature*, 591–6; Gunderson, 'Ecological Resilience', 426–30, 433; Chapin III et al., 'Terrestrial Ecosystem Ecology', pp. 340–1.

(and indeed desirable in some instances for their renewal) that ecosystems will undergo change.[22] This is not necessarily problematic for the biotic communities that form part of the system if it occurs in a way that does not cause a qualitative shift in its structure and functionality. However, if forces impact on an ecosystem which is already weakened because, for example, of a decline in its biodiversity, major change may occur from which a fundamentally different system emerges.[23]

The ability of an ecosystem to remain in a particular state or domain of attraction is related to the slow variables that configure the system and define the boundaries of the domain that it occupies.[24] Variables have thresholds which, if exceeded, can result in the system entering a different domain in which its determining variables, structures and functions differ substantially from those of the preceding state.[25] Walker and Salt use the example of the capacity of sediments in a lake to absorb levels of phosphorus to illustrate how going beyond the threshold of a variable can affect a system's condition.[26] The lake ecosystem is at risk of entering a new domain in which a clear water environment is replaced by the domination of algal growth where levels of phosphorus exceed the capacity of sediments to absorb them.

The phenomenon of ecological regime shifts is of major concern for human well-being because it can result in the replacement of systems that have hitherto provided humanity with essential services with 'poverty trap' systems that are in an impoverished state and are therefore unable to function as they did in their previous states or to support a diversity of species.[27] Norse refers to changes of this nature having occurred in marine ecosystems that once supported a rich biodiversity, but which, as a result of overfishing, have become dominated by

[22] C. S. Holling and L. H. Gunderson, 'Resilience and Adaptive Cycles' in L. H. Gunderson and C. S. Holling (eds) *Panarchy: Understanding Transformations in Human and Natural Systems* (Washington, DC: Island Press, 2002), p. 26.

[23] C. S. Holling, 'Understanding the Complexity of Economic, Ecological and Social Systems' (2001) 4 *Ecosystems*, 400; Scheffer et al., 'Catastrophic Shifts', 591–2; Chapin III et al., 'Terrestrial Ecosystem Ecology', pp. 342–6.

[24] Walker and Salt, 'Resilience Thinking', pp. 53–5, 59–62; S. R. Carpenter and C. Folke, 'Ecology for Transformation' (2006) 21 *Trends in Ecology and Evolution*, 311.

[25] Ibid.; B. Walker and D. Salt, *Resilience Practice: Building Capacity to Absorb Disturbance and Maintain Function* (Washington, DC: Island Press, 2012), pp. 4–9; Chapin III et al., 'Terrestrial Ecosystem Ecology', pp. 343–6.

[26] Walker and Salt, 'Resilience Thinking', pp. 55–8.

[27] Holling, 'Understanding the Complexity', 400; C. Folke, 'Resilience: The Emergence of a Perspective for Social-Ecological Systems Analyses' (2006) 16 *Global Environmental Change*, 257. See also Chapter 2, Section 2.3.

bacterioplankton and invertebrates.[28] Studies of ecosystems where such change has occurred reveal that it may not be possible to restore an ecosystem to its former state simply by reducing the drivers of change to below the level of the thresholds whose crossing triggered the shift.[29] Reduction to much lower levels than those that led to change may be necessary in some cases whilst Walker and Salt fear that, in others, the crossing of a threshold may represent 'a one-way trip'.[30] An additional problem is that the complexity of ecosystems and the multiplicity of sources of human and natural disturbances that affect them may make it extremely difficult to develop plausible hypotheses for the causes of change.[31]

2.2.3 *Interaction between ecosystems and the Earth System*

It is not sufficient, when assessing the ecological consequences of human activities, to examine direct effects on ecosystems alone. We must also consider the relationship between ecosystems and the Earth System. Could the deterioration of ecosystem functionality affect Earth System processes? If so, what feedback effects could change at the global scale have on the functioning of ecosystems?

Steffen and his colleagues define the Earth System as 'the suite of interacting physical, chemical and biological global-scale cycles. . .and energy fluxes which provide the conditions necessary for life on the planet'.[32] Earth System processes include the climatic system, the hydrologic cycle and the biogeochemical cycling of gaseous elements that regulates atmospheric composition.[33] Their influence on the functioning of ecosystems has long been recognised.[34] The cycling of elements and water impacts significantly on how ecosystem structures, functions and properties evolve. In contrast, recognition of the influence of ecological processes at the planetary scale is relatively recent although it is now widely thought that these play a significant role in shaping elements

28 E. A. Norse, 'Ending the Range Wars on the Last Frontier: Zoning the Sea' in E. A. Norse and L. B. Crowder (eds) *Marine Conservation Biology: The Science of Maintaining the Sea's Biodiversity* (Washington, DC: Island Press, 2005), p. 423.

29 Walker and Salt, 'Resilience Practice', pp. 6–9; C. R. Allen et al., 'Commentary on Part One Articles' in L. H. Gunderson, C. R. Allen and C. S. Holling (eds) *Foundations of Ecological Resilience* (Washington, DC: Island Press, 2010), pp. 7, 10–11.

30 Walker and Salt, 'Resilience Practice', p. 9.

31 S. R. Carpenter, 'Ecological Futures: Building an Ecology of the Long Now' (2002) 83 *Ecology*, 2074.

32 Steffen et al., 'Global Change', p. 7. 33 Ibid. 34 Ibid., p. 24.

of the Earth System, and therefore that the cumulative behaviour of individual ecosystems can have knock-on effects on all of the planet's ecosystems.[35]

Rockström and his colleagues recognise this relationship by including land-use change and rates of biodiversity loss amongst nine 'planetary boundaries' which must not be crossed if the Earth is to remain in a safe operating space for humans living on the planet.[36] They argue that the crossing of thresholds could move Earth out of the Holocene era, a period of relatively benign environmental conditions that has prevailed during humanity's evolution, into the less hospitable domain of the 'anthropocene'.[37] Land-use change and biodiversity loss are described as local/regional scale processes that could become of global concern where the aggregate impacts of deteriorating ecosystem function increases the likelihood that other thresholds at the global scale will be breached.[38] For example, deterioration in the capacities of ecosystems to absorb carbon reduces the threshold for greenhouse gases that humans can emit into the Earth's atmosphere without triggering potentially catastrophic change.

The relationship between ecosystems and Earth System processes adds a further layer of complexity to assessing the effects that human activities may have on ecosystem functionality. It means that we must be mindful not only of possible impacts on particular ecosystems when assessing the cumulative effects of activities, but on all ecosystems due to feedback effects from global change.[39] Unfortunately, we are no more able to predict how deterioration in ecosystem functionality could affect processes at the planetary scale, or how this may affect ecosystem functionality in turn, than we are able to identify how ecosystems themselves may react to disturbance. The degree to which a collapse in ecosystem functionality may be required before this starts to have a global effect is not known.[40] Planetary systems also display non-linearity in their behavioural patterns, with the study of them being described by Boardman as

[35] Ibid., pp. 24–35; Chapin III et al., 'Terrestrial Ecosystem Ecology', p. 11.

[36] J. Rockström et al., 'A Safe Operating Space for Humanity' (2009) 461 *Nature*, 472–5; J. Rockström et al., 'Planetary Boundaries: Exploring the Safe Operating Space for Humanity' (2009) 14(2): 32 *Ecology and Society*.

[37] Ibid. See also W. Steffen et al., 'The Anthropocene: Are Humans Now Overwhelming the Great Forces of Nature?' (2007) 36 *Ambio*, 614–22.

[38] Rockström et al., 'A Safe Operating Space', 473–4; Rockström et al., 'Planetary Boundaries', under 'Categorizing Planetary Boundaries'.

[39] Rockström et al., 'A Safe Operating Space', 474–5.

[40] Rockström et al., 'Planetary Boundaries', under 'Rate of Biodiversity Loss', 'Land-system Change' and 'Discussion'.

'inescapably characterized by high levels of uncertainty'.[41] Even so, knowledge of the potentially global scale of impacts that ecosystem failure could have underlines the need for new approaches to governance that seek to prevent the deterioration of those properties that enable ecosystems to remain in states of value to biotic communities. As will be clear from the above, these approaches will need to find some justifiable basis for governing activities that do not depend on prediction of their likely impacts when deployed in particular circumstances.

2.2.4 Complexity, regime shifts and environmental decision-making

Current approaches to environmental decision-making employed throughout the developed, and much of the developing, world rely on prediction of the effects of activities in assessing whether or not they should be permitted and on what terms.[42] The predicted impacts on the environment are weighed against the benefits that a proposal may yield. In the debate over how development can be made sustainable, a recurring theme is that economic benefits, because of their tangibility and quantifiability, tend to be given greater weight in these balancing exercises than the often less tangible or immediate benefits for society of environmental protection.[43] It is difficult to justify the prevention of harm to a species or habitat in the monetary and hard evidence-demanding terms on which these debates are often conducted. Proponents of a stronger approach to sustainability argue that formal limits on economic growth, perhaps related to the preservation of substantive elements of the environment, must be identified and established in law to overcome this handicap both for environmental protection in current decision-making practices and for making development sustainable.[44]

The features of ecosystems as complex adaptive systems that I consider in this section reveal the inadequacy of decision-making processes that *rely* on the prediction of environmental effects for ecological

41 R. Boardman, *Governance of Earth Systems: Science and its Uses* (Basingstoke: Palgrave Macmillan, 2010), pp. 39–43; Steffen et al., 'Global Change', pp. 71–2.

42 R. K. Morgan, 'Environmental Impact Assessment: the State of the Art' (2012) 30 *Impact Assessment and Project Appraisal*, 5–14; J. Holder and M. Lee, *Environmental Protection, Law and Policy*, 2nd edn (Cambridge: Cambridge University Press, 2007), pp. 548–51.

43 This tendency is considered further in Section 5.2 of Chapter 5.

44 Ibid. See also A. Ross, 'Modern Interpretations of Sustainable Development' (2009) 36 *Journal of Law and Society*, 32–54.

protection. The complexity of ecosystems and the combined effects of contemporaneous human and natural disturbances prevent the identification of impacts at the systemic level that may flow from harm to their components. They also prevent the accurate prediction of harm to components themselves as outcomes depend on resulting change in the structure and function of the ecosystems of which they form part. However, knowledge of the propensity of systems to change state also points the way to an alternative approach to decision-making, and one that may provide stronger justification for constraining economic growth on environmental grounds. The key information is that ecosystems can, if the cumulative stresses placed on them prove too great, withdraw the support that they provide to dependent humans by shifting to subsistence states. This may occur with little or no notice and in ways that are irreversible. The significance of regime shifts is reinforced by knowledge of the impact that widespread ecological deterioration could have on Earth System processes with knock-on effects for the functioning of all ecosystems. In view of this, the goal of efforts to preserve ecosystem functionality should be to identify and sustain those elements of ecosystems that enable them to maintain their structures and functions. Proposals for development or resource exploitation under consideration should not be permitted when they could jeopardise the capacity of ecosystems to resist external disturbance.

Two aspects of ecosystem functionality must be considered further to establish whether an ecological perspective in decision-making would enable a clearer line to be drawn between environmentally tolerable and intolerable actions and modes of human behaviour, and if so, how. First, what elements of ecosystems enable them to remain in states that provide support for human living? Second, how are ecosystems placed at risk of failure? This information is required to be able to determine how activities should be governed to try and reduce risks of regime shifts occurring. To explore these matters, it is necessary to consider the systemic property of resilience that ecological scientists have identified as being of central importance for preventing regime shifts in ecosystems. I examine aspects of this property that we need to be clear about if resilience is to provide a focal point for the development of legal structures to protect ecosystems in the following sections. These include: its meaning when used in the context of ecosystem functionality; what is it that makes an ecosystem resilient; whether resilience is a property that can be quantified; and, if so, can controls be imposed on activities by reference to measurement of the resilience that a system possesses?

I conclude from this examination that prediction of the effects that activities may have on the resilience of particular systems would not provide a valid basis for determining the acceptability of actions. The complex systemic behaviour that gives rise to resilience, and the impossibility of knowing whether a system is resilient enough to withstand disturbance, preclude the use of an approach to decision-making whose credibility depends on reliable identification of the environmental risks to which a proposal may expose society. However, an understanding of the nature of resilience does provide a starting point for developing a system of governance that is better equipped to improve ecosystem protection by adopting a holistic and precautionary approach to governing human activities.

2.3 The meaning of resilience

The term resilience has been used in two different ways to describe an ecosystem's response to external events. The first refers to a system's resistance to disturbance and its ability to return to an equilibrium state following perturbation.[45] However, it is its second and more recent use which better captures its role in promoting the long-term survival of ecosystems. This, as it was first defined by Holling, is concerned with the magnitude of disturbance that a system can experience before it shifts into a different state.[46] A more recent explanation of this property also emphasises the ability of an ecosystem to 'reorganize while undergoing change so as to retain essentially the same function, structure, identity, and feedbacks'.[47] These definitions do not equate resilience with a total immunity to change as this, although it may preserve an ecosystem in the short-term, would ultimately result in its collapse due to an inability to react to changing conditions.[48] Rather, they place emphasis on the adaptive capacity of ecosystems as the characteristic that allows them to

[45] Holling and Gunderson, 'Resilience and Adaptive Cycles', p. 27; Gunderson, 'Ecological Resilience', 426; Allen et al., 'Commentary on Part One Articles', pp. 5–6; Folke, 'Resilience', 256–7.

[46] C. S. Holling, 'Resilience and Stability of Ecological Systems' (1973) 4 *Annual Review of Ecology and Systematics*, 1–23; Gunderson, 'Ecological Resilience', 426–8; C. Folke et al., 'Regime Shifts, Resilience and Biodiversity in Ecosystem Management' (2004) 35 *Annual Review of Ecology, Evolution and Systematics*, 558; Folke, 'Resilience', 254–7; Allen et al., 'Commentary on Part One Articles', pp. 4–7.

[47] Folke et al., 'Regime Shifts', 558.

[48] Holling, 'Understanding the Complexity', 400.

retain their structure and functionality in the face of challenges because they are 'able to respond in a flexible way to uncertainty and surprises'.[49]

Resilience, when it is understood as a system's capacity to adapt without undergoing a qualitative shift, has ramifications for the way in which we should control our activities. Changes in state occur when an ecosystem, whilst undergoing renewal and reorganisation in response to disturbance, lacks the resilience to maintain its existing regime.[50] It is well-established that the cumulative effects of human actions tend to erode the ability of ecosystems to cope with change, including through a combination of eradicating important systemic components (e.g., top predators), altering conditions (e.g., through an excess of nutrients) and modifying patterns of disturbance (e.g., through anthropogenic climate change).[51] Folke et al. refer to a wide range of regime shifts in terrestrial, freshwater and marine ecosystems, all of which, it has been argued, were associated with a loss of resilience due to factors including over-exploitation, pollution and the destruction of habitat.[52] Many of these shifts, because the ecosystems lacked the capacity to retain the trappings of their prior state, resulted in systems that were 'simplified' and consequently unable to support a diverse biotic community.[53] The clear conclusion from this is that we need both to reflect on how our acts combine to undermine the ability of ecosystems to remain in states that provide support for our own existence, and also to start determining what we do by reference to the potential for activities, individually or in combination, to erode resilience.

2.3.1 *Specified and general resilience*

The term resilience captures a variety of respects in which an ecosystem's exposure to risks of regime change can be evaluated. Accordingly, answers to questions concerning systemic resilience depend on the risk under consideration. Ecological scientific literature simplifies the position somewhat by using two categories to distinguish between sources of resilience and approaches that should be adopted to prevent their erosion: specified

[49] Holling and Gunderson, 'Resilience and Adaptive Cycles', p. 32; Gunderson, 'Ecological Resilience', 428.

[50] See Chapter 2, Section 2.2.2.

[51] Folke et al., 'Regime Shifts', 568; Gunderson, 'Ecological Resilience', 428–30; Folke, 'Resilience', 257–8; Allen et al., 'Commentary on Part One Articles', pp. 10–11.

[52] Folke et al., 'Regime Shifts', 568. [53] Ibid., 568.

and general resilience.[54] I consider the meaning of these terms and the respective roles of these types of resilience in maintaining ecosystem functionality in the following paragraphs.

The term 'specified resilience' is used to describe the reaction of some specific part of a system to a specific threat.[55] It is concerned with the key slow variables that determine a system's configuration, and with considering how impacts on them may affect the ability of an ecosystem as a whole to retain its structure and functions.[56] For example, Walker and Salt's example of a lake ecosystem examines its potential to flip into an alternative algae-clogged state if a threshold of one key variable, phosphorus content in nutrients, is crossed.[57] The resilience of the lake declines as levels of phosphorus increase, pushing sediments to the point where it can no longer be absorbed. A specified resilience response to this situation could include efforts to reduce the content of phosphorus in agricultural run-off waters or the introduction of filtering plants or algae-consuming zooplankton to the system.[58]

Knowledge of variables of ecosystems and of stressors that may drive them towards thresholds if they are not controlled is valuable for efforts to prevent or address known threats to ecosystem functionality.[59] However, there are three respects in which governing activities to maintain specified resilience is insufficient for reducing risks that ecosystems will shift into undesirable alternative states, and may even heighten them. The first is that it is extremely hard in practice to detect when an ecosystem is vulnerable to undergoing a regime change.[60] The existence of key variables for ecosystem structure or of thresholds for them may not be known.[61] Changes in state have often been unexpected with their

54 Walker and Salt, 'Resilience Thinking', pp. 120–2; Walker and Salt, 'Resilience Practice', pp. 67–105; C. Folke et al., 'Resilience Thinking: Integrating Resilience, Adaptability and Transformability' (2010) 15(4):20 *Ecology and Society*; S. R. Carpenter et al., 'General Resilience to Cope with Extreme Events' (2012) 4 *Sustainability*, 3250.

55 Walker and Salt, 'Resilience Thinking', pp. 120–1; Walker and Salt, 'Resilience Practice', p. 68.

56 Walker and Salt, 'Resilience Thinking', pp. 120–1; Walker and Salt, 'Resilience Practice', pp. 68–74.

57 Walker and Salt, 'Resilience Thinking', pp. 55–8.

58 Ibid., p. 59.

59 Ibid., pp. 120–1; Walker and Salt, 'Resilience Practice', pp. 18–20.

60 Scheffer et al., 'Catastrophic Shifts', 591, 595–6; R. Biggs et al., 'Turning Back From the Brink: Detecting an Impending Regime Shift in Time to Avert It' (2009) 106 *Proceedings of the National Academy of Sciences of the United States of America*, 826.

61 Walker and Salt, 'Resilience Practice', p. 90; B. Walker et al., 'Resilience, Adaptability, and Transformability in the Goulburn-Broken Catchment, Australia' (2009) 14(1):12 *Ecology and Society*.

occurrence becoming apparent only after the event and with lengthy scientific debate being required to reach a consensus on why the shift may have occurred.[62]

Even if key variables and thresholds are known, systemic conditions may afford little or no evidence that change is imminent.[63] Some recent research challenges the view that the imminence of regime change cannot be recognised by suggesting that changing dynamics as a system approaches a threshold could provide an early warning of this.[64] However, the value of that information, whilst it may allow an urgent precautionary response, is questionable in other respects. It does not provide any indication either of where the suspected threshold lies or of how close the system lies to it.[65] In addition, it assumes that socioeconomic systems will be able to respond to a warning with sufficient speed to prevent a change in state from happening.[66] This may be possible if the causes of change are identifiable and can be halted quickly. However, it may not be possible where the causes of movement towards thresholds cannot be established or where this is being driven by activities in which substantial sums have been invested, that use infrastructure with large upfront development costs and a long-term lifespan, and that have become embedded in national, regional and local economies. These considerations place the emphasis on the initial decision rather than waiting on evidence of a potential environmental disaster before acting.[67]

Second, the complexity of ecosystems and our poor understanding of them present obvious risks that the use of targeted interventions to bolster some specific aspect of their resilience may itself create risks of failure. Writers on resilience criticise managerial approaches that seek to maximise an ecosystem's productivity by reducing its vulnerability to some specific disturbance (e.g., through the use of pesticides) because this tends to make them vulnerable in other respects by preventing natural cycles of change from taking their course.[68] In the same way, risks arise that the manipulation of an ecosystem to make it more robust

[62] Scheffer et al., 'Catastrophic Shifts', 591, 595–6; Biggs et al., 'Turning Back', 826; Carpenter, 'Ecological Futures', 2074, 2080–1.

[63] Scheffer et al., 'Catastrophic Shifts', 591; Biggs et al., 'Turning Back', 826.

[64] Biggs et al., 'Turning Back', 826; Walker and Salt, 'Resilience Practice', p. 86.

[65] Biggs et al., 'Turning Back', 829–30. [66] Ibid.

[67] See also Chapter 2, Section 2.3.2.2.

[68] Walker and Salt, 'Resilience Thinking', pp. 5–8; Gunderson, 'Ecological Resilience', 432–3; C. S. Holling, 'The Resilience of Terrestrial Ecosystems: Local Surprise and Global Change' in W. C. Clark and R. E. Munn (eds) *Sustainable Development of the Biosphere* (Cambridge: Cambridge University Press, 1986), pp. 310–11.

to a particular disturbance may impair its resilience to others.[69] However, the knock-on effects of bolstering one feature of an ecosystem cannot be predicted reliably.[70]

Third, and most importantly, it is impossible to reach a level of sufficient resilience to externalities.[71] The resilience of an ecosystem is not, as Holling and Gunderson note, 'a fixed quantity that defines a system'.[72] Rather, it is relative to the magnitude of the challenges with which the system is presented, and its condition at the time a challenge arises. An ecosystem that is already degraded may undergo a regime shift as a consequence of external events which, if its resilience had not been eroded, would not have perturbed it unduly.[73] Conversely, a highly resilient ecosystem may still be altered if the strength of external forces acting on it is sufficient to overwhelm its capacity for adaptation. In this regard, Brierley and Kingsford suggest that the resilience of marine ecosystems would need to be 'very great indeed' to withstand the effects of the temperature increases that are already seen as an inevitable consequence of climate change.[74]

In conclusion, a specified resilience approach may be useful in circumstances where known variables of an ecosystem are under threat from a known stressor. However, it does not assist with sustaining sources of resilience in ecosystems of which we are ignorant or with addressing threats of harm to them that could not have been anticipated. In this regard, the best means of protecting ecosystem functionality against the unknown is to employ a *general resilience* approach. This seeks to reduce risks of regime shifts as far as possible by reducing the cumulative pressures that human activities place on them.[75] As Walker and Salt observe, it is

[69] Walker and Salt, 'Resilience Thinking', p. 121; Walker and Salt, 'Resilience Practice', pp. 19, 90; Folke et al., 'Resilience Thinking', under 'Specified and General Resilience'; F. Miller et al., 'Resilience and Vulnerability: Complementary or Conflicting Concepts?' (2010) 15(3): 11 *Ecology and Society* under 'Defining Concepts: Responses to Stress'; B. Walker and F. Westley, 'Perspectives on Resilience to Disasters across Sectors and Cultures' (2011) 16(2): 4 *Ecology and Society* under 'Trading Risks: Specified vs. General Resilience'.

[70] Gunderson, 'Ecological Resilience', 433.

[71] Scheffer et al., 'Catastrophic Shifts', 595–6; Carpenter, 'Ecological Futures', 2080–1.

[72] Holling and Gunderson, 'Resilience and Adaptive Cycles', p. 32.

[73] Folke et al., 'Regime Shifts', 575.

[74] A. S. Brierley and M. J. Kingsford, 'Impacts of Climate Change on Marine Organisms and Ecosystems' (2009) 19 *Current Biology*, R607.

[75] Walker and Salt, 'Resilience Practice', pp. 18–20, 90–100; Folke et al., 'Resilience Thinking', under 'Specified and General Resilience'. See also the analogy drawn between a general resilience approach and the call in Rockström et al., 'A safe operating space', for humanity to avoid crossing planetary boundaries in Walker and Salt, 'Resilience Practice', pp. 186–91.

preferable to avoid the need for interventions to support specified sources of an ecosystem's resilience that may themselves have negative consequences by doing what we can to keep ecosystems away from thresholds in the first place.[76]

2.3.2 *What makes an ecosystem generally resilient?*

General resilience concerns the ability of systems to 'absorb disturbances of all kinds' including those due to unexpected events, and to phenomena that are expected (such as climate change), but for which the scale of disturbance and consequences are unknown.[77] It also provides cover for our ignorance of the structuring variables of ecosystems and their thresholds, and for the unanticipated effects of interventions into ecosystems. The specified resilience of ecosystems to particular risks contributes to their general resilience. However, it is otherwise difficult to locate general resilience in specific components of ecosystems. The fact that systemic properties are the product of highly complex interrelationships between the biotic and abiotic components of ecosystems makes it impossible to identify the sources of a system's resilience with precision, whilst the reliability of any snapshot of key components will reduce over time because of systemic dynamism.

In view of these difficulties, commentators on general resilience tend to equate this property with the possession of certain attributes that are collectively thought to enhance the ability of ecosystems to withstand disturbance.[78] The diversity of species that a system contains provides 'insurance' for its ability to retain its existing state in the event that species that perform systemic functions are lost. The existence of subcomponents within systems which, whilst they are connected, are not tightly linked ('modularity') enhances the capacity of ecosystems to reorganise in the face of disturbance. The existence of corridors between biodiverse hotspots enables the interchange of biotic communities

[76] Walker and Salt, 'Resilience Practice', p. 100.

[77] Walker and Salt, 'Resilience Practice', pp. 90–1, 185–9; Folke et al., 'Resilience Thinking', under 'General and Specified Resilience'; Carpenter et al., 'General Resilience', 3250–1.

[78] Walker and Salt, 'Resilience Thinking', pp. 121–2; Walker and Salt, 'Resilience Practice', pp. 92–8; Carpenter et al., 'General Resilience', 3251–3; H.M. Leslie and A.P. Kinzig, 'Resilience Science' in K. McLeod and H. Leslie (eds) *Ecosystem-based Management for the Oceans* (Washington, DC: Island Press, 2009), pp. 62–5; S.A. Levin and J. Lubchenco, 'Resilience, Robustness, and Marine Ecosystem-based Management' (2008) 58 *BioScience*, 30–1; R. Biggs et al., 'Toward Principles for Enhancing the Resilience of Ecosystem Services' (2012) 37 *Annual Review of Environment and Resources*, 421–48.

between them, thereby preventing genetic stagnation that undermines the resilience of isolated pockets of species over time ('openness'), and allowing the passage of migratory species. Finally, broad qualities such as the possession of 'reserves' and 'capital assets' buffer systems against negative impacts.

Collectively, these attributes are viewed as conferring flexibility, adaptability and an enhanced ability to absorb shock on systems. They are described in general terms and, as with resilience itself, cannot be quantified or judged to be at a sufficient level. They are also referred to as characteristics that 'social-ecological' systems should acquire to enhance their resilience. The 'social-ecological' perspective is used by writers on general resilience rather than an ecological one alone because they regard the human and natural worlds as having become so interconnected that effective solutions to problems caused by resource exploitation cannot be identified by looking only at one side of this equation.[79] I agree that the growing vulnerability of socioeconomic systems, due to the pressures they place on a deteriorating environment, is a perilous situation that demands an immediate and drastic response. I also agree that placing so much weight for so long on the functioning of ecosystems, an unknown quantity, for the continued functioning of human societies has proved to be deeply unwise, and that there is an obvious and pressing need, now that we are conscious of the risks presented by 'anthropogenic overshoot', to move rapidly and permanently to a less-exposed position. Even so, my preferred focus remains on exploring what makes ecosystems resilient and how this can be enhanced. The aim of my research is to explore possible legal responses to the growing threat of ecological degradation for human well-being. The starting point for this analysis must be to understand the nature of the threat and how human activities are contributing to it so that appropriate reforms to governance for 'socioeconomic' systems can be identified. In this regard, the 'social-ecological' literature on general resilience often refers to desirable attributes of social and ecological systems together and sometimes conflates them. This can make it difficult to identify exactly how the cultivation of a capacity on the social side over time would assist with addressing the ecological crisis that confronts humanity in the present.

Less attention has been devoted to exploring the contours of a general resilience approach to ecosystem protection to date than has been given

[79] Walker and Salt, 'Resilience Thinking', pp. 31–4.

to addressing specific problems through specified resilience responses.[80] Walker and Salt describe research into the 'erosion of general resilience, worldwide, at all scales' as being the biggest challenge for ecological scientists, but also as the 'weakest part of current resilience practice'.[81] However, a substantial body of research conducted during the last twenty years indicates that the diversity of biotic components of ecosystems makes a significant contribution to their functionality and resilience. This attribute overlaps with most of the other attributes referred to above in some respect. A system with a high degree of biodiversity is likely to be regarded as possessing healthy reserves or stocks of natural capital, whilst reduced modularity and connectedness due to human actions may well impact negatively on the diversity of species and habitats that a system can sustain. In view of this, a review of research in this area enables broader conclusions to be drawn about the efficacy of using general resilience and its preservation as the object of ecological governance. Research on biodiversity and general resilience is considered in the following section. I then go on to consider 'tightness of feedbacks', a characteristic which has also been identified as a key feature of resilient systems and one which illustrates well the desirability of adopting a cautious approach in a system of governance that seeks to preserve this property.

2.3.2.1 Biodiversity

Biodiversity is an umbrella term that captures several aspects of the diversity of biotic components of ecosystems.[82] These include the variety of individual species and groups of species that a system sustains and genetic differences between and within their populations. Research conducted since the 1990s has consistently identified both that the biodiversity of ecosystems is central to their functioning and resilience, and that deterioration of this attribute reduces their ability to reorganise after disturbance.[83] It also identifies the need for urgent action to halt the loss

[80] Walker and Salt, 'Resilience Practice', pp. 188, 197. [81] Ibid., p. 197.

[82] Chapin III et al., 'Terrestrial Ecosystem Ecology', pp. 322–4.

[83] For example see N. Myers, 'Biodiversity and the Precautionary Principle' (1993) 22 *Ambio*, 74–9; C. Folke et al., 'Biological Diversity, Ecosystems, and the Human Scale' (1996) 6 *Ecological Applications*, 1018–24; A. Purvis and A. Hector, 'Getting the Measure of Biodiversity' (2000) 405 *Nature*, 212–19; F. S. Chapin III et al., 'Consequences of Changing Biodiversity' (2000) 405 *Nature*, 234–42; Folke et al., 'Regime Shifts'; D. U. Hooper et al., 'Effects of Biodiversity on Ecosystem Functioning: A Consensus of Current Knowledge' (2005) 75 *Ecological Monographs*, 3–35; Chapin III et al., 'Terrestrial Ecosystem Ecology', pp. 333–5.

of species due to human actions. This is currently occurring 'at a rate that has not been seen since the last global mass extinction event'.[84]

The resilience of an ecosystem is not directly correlated with the numbers of different species that it supports, but lies in the variety of species belonging to groups that have roles in maintaining its functionality.[85] For example, certain functional groups enable the renewal of coral reefs following disturbance by removing dead corals and by grazing on algae that would otherwise prevent new corals from taking root.[86] The complete loss of a group reduces the ability of ecosystems to maintain existing structures and functions in the face of disturbance.[87] It is an outcome that specified resilience measures could be used to prevent although a general resilience back up will always be required to account for ignorance of species that are, or could form part of, a grouping.

Research into the role of biodiversity in maintaining ecosystem functionality has identified the critical importance of response diversity in functional groups.[88] Response diversity entails that a group whose members respond differently to changes in conditions maximises the possibility that functions will continue to be performed despite the inability of particular species within a functional group to withstand systemic change.[89] The term redundancy is also used to refer to species whose loss may appear unimportant at a point in time, but which may become of immense value in different circumstances.[90] These concepts point to the desirability of maximising diversity in functional groups as we cannot know which species will respond well to particular conditions or, indeed, what conditions will be encountered in the future.[91]

It would be prudent where we are aware of the importance of certain functional groupings to devote attention to their protection. However, this

[84] Rockström et al., 'A Safe Operating Space', 473–4. See also N. Myers, 'Biodiversity', 74–5; Chapin III et al., 'Consequences of Changing Biodiversity', 234; Chapin III et al., 'Terrestrial Ecosystem Ecology', p. 333.

[85] Folke et al., 'Biological Diversity', 1019–20; Folke et al., 'Regime Shifts', 570; Folke, 'Resilience', 258; Chapin III et al., 'Terrestrial Ecosystem Ecology', pp. 323–4.

[86] Walker and Salt, 'Resilience Thinking', pp. 64–73.

[87] Ibid.; Folke et al., 'Regime Shifts', 570.

[88] Chapin III et al., 'Consequences of Changing Biodiversity', 238; Gunderson, 'Ecological Resilience', 431–2; Folke et al., 'Regime Shifts', 570–1; Folke, 'Resilience', 258; Rockström et al., 'A Safe Operating space', 473–4.

[89] Ibid.

[90] Folke et al., 'Regime Shifts', 570–1; Levin and Lubchenco, 'Resilience', 30–1; Walker and Salt, 'Resilience Thinking', p. 71.

[91] Chapin III et al., 'Terrestrial Ecosystem Ecology', pp. 333–4; Walker and Salt, 'Resilience Practice', pp. 93–4.

does not mean that we can distinguish when governing activities between species belonging to them and others that, to our limited knowledge, do not. A general resilience approach is required at all times in respect of actions that may affect biodiversity because of human ignorance of the behaviour of highly complex systems and of the dynamism and unpredictability of ecosystems and Earth System processes that a general resilience approach is meant to guard against. In this regard, we do not know definitively which species are, or may become, important for ecosystem functionality.[92] In addition, no species can be regarded as dispensable because all of them contribute in ways that we may not be able to divine to ecosystem functioning through their interactions with each other and the abiotic environments they inhabit.[93] The complexity of relationships between systemic components makes it impossible to identify what effect the removal of an apparently unimportant species may have on the behaviour of the system as a whole.[94] The only prudent approach when facing such an array of unknowns and unknowables in circumstances where human action has already weakened biodiversity significantly is to engender ecological conditions that will henceforth support as diverse a range of species as possible.

2.3.2.2 Tightness of feedbacks

Walker and Salt use the term 'tightness of feedbacks' to refer to the speed and clarity with which change in one part of a social-ecological system becomes apparent in other parts, and the strength with which the parts that become aware of this respond to evidence of change.[95] Clear feedbacks enable a prompt and appropriate reaction in systems that have the flexibility to alter their practices. Conversely, it may not be apparent where feedbacks are loose that an underlying activity threatens harm or that alteration of other parts of the system concerned is necessary.

Walker and Salt refer to the growing complexity of social-ecological interactions and globalisation as factors that lessen the ability of socio-economic systems to appreciate and address the consequences of their behaviours.[96] However, the fundamental problem when considering

92 Myers, 'Biodiversity', 76–7.

93 Chapin III et al., 'Consequences of Changing Biodiversity', 237–8; Chapin III et al., 'Terrestrial Ecosystem Ecology', p. 334.

94 Folke et al., 'Biological Diversity', 1019; Chapin III et al., 'Terrestrial Ecosystem Ecology', p. 334.

95 Walker and Salt, 'Resilience Thinking', pp. 121–2; Walker and Salt, 'Resilience Practice', p. 95.

96 Ibid.

how to improve ecological governance of human activities lies with the lack of signals, or at least signals that humans can recognise, that ecosystems are losing resilience or that resilience has been eroded to such a degree that further disturbance may cause a regime change. Rockström and his colleagues describe the non-linearity and dynamism of ecosystems and the Earth System processes with which they interact as having lulled humanity into a false sense of security, but one which can be withdrawn unexpectedly as the crossing of thresholds trigger changes in state.[97] A by-product of this ignorance of hazard is that socioeconomic systems have unwittingly become ever more vulnerable as the pressures they place on the functioning of ecosystems increase. In the meantime, natural systems, whose resilience is being eroded by unrelenting human disturbance, have become increasing fragile.[98]

Awareness of their vulnerability to environmental change places the emphasis firmly on remaking human societies to try and reduce their exposure.[99] This can best be achieved, as the analysis in this section reveals, by reducing the pressures that we place on the functioning of ecosystems with a view to supporting their ability to withstand the disturbances with which they may be confronted. One difficulty with governing actions on this basis, alongside the small matter of altering the course of societies that have invested so much capital in particular ways of living,[100] is that there is no answer to the question 'by how far must we reduce stresses to be safe?' The ultimate conclusion of this enquiry into whether resilience can be used as a focal point for governance is that human societies cannot make themselves invulnerable. What they can do, however, is to try and lessen risks of harm by adhering to a new code of living that reflects the importance of ecological resilience for humanity's well-being whilst acknowledging our limited understanding of this and of how our activities affect it.

2.4 A legal framework for ecological protection

The account in this chapter of the current understanding of ecosystems highlights four aspects that are key to the design of a legal system for

[97] Rockström et al., 'Planetary Boundaries', under 'Discussion'.
[98] Holling, 'The Resilience of Terrestrial Ecosystems', pp. 310–3.
[99] S. E. van der Leeuw, 'Climate and Society: Lessons from the Past 10000 Years' (2008) 37 *Ambio*, 481.
[100] Ibid.

their protection. The first is that the complexity of ecosystems makes it extremely difficult to predict how actions may affect their behaviour. The second is that they may undergo changes in state that can result in the replacement of systems that provide services of importance for human living with other systems that do not. The third is that the resilience of ecosystems enables them to maintain their structures and functions when confronted with disturbances, and therefore the best means available of keeping ecosystems in states that we regard as desirable is to act in ways that do not undermine this systemic property. However, their complexity prevents us from establishing with precision how the interaction of components gives rise to resilience or of how this is eroded. Finally, as the sufficiency of a system's resilience is relative to the challenges that it faces, it does not lend itself to the control of activities with a view to preventing its erosion beyond a particular point. Rather, its qualitative nature places the emphasis on building up what contributes to a system's capacity to adapt as far as possible because we do not know how much resilience it will require to survive future challenges that it may encounter.

The principal conclusion that follows from these considerations is that requirements for protecting ecosystems should be observed at all levels of decision-making. Legal approaches for controlling the negative impacts of development currently operate primarily at the micro-level of regulation. The potential environmental impacts of plans, programmes and projects for the implementation of policy concerning development types that have been governmentally endorsed are required to be assessed so that decision-makers can balance risks of environmental harm against the desirability of the objectives which the assessed proposal represents. Environmental assessment does have an important role to play in identifying risks of harm to systemic components which may impact on the health of an ecosystem as a whole. However, it is not realistic, because of the significant uncertainty over how the consequences of activities may manifest themselves at systemic levels, to prevent regime shifts by focusing on the impacts of individual developments or plans and programmes for sectors in isolation. Ecological protection is more likely to be advanced through applying holistic controls to all of our activities with a view to reducing their collective impacts on, and bolstering, systemic resilience. Broad precautionary measures should be employed that are not reliant on accurate prediction of the effects of activities, but which seek to reduce risks of systemic collapse by reducing the stresses we place on the natural world. For approaches of this nature to be made effective, legal controls are necessary that operate at the macro-level of policy-making.

This need for ecological protection to be made effective through the application of higher-level controls has, in part, been recognised in recent moves towards the formation of marine policies, including in the United States, Canada and Australia,[101] and in member states of the EU acting under the stimulus of the Marine Framework Strategy Directive.[102] The development of single policies for use of the marine environment is certainly an advance on the prior fragmentation of governance for sea uses in these jurisdictions. However, the focus in legislative structures, which have been developed for their implementation, remains on the management of activities rather than on requiring that the resilience of marine ecosystems be taken into account in the formation of policies for sea uses.

This indicates residual confidence in the ability of science to improve our understanding of how ecosystems function, and thereby to reduce the ecological impacts of our activities to acceptable levels without having to make difficult choices about the way we live and the resources we exploit to maintain lifestyles. However, the picture of uncertainty, unpredictability, complexity and human ignorance that emerges from a review of the shifts which the understanding of ecosystems has undergone does not engender confidence that efforts to improve our knowledge of ecosystems and the impacts of activities on them can, on their own, deliver effective ecological protection. Rather, what is needed is a legal framework for making policy which requires that its contents are informed by the ultimate objective of maintaining those aspects of ecosystems from which they derive resilience. The overarching objective of such a framework would be to engender the conditions that allow ecosystems to adapt to change rather than controlling the impacts of activities by reference to fixed indicators of their health. The emphasis would be on the broad review of policy proposals and the cumulative effects of how we act with a view to reducing stresses we place on natural systems 'across the board'.

In the final section of this chapter, I set out a range of principles which, I argue, should inform the development of macro-level controls on what activities receive governmental endorsement. In Chapter 3,

[101] A. A. Rosenberg et al., 'Lessons from National-Level Implementation Across the World' in K. McLeod and H. M. Leslie (eds) *Ecosystem-based Management for the Oceans* (Washington, DC: Island Press, 2009), p. 294.

[102] Council Directive 2008/56/EC of 17 June 2008 establishing a framework for community action in the field of marine environmental policy [2008] OJ L 164/19.

I make detailed proposals for a legal framework within which ecologically oriented policy-making might be conducted.

2.5 Ethical foundations for ecological law

The significant changes in scientific understanding of the natural world and the mounting mass of evidence that current laws are inadequate for restraining ecological degradation invite a reconsideration of how, ethically, we ought to behave in relation to the world around us. This has been recognised in a substantial body of literature that has been produced since the early 1970s with the aim of developing ethical principles to guide humanity's relationship with nature.[103] Much of this literature has been concerned with the question of whether individual creatures, species, ecosystems or the entire biosphere can be said to have value in themselves.[104] Different views on what the possession of intrinsic value entails are presented in the literature, with some authors suggesting that this may preclude us from harming the valued entity except to fulfil our essential needs whilst others see it as one value to be considered alongside others in decision-making.[105]

Whatever consequences are understood to flow from valuing nature intrinsically, arguments that this is necessary have been at the forefront of environmental ethics because of the widespread view that something further than enlightened human self-interest is required for environmental protection.[106] The argument consistently advanced against the adequacy of such a valuation is that an anthropocentric viewpoint cannot provide a reliable platform for protecting the environment because actions that may yield economic and social benefits in the short-term will always seem more desirable to us than seeking to preserve the environment in the long-term interests of humanity.[107] It is suggested that this will particularly be the case when the environmental consequences of our actions seem remote or are hard to establish causally.[108]

[103] Curry, 'Ecological Ethics', pp. 61–149 provides a thorough overview of academic debate over environmental values and of the different viewpoints of participants on why and how the environment should be valued.

[104] Ibid. [105] Ibid., 52–4.

[106] D. Wilkinson, 'Using Environmental Ethics to Create Ecological Law' in J. Holder and D. McGillivray (eds) *Locality and Identity: Environmental Issues in Law and Society* (Aldershot: Ashgate, 1999), p. 19; Curry, 'Ecological Ethics', pp. 61–6.

[107] Wilkinson, 'Using Environmental Ethics', pp. 18–19; Curry, 'Ecological Ethics', pp. 62–3.

[108] J. Alder and D. Wilkinson, *Environmental Law and Ethics* (Basingstoke: Macmillan Press, 1999), p. 54.

I agree that we need to look again at what is valuable in the natural world and at why nature should be valued by us. However, I also agree with Norton that the abstract search for intrinsic value is unlikely to advance the development of an effective ethical position for environmental protection based on which decisions might be made and laws devised, because the arguments advanced are too remote from the way in which people make value judgments.[109] A better approach, and one that would be more likely to result in an ethic to which people can relate, would be to revisit and challenge long-standing perspectives of humanity as having the right to dominate nature and the knowledge to do so by reference to our new appreciation of our dependence on natural systems, the significant limits on our understanding of them and the ease with which our actions can cause them to lose what is important for their functionality. I argue that a proper comprehension of our relationship with ecosystems would provide a basis from which we can appreciate their value to us and develop ethical positions and principles for guiding our conduct in relation to them. Indeed, it would be difficult for us to value ecosystems intrinsically because the way in which we attach value to them is inevitably connected with their ability to provide a support mechanism for our own existence.

A difficulty with seeking to derive ethical theories from the perception of nature in ecological science is the maxim that there is no logical connection between what is and what we ought to do.[110] The fact that scientists consider the preservation of an ecosystem's resilience to be desirable does not necessarily mean that we ought, from an ethical perspective, to act in ways that may preserve it. However, it is also recognised by environmental ethicists that dogmatic adherence to a divide between facts and determining what is the right way to behave is not practicable if ethical guidance of any value for reducing our negative ecological impacts is to be produced.[111] Curry argues that the goal of environmental ethicists should not be to produce a theory whose rationality is unassailable, but to 'articulate a reasonably coherent, consistent and clear set of ethical principles, informed by and conveying ecocentric values, which will lend themselves to incorporation

[109] B. G. Norton, 'Marine Environmental Ethics: Where We Might Start' in D. G. Dallmeyer (ed.) *Values at Sea: Ethics for the Marine* Environment (Athens, GA: The University of Georgia Press, 2003), pp. 38–9. See also B. G. Norton, *Sustainability: A Philosophy of Adaptive Ecosystem Management* (Chicago: University of Chicago Press, 2005), pp. 161–2, 180–90 for a fuller critique of intrinsic value theory.

[110] Alder and Wilkinson, 'Environmental Law and Ethics', pp. 46–7; Curry, 'Ecological Ethics', pp. 31–2.

[111] Curry, 'Ecological Ethics', p. 96.

into people's attitudes and ways of life'.[112] I follow a similar approach in this section in that I do not seek to develop a logically impeccable position, but to devise an appropriate set of propositions to guide our relations with the non-human world in a way that will be beneficial for the health of ecosystems.

2.5.1 The dominion perspective of nature

In a ground-breaking critique of western attitudes towards the environment, Lynn White Jr identified two aspects of humankind's relationship with nature as the source of environmental crises that were beginning to manifest themselves in the late 1960s.[113] The first is that nature has been seen predominantly as having value only to the extent that it can be used by us to advance our economic and social goals.[114] Efforts to move away from this valuation by arguing that nature should be valued intrinsically have, as I noted above, provided a recurring theme in environmental ethical literature.

The second is that the ultimate source of instrumental value, and therefore of the environmental degradation for which we are responsible, is humanity's hubristic perception of itself as a species apart from nature.[115] This perspective was born initially from the 'dominion' view in Judaeo-Christian theology of the natural world as having been created for humankind's use.[116] Growing confidence in our ability to understand nature and manipulate it to our own ends during the early modern and enlightenment periods of the 17th and 18th centuries and the technological revolutions that followed enabled us to give practical effect 'to that which Christianity had already sanctioned'.[117] Notwithstanding the

[112] Ibid.

[113] L. White Jr., 'The Historical Roots of Our Ecologic Crisis' (1967) 155 *Science*, 1203.

[114] Ibid.; Curry, 'Ecological Ethics', pp. 54–6.

[115] Norton, 'Marine Environmental Ethics', pp. 78–9.

[116] Alder and Wilkinson, 'Environmental Law and Ethics', p. 51; G. L. Schaab, 'Beyond Dominion and Stewardship' in P. Burdon (ed.) *Exploring Wild Law: The Philosophy of Earth Jurisprudence* (Kent Town: Wakefield Press, 2011), pp. 107–9; Curry, 'Ecological Ethics', pp. 33–4.

[117] Alder and Wilkinson, 'Environmental Law and Ethics', pp. 51–2; P. Burdon, 'Eco-centric Paradigm' in P. Burdon (ed.) *Exploring Wild Law: The Philosophy of Earth Jurisprudence* (Kent Town: Wakefield Press, 2011), pp. 85–6; B. Vitek and W. Jackson, 'Introduction: Taking Ignorance Seriously' in B. Vitek and W. Jackson (eds) *The Virtues of Ignorance: Complexity, Sustainability and the Limits of Knowledge* (Lexington: University Press of Kentucky, 2008), pp. 1–5; J. Marocco, 'Climate Change and the Limits of Knowledge' in B. Vitek and W. Jackson (eds) *The Virtues of Ignorance: Complexity, Sustainability and the*

environmental crises that now confront us, its influence remains apparent in the optimism that we can address them by identifying technological fixes that will allow economic growth to continue unabated.[118]

It is from this perspective that values associated exclusively with the utility of the natural world have developed. In light of this, a focus on its sources and their validity should be the starting point for forming an ethic that is capable of securing adherents and promoting strong environmental protection because it reflects the reality of our relationship with nature.

Changes in our understanding of ecosystems challenge the 'dominion' perspective and the belief that our powers of reasoning will enable us to manipulate nature to our benefit in two respects. The first challenge relates to the reality of our position in the world. The development of ecological science as a discipline and its emphasis on relationships between species has directed attention away from our characteristics and towards our interactions with biotic communities and the importance of maintaining their health for our well-being. However, it is the application of complex adaptive system theory to the analysis of ecosystems which most clearly reveals the bankruptcy of the notion that humanity is a species apart from nature. This shows us that we are not, in any respect, dominant, but that we, along with other species are the beneficiaries of enormous good fortune that has resulted in the evolution and interaction of ecological and earth systems in ways that generate the conditions which enable us to survive.[119] The dynamic nature of ecosystems and their potential to flip into alternative states that may not be beneficial for us, whether as a consequence of human actions or, more importantly, from natural events over which we have no control, reveals the reality of our position: that we are not and will never be the masters of nature, but that we are dependent on its resilience to fundamental change for our continued existence as a species.

The second challenge is concerned with the confidence we retain in our ability to understand how our activities affect the natural world, and thereby to develop technological solutions that will either reduce the risk of environmental problems arising from what we do or fix the problems we cause. Although this perspective remains stubbornly entrenched, the enormity of the changes in the way we perceive nature during the last

Limits of Knowledge (Lexington: University Press of Kentucky, 2008), pp. 308–12; Curry, 'Ecological Ethics', pp. 35–8.

118 J.Marocco, 'Climate Change', pp. 312–5; Curry, 'Ecological Ethics', pp. 24–7.

119 Steffen et al., 'The Anthropocene', 614–21; Walker and Salt, 'Resilience Practice', p. 195.

eighty years must undermine the belief that we can attain sufficient understanding of how ecosystems respond to human intervention to devise technologies and controls for preventing ecological harm. In addition, to the extent that we can rely on current theories in ecology, they indicate that our traditional use of science to inform us about what we can do without causing environmental harm is not viable for ecological protection. This is because we cannot predict with any confidence how ecosystems will react to disturbances or identify points at which an ecosystem is at risk of undergoing a change in state. Furthermore, we do not know how the fixes that we employ to address extant problems of our creation will affect ecosystem functionality in other respects. These considerations suggest that we should move towards basing our decisions on broad principles as to how we should act in relation to ecosystems rather than retaining an ill-founded faith in science's predictive capacities, stemming as this does from discredited assumptions that the functioning of the natural world as a whole can be understood through the study of its components.[120]

2.5.2 *Revaluing nature*

How would the way in which we value nature change if perception of humanity's relationship with it were based on our new understanding of the natural world rather than on the historical perception which this reveals to be erroneous? Environmental ethicists of the 'deep green' school have argued that comprehension of the reality of our place in the world must lead to an intrinsic valuation of nature.[121] My view is that this is not necessarily the case. Nor would it be desirable if the aim is to develop an ethic with practical effects. Having a clear grasp of our reliance on the benignity of natural systems for our own existence and awareness of the way in which our actions undermine them would enable us to develop values and ethical positions that would provide a high level of environmental protection without resorting to arguments that we should value and therefore preserve nature whether or not it is in our interests to do so.

As I have already noted, the concern of ecocentric ethicists with an 'anthropocentric' or a 'shallow' ethics is that humanity's self-interest

[120] Marocco, 'Climate Change', pp. 316–8; Burdon, 'Eco-centric Paradigm', p. 88; D. Ludwig et al., 'Uncertainty, Resource Exploitation, and Conservation: Lessons from History' (1993) 260 *Science*, 17 and 36.

[121] Curry, 'Ecological Ethics', pp. 92–4.

inevitably makes protection of the environment contingent on other human values not taking precedence.[122] This objection is based on an assumption that an ethic which is human-centred is synonymous with one that holds only instrumental value in nature. However, there is no reason why an anthropocentric position should automatically lead to such a valuation. Indeed, I suggest that an altered perspective would result in a valuation of nature not simply for what we can extract from it, but for its *existence*. The health of ecosystems should be seen as being of supervening value because what is valuable for our existence ultimately derives from their continued functionality.

In this regard, Callicott provides a useful analogy between the condition of ecosystems and our own health.[123] The latter is something we value, in the first instance, for its own existence. In the same way the health of ecosystems is something that we should value because it provides a cradle and support mechanism for our survival as a species.[124] In both cases, 'health' also has instrumental value in that it enables us to pursue our own ends.[125] However, consciousness of its importance for this secondary value to be realised establishes, in principle at least, a clear hierarchy between the valuations.

A perspective of humanity as one element within complex larger dynamic ecological and physical systems, whose well-being is essential for our own, advocates that we should hold value in the continued functionality of the systems of which we form part. However, what is it about ecosystems that we should value and seek to preserve in the ethical positions we adopt? It is not simply the existence of ecosystems that is valuable to us. Indeed, valuing ecosystems as if they were clearly distinct entities is recognised to present difficulties because of their lack of well-defined spatial boundaries.[126] A better focus is on the processes, properties and resilience that contribute to, and maintain, the ecological functions from which we derive benefit. Norton concurs with this view in arguing that true value is to be found in 'nature's creativity' and in the processes that sustain the species and the elements that exist currently

[122] Wilkinson, 'Using Environmental Ethics', p. 19.

[123] J. B. Callicott, 'Aldo Leopold's Concept of Ecosystem Health' in J. B. Callicott (ed.) *Beyond the Land Ethic: More Essays in Environmental Philosophy* (Albany: State University of New York Press, 1999), pp. 334–5.

[124] J. B. Callicott, 'The Value of Ecosystem Health' in J. B. Callicott (ed.) *Beyond the Land Ethic: More Essays in Environmental Philosophy* (Albany: State University of New York Press, 1999), p. 355.

[125] Ibid. [126] Callicott, 'The Value of Ecosystem Health', pp. 348–9.

and populate the world.[127] He also argues that resilience is something that we should value because it enables an ecosystem to maintain 'its creative force by maintaining its self-organizing, auto-poietic (literally 'self-making') structure'.[128]

An ethical system that finds ultimate value in ecological processes and properties and in system-wide resilience would, if translated into a legal system for ecological protection, have significant ramifications for how we use law to protect the environment. The focus in environmental law hitherto has been either on assessing potential impacts on specific areas (predominantly the location in which development will be conducted and its vicinity) or on creating protected areas. However, a geographical approach is not useful for drafting laws that are intended to reflect values held in dynamic events and their outcomes, which cannot be pinpointed to a particular location but are the product of multiple interactions between different ecological levels. Rather, such a valuation would require correspondingly broad controls on our activities to prevent them from undermining the complex occurrences that produce and maintain ecological functionality. We must match the importance of what happens at the systemic level for our well-being with laws that regulate what we do at the macro-level of policy formation.

One further issue we must consider in connection with valuation is the basis on which we should value ecological processes, properties and resilience. A revised perspective that is informed by a new understanding of humanity's place in nature would provide a sufficient basis for an anthropocentric ethic for ecological protection. In any event, I believe that an attempt to form such an ethic through an intrinsic valuation of ecosystems would encounter two difficulties. The first is that the basis on which we value ecosystems is unavoidably anthropocentric. The concepts that we use to indicate whether an ecosystem is in a desirable state are intrinsically connected with whether it remains in a condition that sustains us. In this regard, the very notion of maintaining resilience is bound up with keeping ecosystems in states that we would regard as 'healthy'. Conversely, locating intrinsic value in ecological processes would suggest that we should value them even if they operate to promote a change in state which deprives us of the support that a 'healthy' ecosystem delivers. Such a valuation would be far removed from the

[127] B. G. Norton, 'Biodiversity and environmental values: in search of a universal earth ethic' (2000) 9 *Biodiversity and Conservation*, 1039–40.

[128] Ibid., 1041.

reality of why we would choose to regard the protection of ecosystems as desirable for us.

The second and related difficulty is that ecological processes are not necessarily benign. Resilience may also, as we have already noted, not be a desirable property in a system that has undergone a change in state. It would fly in the face of the benefit that we and a broad diversity of species derive from ecosystems to suggest that we should value ecological processes irrespective of whether they provide us with support or remove it from us. Again, the unavoidable conclusion is that the only realistic way in which we can find value in ecosystems, and therefore the motivation to protect them, is from an anthropocentric perspective.

2.6 Duties and principles for ecologically oriented decision-making

I have advanced broad arguments about the need for humanity to forge a different perspective and to alter its values in light of the changed understanding of the natural world. In this final section, I apply these arguments in proposing a set of principles that might be applied by governments for determining what actions are consistent with ecological values, and how those which are judged to be compatible with preserving ecosystem functionality might be implemented.

Aldo Leopold's famous maxim that a 'thing is right when it tends to preserve the integrity, stability, and beauty of the biotic community' has been used as a starting point for many attempts to develop an ecologically oriented ethics.[129] However, notwithstanding its widespread appeal, Leopold's maxim does not provide a useful basis for establishing principles to govern our relations with ecosystems as we now understand them to be. As our activities inevitably tend to undermine the properties that enable ecosystems to maintain their state to some degree, the great majority of what we do would not be regarded as 'right' according to Leopold's statement. An adaptation of Leopold's position that would come closer to what we now know about ecosystems might adjudge that a thing is right when it tends to have the least erosive effects on systemic resilience and the properties which contribute to it when compared with available alternatives. However, this statement, as with Leopold's, presupposes an ability to

[129] A. Leopold, *A Sand County Almanac* (Oxford University Press: New York, 1949) quoted in Curry, 'Ecological Ethics', pp. 94–5.

establish the effects of actions at the systemic level which, in practice, we do not possess.

I suggest that a more effective ethical position would be based around a clear statement of basic obligations towards ecosystems and supported by principles comprising a virtue ethic for decision-making. The school of virtue ethics has been ignored largely as a route for developing environmental ethics.[130] However, its concern with cultivating behaviours whose practice are more likely than not to result in good outcomes for humanity offers a way forward in circumstances where it is difficult to identify what the consequences of our activities may be, and where we do not understand ecosystems sufficiently to go beyond broad statements of duty as to how we should act towards them.[131] A set of guiding principles for political decision-making that reflects the value of ecosystem functionality for human well-being seems more likely to yield an effective way forward than reliance on consequentialist or deontological solutions alone.

The main duty that flows from values held in ecological processes, properties and resilience is that we should control our activities with the aim of reducing their erosive effects on resilience and the systemic processes and properties that contribute to and maintain it. This duty applies both to the macro-level of determining what activities we should pursue and the micro-level of deciding whether plans, programmes and proposals for development and resource exploitation should be endorsed. It should provide, as argued in Chapter 3, the primary objective for a legal system for ecological protection.

A second duty is that we should make every effort to increase our knowledge and understanding of ecosystems so that we are better able to observe the primary duty of maintaining ecosystem health. Whilst acquiring sufficient knowledge to know exactly how ecosystems will evolve is an unattainable goal, we can at least attempt to reduce uncertainty over the ecological impacts of our activities by seeking to move beyond what Simon Levin describes as 'our shocking ignorance of many of the most fundamental features of the world around us'.[132] The knowledge-gathering I envisage here is distinct from the periodic environmental assessment of the impacts that development proposals may have to aid decision-makers

[130] P. Carfaro, 'Thoreau, Leopold, and Carson: Toward an Environmental Virtue Ethics' in R. J. Goldstein (ed.) *Environmental Ethics and Law* (Aldershot: Ashgate, 2004), p. 23.

[131] Curry, 'Ecological Ethics', pp. 45–51.

[132] S. A. Levin, *Fragile Dominion: Complexity and the Commons* (Cambridge, MA: Helix Books, 1999), pp. 198–9.

in deciding whether they should be authorised. Its aim is to advance our basic knowledge of ecosystem components, of how their interactions contribute to systemic properties, and of what is important to continued ecological functionality so that we are better able to control the negative impacts we have on them.

A related obligation is that we should put in place mechanisms that will enable us to monitor systemic conditions so that we can adapt to reactions that we failed to predict and to changes that arise naturally in dynamic systems. Such provision is necessary because, if we are to maintain what we value at the systemic level, we must employ the means available to us of compensating for our inability to predict how ecosystems behave or to foresee how they may evolve. The principal thrust is to use a precautionary approach in decision-making, but monitoring can provide a back-up by producing information that may reveal unexpected outcomes or the need to strengthen measures to prevent ecological degradation. In Chapter 7 I consider how legal mechanisms might be developed for improving our knowledge of ecosystems and maintaining a flow of information on ecological conditions.

Whilst the obligations for ecological protection set objectives for controlling the impacts of our activities, they do not themselves provide us with any guidance as to how we should go about this. The following principles are intended to give direction to decision-makers in determining which activities it would be appropriate to authorise and how they might be conducted from an ecological perspective. Their breadth reflects the need for broad controls on what we do to protect properties that are the result of multiple interactions at different systemic scales, and the uncertainty over how our activities combine to undermine them.

The most effective means of bolstering systemic resilience would, on its face, appear to be changing the way in which we live so that we place less stress on ecosystems. The view that we ought to decrease our impacts on living things by leading more simple lifestyles dates back to at least the 19th century and Thoreau's ethic of simplicity.[133] It is also apparent in the call made by ecocentric ethicists that we should exploit nature only to the extent that we need to do so to meet our basic needs.[134] However, the obvious difficulty that the notion of 'necessity' encounters as a reference

[133] P. Cafaro, 'Thoreau, Leopold, and Carson', p. 27.

[134] For example see Naess' and Sessions' '*Eight Platform Principles*' of 'Deep Ecology' quoted in Curry, 'Ecological Ethics' p. 101 and J. P. Sterba, 'Reconciling Anthropocentric and Nonanthropocentric Environmental Ethics' (1994) 3 *Environmental Values*, 229.

point for decision-making is that its meaning is inevitably influenced by the societal context in which it is used.[135] If it is intended by ethicists to denote that we should retreat to subsistence lifestyles, that would not provide a realistic benchmark for the transformation of a society in which a high standard of living is enjoyed, expected and economically embedded. If there is no objective definition of what a human must have to enjoy a reasonable standard of life, broad scope is also left for arguing that the continuity of environmentally unsustainable lifestyles is justified by a host of social and economic considerations.

I suggest that an alternative and more practical approach would be to focus on doing less of what places ecosystems under stress and to develop strategies to reduce or alter patterns of consumption in line with determination of which practices should be approved and which reduced or discontinued in the interests of maintaining ecosystem health. Two principles would assist with decision-making on this basis. The first is the under-utilisation of resources.[136] This entails that we should not use resources if the reasons for employing them can be met by other less ecologically stressful means. A prominent example of its application would be to require a focus on how far we can increase energy efficiency and reduce consumption, and over what timescales, in preference to the use of renewable energy technologies that may have ecological impacts from the manufacture and construction of infrastructure for power production and transmission. On the same basis however, renewable energy generation would almost certainly be preferred to continued fossil fuel generation in light of the significant threat presented to ecosystem health by increased atmospheric carbon and unmitigated climate change. Accordingly, this principle might be applied in a re-evaluation of energy policy with a broad hierarchy of ecologically preferred approaches being established and strategies determined for moving towards the options that are least likely to undermine ecological resilience.

The second principle is that we should minimise our reliance on activities that are most likely to engender changes in ecological states, either because of their effects on systemic resilience or their potential to present external challenges to the structure and functionality of ecosystems.[137] We already have in place sophisticated legal structures for determining which chemicals it would be safe to continue to use from

135 See Chapter 3, Section 3.3.2.1 for a fuller discussion of the difficulties with using 'needs' as a reference point in decision-making.

136 Levin, 'Fragile Dominion', p. 201.

137 Ibid., p. 201.

human health and environmental perspectives.[138] These allow for timetables to be set for their removal from the market and the allocation of permissions for limited continued use enabling adjustment to withdrawal. Whilst decision-making under these structures is highly technical, the legal frameworks under which they operate might be applied and adapted for the identification of activities that present too high a threat to ecosystem health and to establishing a timetable and measures for their reduction or withdrawal. To use the energy example again, an obvious focus would be to devise a firm strategy for the reduction of carbon-emitting energy generation in favour of combinations of energy sources whose collective impacts are less likely either to reduce systemic resilience or create conditions that significantly increase risks of a regime shift.

The concept of 'need', as I note above, would not, because of the difficulty with giving it definition, provide a suitable basis for a generally applicable principle of decision-making on whether activities are ecologically appropriate. It can only be given concrete form, because of its indeterminate nature, through public debate. That said, it would also be important under a programme of stress reduction to consider if it is essential for 'human wants' to be met, and, indeed, to explore what 'needs', as opposed to desired outcomes, are in a modern society. I argue in Chapter 3 that reflection on how consumption can be reduced should be a primary concern of policy-making. In addition, the alteration of patterns of living with a view to alleviating the pressures that these place on natural systems is a key aim of the system of governance I propose in Chapters 4, 5 and 6. However, reductions in consumption under this system would be a product both of discussion and agreement with those whom proposed changes affect, and, ultimately, of their own willingness to change their lifestyles. The question of whether current practices are necessary or whether people would be willing to abandon them should be examined in deliberative processes of the type called for in Chapter 6.

It is hoped that the application of macro-level principles will secure reductions in the cumulative ecological impacts of human actions. Even so, as any activities that are conducted may have some erosive effects on systemic resilience, it is desirable that the focus at the micro-level of regulation (e.g., planning and development controls) should be on the

[138] See for example Council Directive 91/414/EEC of 15 July 1991 concerning the placing of plant protection products on the market [1991] OJ L 230/1. See also the discussion of Swedish chemicals policy and law at Chapter 3, Section 3.3.2.3.

use of land and resources in ways that minimise stress on ecosystems. Accordingly, the main principle for this level of decision-making is that alternatives for implementing policy which are assessed to pose least threat to the properties that maintain systemic resilience should be pursued. As with the principles of minimising reliance on options that potentially present a threat to ecological functionality, activities should not be endorsed where they are judged to be incompatible with the objective of reducing human erosion of the resilience of ecosystems. I examine in Chapters 4, 5 and 6 how a system of governance could be established to advance these principles for policy implementation and, in doing so, to explore how far reductions in stress envisaged in ecologically oriented policies can be realised.

3

Ecologically oriented policy-making

3.1 Introduction

Recognition that it is in humanity's interests to support the resilience of ecosystems brings in its wake a need to consider how the erosive effects of its activities on this vital property might be reduced. It also raises the question of what role law might play in alleviating risks that anthropogenic stresses will trigger unwelcome changes in their states. In this chapter, I examine how law might be used to promote a focus in the formation of policy on maintaining ecological functionality. There has, to date, been strong institutional resistance to the application of environmental constraints on policy-making. However, if the health of ecosystems is accepted as being of supervening value for human well-being, it is essential that the processes by which fundamental decisions are made about the direction that societies take should be oriented towards their protection.

There are two particular difficulties with deciding how activities should be governed with a view to supporting the functioning of ecosystems. These are the pervasive uncertainty over how their cumulative impacts undermine this, and corresponding ignorance of the extent to which they must be reduced to prevent changes in state from occurring. I provide an introduction to these problems and the challenges they present for designing laws for protecting ecosystems in Section 3.1.1. The legal framework for policy-making presented in this chapter addresses them by employing mechanisms to support decision-making that are not dependent on knowledge of the causal effects that actions may have, and by seeking to drive the progressive diminution of risks of ecological harm that they give rise to. It differs significantly from current uses of law that aim to temper the environmental consequences of decisions, but without disturbing the status quo. In contrast, the framework's goals of promoting ecosystem health as an objective of policy-making and establishing precaution as the default approach in environmental decision-making are explicitly normative.

3.1.1 Adapting to endemic uncertainty

Consideration of how negative impacts on ecosystems can be prevented and of law's role in this endeavour meets an immediate difficulty: there is a high degree of uncertainty over how they react to human intervention and concerning the properties that a legal system for ecological protection would aim to protect.[1] This manifests itself in several respects: we are unable to predict what consequences our activities will have, whether individually or cumulatively, on systemic properties of importance for ecosystem functionality;[2] we do not know the causal pathways by which anthropogenic stresses combine to erode resilience or cause shifts in states;[3] we have poor knowledge of what properties are important for the maintenance of resilience apart from an appreciation that diversity is important for this;[4] we *cannot* know what elements of ecosystems will become important for their functionality as they, and relations between species comprising them and the environments they inhabit, change;[5] and, finally, we *cannot* know whether resilience is sufficient for ecosystems to withstand the impacts of events that may confront them in the future.[6]

Application of the precautionary principle as it is currently conceived would suggest that decision-making on matters that may present threats of harm to ecosystems should be delayed or activities halted at least until sufficient knowledge of their behaviour is available to make informed choices over whether the risks concerned are acceptable.[7] However, the reality is that the complexity and unpredictability of ecosystems, when coupled with our poor understanding of them, will prevent us from

[1] See my discussion of the complexity and unpredictability of ecosystems, of the nature of resilience, and of the difficulties that these present for controlling activities at Chapter 2, Sections 2.2 and 2.3. See also the detailed discussion of scientific uncertainty concerning ecological behaviour in R. A. Young, *Uncertainty and the Environment: Implications for Decision-Making and Environmental Policy* (Cheltenham: Edward Elgar Publishing, 2001), pp. 1–10, 46–59.

[2] Chapter 2, Section 2.2; Young, 'Uncertainty and the Environment', p. 1, 7; Walker and Salt, 'Resilience Thinking', pp. 34–6.

[3] Chapter 2, Section 2.2; Young, 'Uncertainty and the Environment', p. 48; Scheffer et al., 'Catastrophic Shifts', 595–6; Biggs et al., 'Turning Back', 826–830.

[4] Chapter 2, Section 2.3; Young, 'Uncertainty and the Environment', pp. 9, 52–3; Walker and Salt, 'Resilience Practice', pp. 89–94, 197; Rockström et al., 'A Safe Operating Space', 473–4.

[5] Chapter 2, Section 2.3; Young, 'Uncertainty and the Environment', pp. 9–10; Myers, 'Biodiversity', 74–9.

[6] Chapter 2, Section 2.3; Young, 'Uncertainty and the Environment', pp. 53–6; Scheffer et al., 'Catastrophic Shifts', 596; Walker and Salt, 'Resilience Practice', pp. 92–3.

[7] See the discussion of the precautionary principle at Chapter 3, Section 3.2.

establishing the causal effects of our pursuits for the foreseeable future. Indeed, there is no guarantee that we will ever be in a position to identify with confidence the mechanisms by which anthropogenic stresses cause ecological degradation, and thereby to found decisions on reasonable levels of confidence that we know what the likely outcomes of an action or combinations of actions will be.

Although we do not know how the disturbance of ecosystems causes their health to deteriorate, we are aware that their degradation is happening at an increasingly rapid rate and that, in all likelihood, this is due to human interference with natural processes.[8] Accordingly, we must find a means of deciding how to control our activities with a view to maintaining systemic properties *despite* our ignorance of how they cause ecosystems to decline and fail. It is argued in Section 3.2 that this situation demands a new conception of the precautionary principle which is attuned to endemic uncertainty. The reconceived principle would require that positive action should be taken as a matter of course to reduce risks of ecological harm, and thereby to address sources of threat to society's well-being. Normative precaution could be put into practice under a legal regime which requires that characteristics of importance for ecosystem functionality should, as far as possible, be preserved, and that options for meeting policy objectives should be evaluated by reference to their propensity to impinge on these characteristics. An introduction to this legal framework is provided at Section 3.1.2.

Resilience should provide a focal point for ecological protection because it is this property that enables ecosystems to maintain their functionality in the face of external challenges. The guiding principle for decision-making should therefore be the avoidance or reduction of reliance on activities that may erode resilience. However, a difficulty with adopting this concept as an object of legal protection is that resilience is not amenable to use as a quantitative benchmark by which we can determine how much human interference an ecosystem can accommodate. This is because the adequacy of an ecosystem's resilience is relative to the scale of challenges that it may meet.[9] This difficulty is also compounded by our currently poor understanding of where resilience lies in ecosystems and of how it is lost.

Regulatory approaches which assume that the acceptability or unacceptability of proposals can be judged by reference to the anthropogenic stresses that the environment can carry are not suitable for ecological

[8] Millennium Ecosystem Assessment, 'Ecosystems and Human Well-Being'.
[9] Chapter 2, Section 2.3.

protection (leaving aside their suitability in other contexts). They do not reflect the reality of how the functionality of ecosystems is placed at risk. Instead, laws are required that replace a 'bottom-line' conception of the environment with a 'top-line' approach to environmental decision-making. This would be based on recognition that we are unable to identify where the 'cliff edge' lies. We should therefore concentrate our efforts on bolstering the health of ecosystems by controlling our impacts on them in the hope that they will be strong enough to withstand the natural and anthropogenic disturbances that they encounter in the future.

3.1.2 *Ecological policy-making*

In Section 3.3 proposals for a legal framework under which ecologically oriented policy-making might be conducted are set out. It is designed to facilitate and, where necessary, to drive the passage from passive management of environmental risks to active risk reduction by promoting practices that reduce the stresses that we place on ecosystems, and by moving away from reliance on those that are likely to erode resilience or trigger regime shifts. It addresses the challenges that uncertainty and the relative nature of resilience present for ecological protection in two main respects. The first is that it places ecological values at its apex by making the preservation of ecosystem functionality the principal objective of policy-making. Policy options are to be assessed and a hierarchy of preferred alternatives established by reference to their compatibility with what is ecologically valuable rather than through prediction of the effects they may have.

The second is that forward-looking strategies are to be prepared with a view to determining how the stresses we place on ecosystems can be diminished. Policy-makers are required, through strategy formation, to develop scenarios in which the ecological impacts of economic and social activity have been lessened and then to explore how governmental action might promote their realisation. Strategies would examine how options that are judged to be too ecologically harmful for continued reliance on them might be replaced. They would also lay down proposals for increasing the use of preferred alternatives in meeting policy objectives. The visions developed would provide a platform for public discussion and debate about what the shift towards an ecologically safer future would entail, of the economic and social impacts that different rates of progress towards this future would have, and the acceptability of policy measures that would be necessary for reaching desired ends. Ultimately, they would also be used to inform final decision-making on policy contents.

The framework applies the two key principles for macro-level decision-making that are proposed in Chapter 2: the under-utilisation of resources and minimising reliance on activities that are most likely to provoke changes in ecological states.[10] It advances the first principle by providing that policy options which place least stress on ecosystems should be prioritised and that strategies should explore how these might be promoted. It encompasses the second principle by requiring that reliance on options which are assessed to present unacceptable risks of ecological harm should be reduced with a view, ultimately, to their cessation. I discuss the application of principles for substitution and sun-setting under the proposed framework and their antecedents in Swedish chemicals policy at sections 3.3.2.3 and 3.3.2.4.

The introduction of such a legal framework would require reform of the processes by which policy is made. Historical and current opposition to extending environmental assessment to policy-making indicates that this would encounter institutional resistance.[11] It has been argued that it would be inappropriate, and, indeed, unrealistic to constrain complex practices involved with weighing up a multitude of conflicting values and determining what actions should be taken in the national interest within an environmental 'strait jacket'.[12] However, my response to this argument is that the prized flexibility of policy formation is incompatible with the rigour that is required in decision-making if the degradation of ecosystems is to be halted, and that it must, to an extent, be sacrificed to ensure that policies contribute to reducing risks of ecological harm.

I make proposals in Section 3.4 as to how the loose and informal approach that prevails in policy-making might be reformed with a view to ensuring that ecological considerations are prioritised. Aspects of current practices that my proposals address include the lack of systematisation that results in policies that are implicit as well as those which are formally presented as representing governmental positions, and the division of responsibilities amongst ministries which makes it difficult to achieve a coherent response to issues whose resolution requires national direction. These might be addressed by adopting a 'whole of government' approach involving the review and periodic reappraisal of options for action in different policy areas under the leadership of a

[10] Chapter 2, Section 2.6. [11] Chapter 3, Section 3.4. [12] Ibid.

cross-governmental body with responsibility for coordinating the shift towards a low-risk society.

In addition, the anticipated resistance may make it difficult, until an ecological focus becomes part of the culture of policy-making, to ensure that assessments and strategies have an influence on policy contents. To address this concern, I propose that an independent body should be established with the authority to review proposed policy and to advise the government on how it might be revised to ensure consistency with statutory objectives for protecting ecosystems. This mechanism would be supported by rights of standing that would allow the government to be challenged in the event that the body's guidance is not followed.

3.1.3 Political will

Several significant issues would need to be addressed for the introduction of an ecologically oriented approach to policy-making. However, perhaps the most substantial obstacle to this is that sufficient political will would be required for politicians to introduce measures that would involve a re-evaluation of economic and social goals, to take actions that may well be electorally unpopular, and to accept constraints on the policy-making process.[13] The importance of respecting ecological limits for society's well-being has been recognised in the policies and legislation of some developed states.[14] However, as experience with New Zealand's Resource Management Act suggests, even statutory recognition of the need for ecologically responsible resource use is no guarantee that the political preparedness to control activities will follow.[15]

Despite this, I believe that there are good reasons for presenting proposals for the legal and institutional reforms that would be required for prioritising ecological considerations in policy-making whether or

[13] A. Jordan and A. Lenschow, 'Environmental Policy Integration: A State of the Art Review' (2010) 20 *Environmental Policy and Governance*, 150–1, 153–4.

[14] See for example Resource Management Act 1991 (NZ); The Council of Australian Governments, *National Strategy for Ecologically Sustainable Development* (Australian Government, 1992), http://www.environment.gov.au/about/esd/publications/strategy/index.html; Department for Environment, Food and Rural Affairs, *Securing the Future: The UK Government Sustainable Development Strategy* (HM Government, 2005).

[15] R. Connor and S. Dovers, 'Sustainable Management of Natural and Physical Resources: The New Zealand Resource Management Act 1991' in R. Connor and S. Dovers (eds) *Institutional Change for Sustainable Development* (Cheltenham: Edward Elgar Publishing, 2004), pp. 108–12; I. H. Williams, 'The Resource Management Act 1991: Well Meant But Hardly Done' (2000) 9 *Otago Law Review*, 673.

not the political will to implement them is present. The first is that, whilst the appetite for change may now be lacking, further evidence of global deterioration in the condition of ecosystems and its consequences may open windows of opportunity during which changes to the status quo would be possible.[16] It is important that templates for change should be available in the event that it is seen as politically important to take active steps for reducing stresses on the natural world.

The second is that, without a vision of how change could be effected, possibilities for a shift in society's course might be dismissed by decision-makers as unfeasible. Ecological sustainability may appear so far removed from present realities that even minor steps towards it would be dismissed as impossible. However, it may be the case, as Dreborg suggests, that 'our perceptions of what is possible or reasonable may be a major obstacle to real change'.[17] Dreborg argues that the planning technique of back-casting (see Section 3.3.4) can be used to show policy-forming authorities that the strengthening or weakening of unsustainable trends that appear from forecasting studies to be 'laws of nature' is, in fact, a matter of policy choice.[18] In the same way, the availability of credible proposals for decision-making in the face of uncertainty, for protecting ecosystems, and for reforming institutional practices would at least help decision-makers with recognising that, although the changes involved would be challenging, they are not impracticable.

3.2 Decision-making in the face of uncertainty

Situations in which we do not know what environmental impacts an action may have are frequently referred to as involving uncertainty. However, this catch-all term covers a variety of circumstances in which information about causal effects is unavailable and that have varying ramifications for the conduct of decision-making. Some commentators have argued that the different degrees of uncertainty should be categorised.[19] Their contention is that having an appreciation of how far removed we are from knowledge of the possible consequences that an

[16] M. Averill, 'Introduction: Resilience, Law, and Natural Resource Management' (2008) 87 *Nebraska Law Review*, 831–2; S. Dovers, 'Precautionary policy assessment for sustainability' in E. Fisher, J. Jones and R. von Schomberg (eds) *Implementing the Precautionary Principle: Perspectives and Prospects* (Cheltenham: Edward Elgar, 2006), p. 104.

[17] K. H. Dreborg, 'Essence of Backcasting' (1996) 28 *Futures*, 816. [18] Ibid., 822.

[19] B. Wynne, 'Uncertainty and Environmental Learning: Reconceiving Science and Policy in the Preventative Paradigm' (1992) 2 *Global Environmental Change*, 111; P. Harremoës et al.,

activity may have is fundamental to deciding how we should manage a risk that harm will be caused. For example, an inability to predict outcomes that is due to a lack of data may be addressed through monitoring and observation. Conversely, waiting on new information may be of no assistance where present ignorance of likely outcomes is due both to an inability to understand how natural systems behave and to their inherent unpredictability.[20]

Uncertainty over how human intervention may affect ecosystem health lies predominantly at this latter extreme of the term's spectral range. Our ignorance is such that it effectively precludes the meaningful use of risk assessment to decide whether action to advance economic and social objectives would be environmentally tolerable, and therefore of approaches to environmental decision-making that depend on the credible prediction of likely systemic reactions to human disturbance.[21] Accordingly, a decision-making approach over how activities should be controlled to reduce their cumulative impacts on ecosystem health is required which is not dependent on information about their causal consequences.

The question of how choices might be made where knowledge of their likely environmental effects is lacking has been and remains the subject of extensive debate. It is a key consideration in the sustainable development discourse. A broad consensus has emerged, as reflected in the influence of the precautionary principle, that a lack of scientific certainty should not provide a reason for inaction when threats of environmental harm are present.[22] I consider in this section whether the precautionary

'Twelve Late Lessons' in P. Harremoës et al. (eds) *The Precautionary Principle in the 20th Century: Late Lessons from Early Warnings* (London: Earthscan, 2002), pp. 185–90; S. R. Dovers and J. W. Handmer, 'Ignorance, Sustainability, and the Precautionary Principle: Towards an Analytical Framework' in R. Harding and E. Fisher (eds) *Perspectives on the Precautionary Principle* (Sydney: The Federation Press, 1999), pp. 167–83; J. Zander, *The Application of the Precautionary Principle in Practice: Comparative Dimensions* (Cambridge: Cambridge University Press, 2010), pp. 14–17; A. Klinke and O. Renn, 'Adaptive and Integrative Governance on Risk and Uncertainty' (2012) 15 *Journal of Risk Research*, 276–7.

20 Zander, 'Precautionary Principle in Practice', pp. 16–17; Klinke and Renn, 'Adaptive and Integrative Governance', 276–7.

21 Young, 'Uncertainty and the Environment', pp. 41–2; A. Stirling, 'Participation, Precaution and Reflexive Governance for Sustainable Development' in W. N. Adger and A. Jordan (eds) *Governing Sustainability* (Cambridge: Cambridge University Press, 2009), pp. 203–4; O. Renn, 'Precaution and the Governance of Risk' in W.N. Adger and A. Jordan (eds) *Governing Sustainability* (Cambridge: Cambridge University Press, 2009), pp. 232–5.

22 J. Wiener, 'Precaution' in D. Bodansky, J. Brunnée and E. Hey (eds) *The Oxford Handbook of International Environmental Law* (Oxford: Oxford University Press, 2007), p. 597; A. Trouwborst, 'The Precautionary Principle in General International

principle and the debate over its meaning and contents provide guidance on using law to protect ecosystems. I conclude that the principle as it is currently characterised does not assist with this task. It remains too rooted in assumptions concerning both the continued dominance of decision-making based on the prediction of cause and effect and that uncertainty is a temporary state of affairs that research will overcome to assist with decision-making for ecological protection. However, discussion of the principle is useful as analysis of its inadequacies for meeting the epistemic challenges that the protection of ecosystems presents points towards new conceptions of precaution and of precautionary action on which a legal framework for ecological policy-making can be founded.

3.2.1 Precaution under an ecological paradigm

There is significant controversy over the precise meaning and contents of the precautionary principle.[23] Many different formulations of the principle have been used in international and national instruments and argued for in the literature concerning its nature.[24] I do not join in the debate as to how, precisely, the principle should be defined, but base my analysis of it on four elementary components of the principle that reviews of its use in legal instruments and of its status in customary international law have identified.[25] These are: a threat of environmental harm should be present for its application; this should be of sufficient magnitude for a precautionary approach to be justified; there should be uncertainty over the environmental effects of the action under consideration; and, in such circumstances, effective but also proportionate steps should be taken at an early stage to prevent unacceptable environmental damage.[26]

Law: Combating the Babylonian Confusion' (2007) 16 *Review of European Community and International Environmental Law*, 185; A. Trouwborst, 'The Precautionary Principle and the Ecosystem Approach in International Law: Differences, Similarities and Linkages' (2009) 18 *Review of European Community and International Environmental Law*, 27.

23 Trouwborst, 'The Precautionary Principle in General International Law', 185–6; Zander, 'Precautionary Principle in Practice', p. 26.

24 Wiener, 'Precaution', p. 597; Zander, 'Precautionary Principle in Practice', pp. 26–32.

25 N. de Sadeleer, *Environmental Principles: From Political Slogans to Legal Rules* (Oxford: Oxford University Press, 2002), pp. 155–72; Trouwborst, 'The Precautionary Principle in General International Law', 187.

26 Ibid.

The first component of the principle restricts the circumstances in which it should be applied to those where there are reasonable grounds for believing that harm may be caused. What level and type of evidence is needed for this requirement to be satisfied is unclear although it is generally accepted that more-than-hypothetical risks should be present.[27] The desire to avoid wholly unnecessary restraint is understandable. However, the need to make a case for precaution in situations that are typically marked by a difficulty with predicting outcomes seems contradictory and likely to result in more instances of harm than of excessive caution. As Dovers and Handmer argue, it is paradoxical to expect that we should become knowledgeable about ignorance before precautionary action is taken to prevent environmental harm that, in better-informed circumstances, we would actively seek to avoid.[28]

Definitions of the precautionary principle in international, European and national law have further restricted its application by stating that possible harm resulting from a hazard should exceed a threshold.[29] Typical requirements are that this should be 'serious' or 'irreversible' or both.[30] Trouwborst advises that, for the precautionary principle to apply in customary international law, the anticipated environmental harm should be 'significant – that is, at a minimum, tangible and appreciable'.[31] Commentators view this as a necessity to prevent precaution being required in law where its use is not merited by the potential consequences of an action.[32] Even so, it could have the counterproductive effect for environmental protection of preventing the precautionary treatment of situations where there is a high degree of uncertainty over outcomes. De Sadeleer echoes Dovers and Handmer in questioning whether 'the desire to determine damage on the basis of these criteria leads to a paradox since its occurrence remains subject to scientific uncertainty'.[33] As he observes, this is particularly the case for ecological

[27] R. von Schomberg, 'The Precautionary Principle and its Normative Challenges' in E. Fisher, J. Jones, and R. von Schomberg (eds) *Implementing the Precautionary Principle: Perspectives and Prospects* (Cheltenham: Edward Elgar Publishing, 2006), p. 40; de Sadeleer, 'Environmental Principles', pp. 157–162; Trouwborst, 'The Precautionary Principle in General International Law', 188.

[28] S. R. Dovers and J. W. Handmer, 'Ignorance, the precautionary principle and sustainability' (1995) 24 *Ambio*, 93; M. B. A. van Asselt and E. Vos, 'The Precautionary Principle and the Uncertainty Paradox' (2006) 9 *Journal of Risk Research*, 317–8.

[29] de Sadeleer, 'Environmental Principles', pp. 161–7. [30] Ibid.

[31] Trouwborst, 'The Precautionary Principle in General International Law', 188–9.

[32] de Sadeleer, 'Environmental Principles', pp. 162–3. [33] Ibid., pp. 166–7.

processes whose complexity means that 'determining what damage may be anticipated is always a gamble'.[34]

Applying these restrictions to questions concerning the appropriateness of action to protect ecosystems provides a good illustration of the problems that they may generate. We know that the stresses which human activities place on ecosystems do erode their resilience and leave them vulnerable to events that may trigger a change in state, but it is often the case that we are not aware of this erosion or that a change in state is a possible outcome until after a regime shift has occurred. Even on an ex post analysis, we may not be able to identify with confidence the causes of change. The principle as it is currently constituted may not require action in respect of these threats because of the extreme difficulty with identifying the causal pathways by which they arise in systems whose complexity is beyond our current understanding. However, this would clearly be an unsatisfactory outcome in view of the possible consequences of ecosystem failure for our own well-being. In addition, factors that leave ecosystems more exposed to regime change without presenting an obvious risk of triggering this may not be regarded as presenting threats of significant damage themselves although they increase the likelihood that a highly undesirable situation will occur. However, bolstering the resilience of ecosystems should (as argued in Chapter 2) provide the focal point for legal regimes that seek to prevent ecological degradation. This conclusion suggests that the precautionary principle and notions of environmental damage on which it rests are ill-suited for ecological governance because this demands a proactive approach to reducing risks that harm will occur.

In view of these considerations, I suggest that a different conception of precaution is required for controlling the potential, but highly uncertain, effects of activities on ecosystem functionality. This would require that precautionary action be taken as a matter of course and despite an inability to point to clear risks of harm in particular circumstances. When confronted with the possibility that risks of 'poorly known' but 'high-impact events' occurring may be exacerbated by our own actions, a rational response would, as Sluijs and Turkenburg argue in the context of climate change, be to form precautionary strategies which seek, as far as possible, to reduce risks that the feared event will occur.[35]

[34] Ibid., p. 166.

[35] J. van der Sluijs and W. Turkenburg, 'Climate Change and the Precautionary Principle' in E. Fisher, J. Jones, and R. von Schomberg (eds) *Implementing the Precautionary*

The assumption that precaution is a departure from the normal condition of decision-making based on knowledge of cause and effect is incompatible with the endemic uncertainty found in connection with predicting the cumulative impacts of our activities on systemic properties such as resilience. Indeed, it is arguable that, for decision-making which takes the preservation of ecosystem health as its objective, precaution should be regarded as the standard approach. In light of this, I suggest that a different understanding of the precautionary principle is needed if environmental decision-making is to adapt to an ecological paradigm. Under this new conception, precaution would be understood to be a normative concept and one around which legal frameworks for ecological protection should be constructed. A trigger for precautionary action would not be required because uncertainty is recognised to be the medium within which decisions that may impact on ecosystems must be made.

3.2.2 Taking precautionary action

The fourth component of the precautionary principle is a requirement that, despite the unavailability of scientific evidence concerning the risks in question, action should be taken in sufficient time to prevent unacceptable environmental harm.[36] This aspect of the principle has been criticised because, in most of its formulations, no guidance is provided as to what precaution is or how we should decide what action to take when we do not know what impacts proposals under consideration may have.[37] Dovers and Handmer describe this as the second paradox of precaution: that, having been told to take anticipatory steps to prevent potential damage, decision-makers are left pondering how to anticipate outcomes that are uncertain, indeterminate or simply unknowable.[38]

One conclusion that might be drawn from this lack of clarity is that, in essence, the principle requires only that holding action be taken pending the generation of information that will allow the resumption of decision-making based on causal knowledge. This is a view that is likely to be

Principle: Perspectives and Prospects (Cheltenham: Edward Elgar Publishing, 2006), pp. 261–2. See also Klinke and Renn, 'Adaptive and Integrative Governance', 284–6.

36 Trouwborst, 'The Precautionary Principle in General International Law', 189.

37 Dovers and Handmer, 'Ignorance, Sustainability and the Precautionary Principle', p. 174; Young, 'Uncertainty and the Environment', p. 17; J. A. Tickner and K. Geiser, 'The Precautionary Principle Stimulus for Solutions – and Alternatives-based Environmental Policy' (2004) 24 *Environmental Impact Assessment Review*, 805.

38 Dovers and Handmer, 'Ignorance and the Precautionary Principle', 94.

favoured by those who have criticised the lack of direction that the principle gives on grounds that it may legitimise arbitrary decision-making,[39] or who are sceptical over the possibility of making valid decisions on precautionary action when a high degree of uncertainty about the risks involved is present.[40] However, such a narrow understanding of the principle is clearly unsuited for addressing situations of uncertainty that are not capable of easy resolution through scientific research, but which, if they are not addressed, may result in serious and potentially irreversible consequences for ecosystems. For issues that raise more than 'soft uncertainty', a conception of precaution is required which recognises the need for action to prevent harm that goes beyond gathering sufficient knowledge to characterise the risks that proposed activities may present.

Trouwborst advises that 'proportionality' has been widely accepted as a guide for precautionary action in international law.[41] A proportionate action is one that would correspond to the probability that harm will be caused and the likely magnitude of that harm.[42] However, as with the trigger for the principle's application, this concept assumes that enough will be known about a situation to assess what risks of damage are present. It provides no direction in circumstances where the range of possible outcomes is unidentifiable.[43] Again, it is clear that a new understanding of precaution is required to replace expectations that scientific knowledge of cause and effect will reveal the way forwards with a clear mandate for action to protect ecosystems despite our ignorance of how human disturbance causes them to fail.

3.2.3 *Normative precaution*

Reluctance to move away from decision-making based on knowledge of cause and effect reflects a prevailing unwillingness to choose between environmental protection and the pursuit of objectives that are seen to be economically and socially advantageous. The hope is that scientific

[39] E. Fisher, J. Jones, and R. von Schomberg, 'Implementing the Precautionary Principle: Perspectives and Prospects' in E. Fisher, J. Jones, and R. von Schomberg (eds) *Implementing the Precautionary Principle: Perspectives and Prospects* (Cheltenham: Edward Elgar Publishing, 2006), pp. 5–6.

[40] A. Kinzig and D. Starrett, 'Coping with Uncertainty: A Call for a New Science-Policy Forum' (2003) 32 *Ambio*, 330.

[41] Trouwborst, 'The Precautionary Principle in General International Law', 189. See also de Sadeleer, 'Environmental Principles', pp. 167–70.

[42] Trouwborst, 'The Precautionary Principle in General International Law', 189.

[43] de Sadeleer, 'Environmental Principles', pp. 167–8.

information will point to solutions that allow economic growth and advance societal wealth whilst leaving natural support systems intact. It is this unwillingness that has prevented the sustainability agenda from presenting a coherent vision of an environmentally desirable future. However, as our focus turns to how the functionality of ecosystems might be preserved, this choice cannot be avoided. This is because of the many difficulties with knowing how ecosystems will react to human intervention that I refer to in this section. It is also due to the nature of resilience which, as it is impossible to identify a level at which this property might be judged sufficient to prevent ecological collapse, precludes the assumption that trade-offs between environmental health and economic and social goals can be made as long as an ecological bottom line is not breached.

As argued in Chapter 2,[44] reflection on what is important for our own well-being should lead to recognition that ecosystem health is of supervening value for us and that we should do what we can to prevent our actions from harming it. This evaluation, when coupled with consciousness of the threats that our activities present for ecosystem functionality, provides the starting point for consideration of what form a precautionary principle that is adapted to the needs of ecological protection would take. I suggest that a principle cast in this mould would require that positive action be taken to address risks of ecological harm. This would involve the exploration of how far the erosive effects that human activities have on resilience and the threats they present to the functionality of ecosystems might be reduced. It would also require the harnessing of our institutional structures to ensure that they contribute to this effort.

An ecological conception of precaution would be strongly normative in driving a societal shift away from reliance on practices that present threats of harm. It would also, in its forward-looking nature, come closer than its reactive forbear to the origins of the principle in the *vorsorge* concept with its emphasis on avoidance of environmental damage by forward planning.[45] The current model of precaution requires only that the need for precautionary action should be considered when concerns

[44] Chapter 2, Section 2.5.

[45] M. O'Brien, 'Science in the Service of Good: The Precautionary Principle and Positive Goals' in J. A. Tickner (ed.) *Precaution, Environmental Science and Preventative Public Policy* (Washington, DC: Island Press, 2003), p. 279; Tickner and Geiser, 'The Precautionary Principle Stimulus', 804–5; T. Aven, *Misconceptions of Risk* (Chichester: John Wiley and Sons, 2010), p. 216.

arise over the effects that action or inaction may have on the environment. In contrast, the model that I propose would require that proactive precautionary action be taken at all times to reduce risks that ecological problems will arise, and that governmental action should be directed towards advancing that end.

3.3 A legal framework for ecologically oriented policy-making

A normative conception of precaution would provide guidance as to how we should respond to unpredictable but potentially catastrophic threats of ecological harm. However, institutional structures that actively promote the reduction of risk are required if this guidance is to be given practical effect. The primary objective of these structures should be to reduce the stresses that we place on ecosystems and which expose them to, and threaten to force the occurrence of, changes in their states. This is identified by several commentators as a necessary response to risks of ecological degradation, including those posed by climate change, in the face of uncertainty over the causes, timing and consequences of ecosystem failure.[46] In addition, they should institute a culture of decision-making that aims, through strategic planning, to reduce the likelihood and, as far as possible, the magnitude of unwelcome environmental surprises.

In this section, I set out proposals for a legal framework for policy-making that seeks, through adopting a precautionary approach, to enhance ecological and societal resilience. It does this by requiring that, in the formation of policy, preference should be given to ways of meeting objectives that, cumulatively, place least stress on ecosystems. In addition, it requires that options which present too great a threat to ecosystem health should be discontinued and plans developed for their replacement. The

[46] M. Nilsson and A. Persson, 'Can Earth System Interactions be Governed? Governance Functions for Linking Climate Change Mitigation with Land Use, Freshwater, and Biodiversity Protection' (2012) 75 *Ecological Economics*, 66; F. S. Chapin III et al., 'A Framework for Understanding Change' in F. S. Chapin III, C. Folke and G. P. Kofinas (eds) *Principles of Ecosystem Stewardship: Resilience-based Natural Resource Management in a Changing World* (New York: Springer, 2009), pp. 18–22; R. K. Craig, '"Stationarity is Dead" – Long Live Transformation: Five Principles for Climate Change Adaptation Law' (2010) 34 *Harvard Environmental Law Review*, 34–9. See also Rockström et al., 'Planetary Boundaries' and G. Garver, 'Introducing the rule of ecological law' in L. Westra, C. L. Soskolne and D. W. Spady (eds) *Human Health and Ecological Integrity: Ethics, Law and Human Rights* (Abingdon: Routledge, 2012), pp. 322–5 in the context of maintaining a safe distance from planetary boundaries.

framework's principal mechanisms for advancing its ends are the assessment of alternatives against criteria by which their compatibility with objectives for ecological protection can be judged and the development of strategies for increasing reliance on preferred alternatives. These mechanisms operate together to produce visions of futures in which anthropogenic stresses on the natural world are lessened, and scenarios that explore how those visions might be realised for use both in public discussion of what actions we should take to reduce risks of ecological harm in the face of uncertainty, and, ultimately, for decision-making on policy contents.

A legal framework that requires an ecological focus in policy-making is desirable in a number of respects. The loss of resilience is, to a large extent, a product of the combined effects of our activities on ecosystems. It is through consideration of the direct impacts that the choices we make have and the preference in all aspects of policy-making for the least ecologically consequential options that anthropogenic stresses might best be controlled. In addition, direct effects are, themselves, the product of unsustainable patterns of consumption. Policy choices can serve either to entrench these patterns or to promote economic and social change. Accordingly, it is at this level of decision-making that most can be done to address the underlying drivers of ecological degradation.

Current practice of environmental policy assessment is far removed from the proposals made in this chapter. The conduct of assessments that examine policy proposals explicitly from an environmental perspective is limited to a small group of developed countries and international institutions.[47] Techniques used are mostly derived from environmental impact assessment and concerned only with predicting the effects of policies rather than exploring whether they are capable of delivering an environmentally desirable future.[48] The assessment processes themselves are, for the most part, not legally required, informal and lacking in transparency.[49] In contrast, some form of general policy assessment has become widespread in the Organisation for Economic Co-operation

[47] K. Ahmed and E. Sánchez-Triana, 'Strategic Environmental Assessment and Policy Formation' in K. Ahmed and E. Sánchez-Triana (eds) *Strategic Environmental Assessment for Policies: An Instrument for Good Governance* (Washington, DC: The World Bank, 2008), pp. 5–6; B. Sadler (ed.) 'Strategic Environmental Assessment at the Policy Level: Recent Progress, Current Status and Future Prospects' (report produced for the United Nations Economic Commission for Europe, 2005), p. 1, pp. 13–14.

[48] Sadler, 'Strategic Environmental Assessment', pp. 15–16.

[49] Ibid., pp. 11–28. See also Jordan and Lenschow, 'Environmental Policy Integration', 152–3.

and Development (OECD) and EU countries during the last two decades.[50] This is a response, in part, to calls for integration of environmental considerations into decision-making in connection with the sustainable development agenda.[51] However, this has not always resulted in a higher profile for environmental objectives in policy formation with Adelle and Weiland reporting in 2012 that these 'may or may not be a significant feature of a policy assessment system, if present at all'.[52] Even where policy assessment processes require that environmental goals and impacts should be taken into account in policy-making, these are often given a much lower profile than analysis of the economic benefits of policy and of regulatory efficiency that have had a stronger influence on the evolution of policy assessment practices.[53]

It is fair to conclude that environmental policy assessment remains, as Boothroyd described it in 1995, 'conceptually, practically and terminologically inchoate'.[54] If there is to be meaningful progress towards ecological sustainability, a new model for policy assessment is required under which policy options are identified and assessed in terms of goals for ecological protection. I concur with Boothroyd's argument that policy assessment should consist not only of exploring policy's unintended impacts, but also of its effectiveness for attaining and consistency with its objectives.[55] The framework I propose provides for the latter in its requirements for alternatives assessment and for the independent review of policy proposals. It also provides for the former at two stages:

[50] C. Adelle and S. Weiland, 'Policy Assessment: The State of the Art' (2012) 30 *Impact Assessment and Project Appraisal*, 25–27.

[51] Ibid., 26.

[52] Ibid., 25 and 27. See also K. Jacob et al., 'Improving the practice of impact assessment', EVIA (Evaluating Integrated Impact Assessments) Policy Briefing, Project No. 028889, European Commission, Sixth Framework Programme (2008).

[53] Adele and Weiland, 'Policy Assessment', 28; D. Russel and J. Turnpenny, 'The Politics of Sustainable Development in UK Government: What Role for Integrated Policy Appraisal?' (2009) 27 *Environment and Planning C: Government and Policy*, 349; J. Hertin, K. Jacob and A. Volkery, 'Policy Appraisal' in A. Jordan and A. Lenschow (eds) *Innovation in Environmental Policy? Integrating the Environment for Sustainability* (Cheltenham: Edward Elgar, 2008), p. 130; Jacob et al., 'Improving Impact Assessment', p. 5.

[54] P. Boothroyd, 'Policy Assessment' in F. Vanclay and D. A. Bronstein (eds) *Environmental and Social Impact Assessment* (Chichester: John Wiley, 1995), p. 93. Similar conclusions are reached in Hertin et al., 'Policy Appraisal', pp. 126–30 and in Jordan and Lenschow, 'Environmental Policy Integration', 152–3.

[55] Boothroyd, 'Policy Assessment', p. 105. See also P. Boothroyd, 'Integrating Economy, Society and Environment through Policy Assessment' in R. Woollard and A. Ostry (eds) *Fatal Consumption: Rethinking Sustainable Development* (Vancouver: University of British Columbia Press, 2000), pp. 130–65.

the assessment of potential restraints on reducing ecological stress as part of strategy formation and the identification of measures by which these might be addressed; and the assessment of economic and social impacts of strategies with a view to providing information for discussion and decision-making on policy contents. However, I depart from Boothroyd's proposals for policy assessment in an important respect. These are concerned with the assessment of extant or proposed policies and their amelioration. A system for ecological governance should go further in requiring that the assessment of options for meeting objectives in different policy areas should be conducted periodically as part of a 'whole of government' review. It calls for policy that is designed to drive societal change rather than seeking the incremental improvement of policy proposals as they arise.

3.3.1 *Ecological protection as a strategic objective*

A legal framework for policy-making must, if it is to result in better ecological outcomes, provide a clear statement at its outset of the ends that policies should achieve. Clarity about the goals of the process gives direction as to how mechanisms for policy formation should be applied. For example, the availability of an overarching vision against which the assessment of policy options might be conducted is essential if the alternatives that are most likely to reach desired ends are to be identified.[56] A statutorily entrenched objective for policy-making will also promote change in the way that decisions on policy contents are made although, as discussed in Section 3.4, statutory entrenchment is not, of itself, sufficient to drive institutional change.

The statement of objectives I propose would make it clear that the purpose of ecologically oriented policy-making is to reduce the erosive effects of human activities on the resilience of ecosystems, and to end reliance on activities that are most likely to trigger change in their states. It would also require that, in light of this, policies should be designed to reduce anthropogenic stresses on ecosystems that may expose them to, or cause, regime shifts as far as possible, and within the quickest feasible timescales for social and economic adaptation.

A statement of this kind would not create substantive goals for policy-making. The reality is that our poor understanding of ecological behaviour

[56] B. F. Noble, 'Strategic Environmental Assessment: What is it and What Makes it Strategic?' (2000) 2 *Journal of Environmental Assessment, Policy, and Management*, 207.

and the relative nature of resilience would prevent us from identifying definitive points at which we could say that a desired level of ecosystem health has been reached. Rather, it would establish enhancing the resilience of ecosystems and reducing the stresses we place on them as ideals to be observed in the conduct of decision-making. This approach can be compared with the use of 'sustainability' in some legal contexts as an ideal of how development should be conducted rather than as an endpoint towards which it is desired that natural systems should evolve.[57] However, the wording I propose differs from typical uses of 'sustainability' in making it clear that ecological values should be prioritised over economic and social goods in determining policy contents. 'Sustainability', save where environmental limits on the pursuit of economic and social goals are made clear in its definition, does not provide an effective guide for improved environmental protection because it presents no vision of the environmental conditions that are desired.[58]

3.3.2 *Principles for ecological policy-making*

As experience with New Zealand's Resource Management Act indicates, a statutory definition of expected outcomes is not itself sufficient to ensure that ecological protection will be advanced.[59] Observance of the Act's requirement that ecological limits should be respected in resource management was hampered by the lack of explanation in the legislation of how it should be applied and of following guidance on how the Act should be implemented.[60] In contrast, the objective I propose is supported by principles that give guidance on how the policy process should be conducted and for the evaluation of policy options. These principles are discussed in the following sections.

3.3.2.1 Reducing consumption

An effective means of alleviating ecological stress would be the significant reduction of existing levels of consumption, and particularly where these drive the use of resources and the conduct of activities that present

[57] A. Bagheri and P. Hjorth, 'Planning for Sustainable Development: A Paradigm Shift Towards a Process-based Approach' (2007) 15 *Sustainable Development*, 84.

[58] A. Ross, *Sustainable Development Law in the UK: From Rhetoric to Reality?* (Abingdon: Earthscan, 2012), p. 292, 299–301; K. Bosselmann, 'From Reductionist Environmental Law to Sustainability Law' in P. Burdon (ed.) *Exploring Wild Law: The Philosophy of Earth Jurisprudence* (Kent Town: The Wakefield Press, 2011), pp. 204–13.

[59] Connor and Dovers, 'Sustainable Management', pp. 108–9.

[60] Ibid.

clear threats to ecosystem health.[61] However, securing change in patterns of consumption is hugely challenging.[62] The fact that consumption is intrinsic to economic growth and to conceptions of what is needed for a good quality of life makes its reduction problematic.[63] It is also something that cannot be addressed through policy alone, but which would require substantial change in everyone's lifestyles and values.[64] Despite this, much can be done through governmental action to influence individual and social behaviour.[65] The provision of appropriate opportunities and fora for participation in ecological governance by the state can, as I argue in Chapters 4 and 6, increase the likelihood that people will come to accept that governmental action to protect ecosystems is both necessary and legitimate, and choose themselves to live in ways that reduce demand on resources. It is also only through decision-making at this level of governance that change might be made to the current economic model so that it is less reliant on continual increases in the amount we consume.[66] The formation of a coherent strategy for reducing consumption must therefore, despite the attendant difficulties, be the first consideration in devising a government-wide programme and associated policies for reducing risks of ecological harm.

The first principle for policy-making that I propose is that the reduction of levels of consumption and consideration of how governmental action might be used to promote this should be prioritised in policy formation. This principle is given practical effect by a requirement at the strategy formation stage that a credible package of measures for tackling consumption should be produced. Whilst this is a 'whole of government' issue in that the factors which drive it are highly interconnected, it might also be considered from the perspective of discrete policy areas. For

[61] Ross, 'Sustainable Development', pp. 302–4; D. Farber, 'Sustainable Consumption, Energy Policy, and Individual Well-being' (2012) 65 *Vanderbilt Law Review*, 1483–6.

[62] D. L. Goldblatt, *Sustainable Energy Consumption and Society: Personal, Technological, or Social Change?* (Dordrecht: Springer, 2005), p. 67.

[63] I. Røpke, 'Ecological Economics: Consumption Drivers and Impacts' in C. Lever-Tracy (ed.) *Routledge Handbook of Climate Change and Society* (Abingdon: Routledge, 2010), pp. 121–30; T. Jackson et al., 'Beyond Insatiability: Needs Theory, Consumption and Sustainability' in L. A. Reisch and I. Røpke (eds) *The Ecological Economics of Consumption* (Cheltenham: Edward Elgar, 2004), pp. 79–110.

[64] Curry, 'Ecological Ethics', pp. 21–3; Røpke, 'Ecological Economics', pp. 123–4, pp. 128–9.

[65] Ross, 'Sustainable Development', pp. 302–4; Farber, 'Sustainable Consumption', 1502–21; T. Jackson, *Prosperity without Growth: Economics for a Finite Planet* (London: Earthscan, 2009), pp. 158–61.

[66] Jackson, 'Prosperity without Growth', pp. 158–61, 166–9.

example, techniques for strategic planning have been used to explore not only how less environmentally harmful means of meeting energy demands might be deployed, but also to examine how far demand for energy might be reduced, over what timescales reductions might be achieved, and what policy measures might be used to promote this.[67]

3.3.2.2 Obviating development

Alleviating the pressures we place on ecosystems by reducing our expectations of the quality of life that natural resources can support is a long-term objective. Its pursuit would operate as a separate initiative although its success or failure would inevitably have major implications for the extent to which permanent reductions in anthropogenic stresses can be achieved. In the meantime, demand should be met in ways that present as little threat of harm as possible to the health of ecosystems. With this end in mind, we must consider whether needs can be satisfied without taking action that will generate additional stress. For example, might the construction of new power plants be avoided by making the products that consume energy more efficient and through the better insulation and more energy-efficient design of existing and new homes, and buildings?

Commentators who have argued for a more environmentally progressive use of strategic environmental assessment contend that its first aim should be to explore whether there are ways of meeting demand or of managing it so that new development might be avoided.[68] The UK Government's guide of 2005 on strategic environmental assessment also advises that the first question in identifying and assessing alternatives should be whether demand can be met without a proposed plan or programme being implemented.[69] I agree that options which would genuinely achieve policy objectives without adding to stresses should be preferred. However, the reality is that, in ecological terms, such possibilities will be

[67] K. L. Anderson, 'Reconciling the Electricity Industry with Sustainable Development: Backcasting – a Strategic Alternative' (2001) 33 *Futures*, 607.

[68] E. Joao, 'Key Principles of Strategic Environmental Assessment' in M. Schmidt, E. Joao, and E. Albrecht (eds) *Implementing Strategic Environmental Assessment* (Berlin: Springer, 2005), p. 7; R. Goodland, 'Strategic Environmental Assessment' in A. L. Porter and J. J. Fittipaldi (eds) *Environmental Methods Review: Retooling Impact Assessment for the New Century* (Fargo: The Press Club, 1998), p. 89.

[69] Office of the Deputy Prime Minister, 'A Practical Guide to the Strategic Environmental Assessment Directive' (HM Government, 2005), pp. 68–9.

unusual.[70] For example, many initiatives for enhanced energy efficiency will require resource consumption to provide new equipment and insulating material. Many of the examples that the UK Government's guidance document gives of options that would avoid major infrastructure development would also require construction to provide better local facilities.[71] Accordingly, I do not propose that preference for options which would obviate development should be a separate principle for policy-making. Instead, the ecological consequences of efficiency measures would fall to be assessed alongside those of other options for meeting demand.

3.3.2.3 Substitution

The second principle for policy-making is that options which are assessed to present the least threat to ecosystem health should be preferred. Needs should be met in ways which, comparatively, are judged as being least likely to erode the resilience of ecosystems or to trigger change in their states. The principle corresponds with and supports normative precaution's aim of risk reduction. Options that are assessed to present the greatest threat of harm would be ranked lowest amongst alternatives for meeting policy objectives and their use discontinued if less-harmful alternatives are available.[72] In addition, it acts as a stimulus for the development of new technologies and, generally, for the identification of ecologically desirable solutions to policy issues. When coupled with a requirement for the rolling review of policy, the principle establishes perpetual movement away from reliance on options that heighten threats of ecological degradation as a central aim of government.[73]

The principle shares parallels with the substitution principle which has been employed in Swedish chemicals policy to promote the

[70] G. Pring et al., 'The Impact of Energy on Health, Environment and Sustainable Development: the TANSTAAFL Problem' in D. N. Zillman, C. Redgwell, Y. O. Omorogbe and L. K. Barrera-Hernández (eds) *Beyond the Carbon Economy* (Oxford: Oxford University Press, 2008), pp. 13–15.

[71] Office of the Deputy Prime Minister, 'A Practical Guide', pp. 70–1.

[72] This approach corresponds with that prescribed by the maximin rule for decision-making under conditions of ignorance. The rule directs that, in such circumstances, a rational decision-maker should choose the option whose worst possible outcome is not worse than that presented by any other option's worst possible outcome. For further discussion of this rule see O. Godard, 'The Precautionary Principle and Catastrophism on Tenterhooks: Lessons from a Constitutional Reform in France' in E. Fisher, J. Jones and R. von Schomberg (eds) *Implementing the Precautionary Principle: Perspectives and Prospects* (Cheltenham: Edward Elgar, 2006), p. 77; and C. Munthe, *The Price of Precaution and the Ethics of Risk* (Dordrecht: Springer, 2011), pp. 44–50.

[73] Chapter 3, Section 3.4.2.1.

development and use of alternatives to hazardous substances.[74] The Swedish Environmental Code requires that chemical products or biotechnical organisms 'that may involve risks to human health or the environment' should not be used or sold 'if products or organisms that are assumed to be less dangerous can be used instead'.[75] This approach is similar to that which would be used under the principle I propose. It is intended to stimulate the invention of new and less-harmful chemicals in the expectation that a market will be available for them as a replacement.[76] However, the existing and proposed principles differ in two important respects. Firstly, the costs involved with substitution under Swedish law are a relevant consideration in determining whether an alternative is 'suitable'.[77] The principle's ability to drive ecological change is therefore limited by economic factors. Conversely, options for ecologically oriented policy are to be chosen and ranked by reference only to the harms they may present for ecosystem health and the technical feasibility of their use. To do otherwise would be to constrain the framework's ability to promote improved ecological protection by rooting consideration of what is achievable in the present. A better approach is (as argued at Section 3.3.4) to form a vision of how needs might be met using preferred alternatives, and then to explore what measures might be taken to address the economic and social impacts that the implementation of 'ideal' strategies may have.

The second is that, in Swedish law, substitution is concerned only with substances that are recognised to present risks of harm to human health or the environment.[78] As discussed in connection with the precautionary

[74] B. Wahlström, 'The Precautionary Approach to Chemicals Management: A Swedish Perspective' in C. Raffensperger and J. Tickner (eds) *Protecting Public Health and the Environment: Implementing the Precautionary Principle* (Washington, DC: Island Press, 1999), p. 51; O. Mont, 'The Swedish Product Choice Principle' (2001) 10 *European Environmental Law Review*, 351; Zander, 'Precautionary Principle in Practice', pp. 334–8; A. Nilsson, 'The Precautionary Principle in Swedish Chemicals Law and Policy' in N. de Sadeleer (ed.) *Implementing the Precautionary Principle: Approaches from the Nordic Countries, the EU and USA* (London: Earthscan, 2007), pp. 307–10; M. Karlsson, 'The Precautionary Principle, Swedish Chemicals Policy and Sustainable Development' (2006) 9 *Journal of Risk Research*, 342–3, 347–8.

[75] Chapter 2, Section 2.6, The Environmental Code [DS 2000: 61] (Sweden, 1999), http://www.sweden.gov.se/content/1/c6/02/28/47/385ef12a.pdf.

[76] Karlsson, 'Precautionary Principle and Swedish Chemicals Policy', 351.

[77] Chapter 2, Section 2.7, The Environmental Code; Mont, 'The Swedish Product Choice Principle', 353; Karlsson, 'Precautionary Principle and Swedish Chemicals Policy', 348.

[78] Chapter 2, Section 2.6, The Environmental Code; Mont, 'The Swedish Product Choice Principle', 352.

principle, a threshold perception of a threat of environmental harm could prevent precautionary action being taken to prevent ecological degradation because of ignorance over how human disturbance affects ecosystem functionality. In contrast, the mechanism for alternatives assessment under the framework requires that the ecological impacts of all options for meeting policy objectives be considered so that policies which are most likely to enhance the protection of ecosystems can be drawn up.

3.3.2.4 Sunsetting

A prudential approach to ecological protection in circumstances of profound uncertainty requires that the least-hazardous alternatives for meeting demand should be preferred and that options which may imperil the things that we value should be avoided.[79] Substitution provides one means of reducing reliance on those of our activities that place most stress on ecosystems. However, it is not, itself, sufficient for dealing with practices that present significant threats to ecosystem health. A separate principle for policy-making is required in respect of those activities that are most likely to engender or be the direct cause of ecological regime shifts.

A practice known as 'sunsetting' has been used in Swedish chemicals policy for the progressive elimination of substances that are regarded as being of high concern because of their potential impacts on environmental and human health.[80] A sunsetting approach has also been adopted by the body responsible for governance of the Great Lakes region to eradicate the use of certain toxic chemicals.[81] A third principle for ecological policy-making would draw from these practices in requiring that options which present unacceptable risks of harm to ecosystem health should be discontinued. This would require that they be phased

[79] R. Gibson et al., *Sustainability Assessment: Criteria and Processes* (London: Earthscan, 2005), p. 117.

[80] Wahlström, 'The Precautionary Approach', p. 62; Tickner and Geiser, 'The Precautionary Principle Stimulus', 812; Zander, 'Precautionary Principle in Practice', pp. 335–6; Nilsson, 'Precautionary Principle in Swedish Chemicals Law', pp. 309–10; Karlsson, 'Precautionary Principle and Swedish Chemicals Policy', 349–50, 352–3. See also information at the Internet site of the Swedish Chemicals Agency (KEMI) concerning its work to achieve a 'non-toxic environment' in line with an environmental quality objective set by the Swedish government in 1999 at: http://www.kemi.se/en/Start/A-Non-Toxic-Environment.

[81] J. A. Tickner (1999) 'A Map Toward Precautionary Decision Making' in C. Raffensperger and J. A. Tickner (eds) *Protecting Public Health and the Environment: Implementing the Precautionary Principle* (Washington, DC: Island Press, 1999), p. 179.

out in the shortest feasible timescale for their replacement with preferred options unless it is judged that the concerns they give rise to are such that earlier discontinuation is required or, exceptionally, that a longer lead-in time is necessary for economic and social adaptation. The proposed principle again corresponds with the precautionary requirements of risk reduction and that forward-looking laws and policies should be used to drive this process. Phasing out activities is likely to provide a particularly effective stimulus for the development of new and more ecologically friendly products, processes, or other means of replacing them.[82]

An obvious difficulty for sunsetting is our uncertainty over the precise effects that activities may have, whether individually or in combination with others, on ecosystem functionality. As argued in the following section, this might be addressed through the use of criteria to assess qualitatively whether an option's characteristics are such that it is or is not tolerable from an ecological perspective. A further complication is how economic and social impacts of phasing out products or activities should be managed. I propose that ways in which phase-outs might be conducted with a view to mitigating these impacts should be explored in the strategy-formation stage. However, it is important if the framework is to drive change in the way we protect ecosystems that decisions on whether an option should be prohibited are made purely on ecological grounds.

3.3.3 *Assessing alternative policy options*

The assessment of alternatives is central to a policy-making approach that seeks to identify the best means available of achieving environmental policy goals.[83] Both Tickner and O'Brien, in their respective calls for a less-reactive conception of the precautionary principle, advocate alternatives assessment as a means of replacing the analysis of risks presented by particular proposals and the determination of causality with the proactive consideration of whether less hazardous alternatives

[82] Karlsson, 'Precautionary Principle and Swedish Chemicals Policy', 350–1.

[83] See the discussion of alternatives assessment in connection with substituting hazardous chemicals in J. A. Tickner et al., 'Alternatives Assessment in Regulatory Policy: History and Future Directions' in R. E. Hester and R. M. Harrison (eds) *Chemical Alternatives Assessment* (Cambridge: The Royal Society of Chemistry, 2013), pp. 256–95.

are available to satisfy needs.[84] Noble, in his argument for a genuinely strategic form of environmental assessment, also emphasises its potential role in aiding the selection of the best alternatives to reach desired ends.[85] I concur with these views in proposing that the assessment of different options should be conducted as the first stage in ecological policy formation.

The practice of assessing alternatives to proposed governmental plans and programmes as part of strategic environmental assessment is well-established.[86] This typically involves comparing a range of 'reasonable' alternatives with extant policies or proposals. The hope is that this will promote ascertainment and adoption of the option that is best from an environmental perspective amongst those considered although not necessarily of the best options for environmental protection.[87] My proposals for alternatives assessment go beyond current practice in requiring that an absolute review be conducted of the different means available for meeting needs in policy areas under consideration. The purpose of this review would be to identify those options that would present the lowest collective threat of harm to ecosystem health. The options to be considered under this process would include means of achieving ends that avoid development or which otherwise depart from typical practices for meeting demand. By way of example, the ecological ramifications of avoiding large power plant construction through promoting decentralised generation would be a relevant consideration in the energy context. The intended output of alternatives assessment is a hierarchy of options ranked according to their propensity to erode resilience and contribute to the triggering of regime shifts which might then be used in the development of strategies for risk reduction and, ultimately, in policy formation.

The key issue for alternatives assessment under the framework is how different options are to be evaluated when we are uncertain about what their causal impacts on ecosystem functionality would be if deployed.

[84] M. O'Brien, 'Alternatives Assessment: Part of Operationalizing and Institutionalizing the Precautionary Principle' in C. Raffensperger and J. A. Tickner (eds) *Protecting Public Health and the Environment: Implementing the Precautionary Principle* (Washington, DC: Island Press, 1999), pp. 207–19; Tickner, 'Precautionary Decision-making', pp. 267–8, 274–6.

[85] Noble, 'Strategic Environmental Assessment', 210.

[86] M. F. Tetlow and M. Hanusch, 'Strategic Environmental Assessment: The State of the Art' (2012) 30 *Impact Assessment and Project Appraisal*, 17–18.

[87] A. J. Bond and A. Morrison-Saunders, 'Sustainability Appraisal: Jack of all Trades, Master of None?' (2009) 27 *Impact Assessment and Project Appraisal*, 326–7.

I suggest that, to overcome this difficulty, qualitative criteria corresponding to characteristics that may undermine ecosystem health should be used as the basis for assessment. The criteria should be formulated to advance the statutory objective of reducing anthropogenic pressures on ecosystem functionality by exploring the extent to which an option would make demands on, or otherwise affect, the natural world. For example, would it require the consumption of resources? Would its use result in the emission of greenhouse gases? This approach provides a means of addressing our inability to identify likely effects of activities on systemic properties. It is, in any event, well-suited to a legal framework concerned with ecological protection as it displays an appropriate level of concern for the preservation of what is ecologically valuable. This can be contrasted with current practices that gamble on the accuracy of prediction in the misplaced hope that opportunities for economic and social gain might be maximised without causing ecological degradation.

Commentators on risk management in the face of uncertainty have argued for decision-making by reference to qualitative criteria. Klinke and Renn suggest that when potential damage and its probabilities are unknown or contested, measures of hazardousness such as ubiquity, irreversibility and pervasiveness should be used 'as proxies for judging severity'.[88] Stirling and Harremoës have argued in the contexts of food and chemicals regulation respectively that assessment should be conducted by reference to 'intrinsic hazard properties' with criteria such as bioaccumulativity and persistence being used to determine the extent of environmental and health concerns presented by a substance.[89] This means of evaluation might also be used for assessing the characteristics of different policy options and their consistency with an objective of ecological protection. Criteria that reflect the importance of diversity in ecosystems and of other properties that are believed to promote resilience might be used to assess the extent to which different alternatives could impinge on the functionality of ecosystems. General criteria such

88 A. Klinke and O. Renn, 'A New Approach to Risk Evaluation and Management: Risk-based, Precaution-based, and Discourse-based Strategies' (2002) 22 *Risk Analysis*, 1091. See also O. Renn, *Risk Governance: Coping with Uncertainty in a Complex World* (London: Earthscan, 2008), pp. 193–6; and Renn, 'Precaution and the Governance of Risk', pp. 238–9.

89 A. Stirling, O. Renn and P. van Zwanenburg, 'A Framework for the Precautionary Governance of Food Safety: Integrating Science and Participation in the Social Appraisal of Risk' in E. Fisher, J. Jones and R. von Schomberg (eds) *Implementing the Precautionary Principle: Perspectives and Prospects* (Cheltenham: Edward Elgar, 2006), p. 294; Harremoës et al., 'Twelve Late Lessons', p. 189.

as the possible duration of effects, their propensity to spread beyond the locus of immediate impacts, and their potential to destabilise patterns of climate and precipitation to which ecosystems in general may be sensitive would be very relevant to the ecological ranking of the various possibilities for policy formation.

Assessment is important not only for establishing a hierarchy of preferred options, but also for the identification of those which present too great a threat of ecological harm for their continued use. The question is how these most harmful of options might be separated from others which, whilst they may have some erosive effects on resilience, are not deemed to be so threatening that they should be phased out. The labelling of developments as unacceptable or acceptable by reference to their potential to further or undermine ecological policy goals is a political decision that should be made by the democratically elected and accountable institutions of a state.[90] Decisions should be made with the statutory objectives of stress reduction and the lessening of risks that human activities will trigger regime change in mind, and should be based on information produced during alternatives assessment about the degree of ecological threat that an option presents. Whilst these broad considerations afford politicians some discretion in decision-making on sunsetting, it is possible to suggest that a political system which recognises the fundamental importance of ecosystem functionality for human well-being should choose to move away from reliance on options that are likely to undermine this because they would involve, or may result in, interference with, or the destruction of, ecologically valuable land, reductions in the diversity and modularity of ecosystems, or the alteration of the chemical composition of the atmosphere and seas with which all ecosystems interact.

In this regard, the EU's adoption of sustainability criteria for biofuels under its Renewable Energy Directive of 2009 provides an example of the use of law to distinguish between activities as being sustainable or unsustainable.[91] Biofuels will not count towards a target set under the

[90] O. Godard, 'Managing Global Risks through "Proportionate" Precaution: The Interplay between States, Civil Society, and International Regulation' in E. Brousseau, T. Dedeurwaerdere and B. Siebenhüner (eds) *Reflexive Governance for Global Public Goods* (Cambridge, MA: MIT Press, 2012), p. 130; Klinke and Renn, 'Adaptive and Integrative Governance', 282–4.

[91] Council Directive 2009/28/EC of 23 April 2009 on the promotion of the use of energy from renewable sources and amending and subsequently repealing Directives 2001/77/EC and 2003/30/EC ('Renewable Energy Directive') [2009] OJ L 140/16, Article 17.

Directive for increasing the proportion of renewable energy in overall energy consumed for transportation to 10 per cent by 2020 or be entitled to receive subsidies if the cultivation of feedstocks used for their production results in the loss of: land with high biodiversity value including primary forests, legally designated areas for nature protection, and highly biodiverse grassland;[92] land with high carbon stocks including wetlands, continuously forested areas and other forested areas meeting certain criteria;[93] and peatland.[94] Some environmental groups have criticised the Directive's definition of ecologically valuable land for being too limited,[95] but its identification of the exploitation of certain types of land as definitively unsustainable represents an important advance in the use of law for protecting ecosystems beyond designating particular habitats for preservation.

An important factor in determining whether an option should be used would be the manageability of impacts.[96] If we have no reliable means of controlling the ecological effects of options, that may provide a strong argument against continued reliance on them. For example, many of the potential ecological effects of offshore wind farm development might be minimised (although not removed) through careful selection of sites for construction. Conversely, we have, at present, no reliable means of controlling the effects of fossil fuel generation on climate or of containing carbon dioxide once it is released. Carbon capture and storage has been proposed as a technology for providing the management that is currently lacking. However, until its reliability and the safety and ecological benignity of storage can be demonstrated, fossil fuel generation provides an obvious candidate for sunsetting. Reversibility is also a key consideration, the 'primary thrust of precaution' being, in Renn's view, 'to avoid irreversibilility'.[97] A prudent approach when assessing an option whose ecological effects are unknown because of its novelty would therefore be to 'pursue a cautious strategy that allows learning by restricted errors'.[98] For example, it may be appropriate in view of our current ignorance of how marine species may be affected by noise from

92 Ibid., Articles 17(3)(a),(b) and (c). 93 Ibid., Article 17(4). 94 Ibid., Article 17(5).

95 J. M. Amezaga, S. L. Boyes and J. A. Harrison, 'Biofuels Policy in the European Union', conference paper presented at the 7th International Biofuels Conference, New Delhi, February 2010, pp. 6–7, http://research.ncl.ac.uk/reimpact/Related%20Documents/Reports/Biofuels%20Policy%20in%20the%20European%20Union.pdf.

96 Klinke and Renn, 'A New Approach to Risk Evaluation', 1074.

97 Renn, 'Precaution and the Governance of Risk', p. 239. 98 Ibid.

offshore wind turbines to restrict the growth of this new energy source until this has been explored further.[99]

As the distinction drawn between sustainable and unsustainable biofuels under the Renewable Energy Directive illustrates, policy options that are ostensibly preferable when compared to each other in isolation may be unacceptable in particular circumstances because of their ecological effects on places where they are deployed. One purpose of the legal framework for planning that I propose in Chapter 5 is to prevent development and actions that would harm ecosystem functionality.[100] The policy-making process should also address this situation in two ways. The first is by making clear, perhaps in a general planning policy statement, that recourse to options which would cause ecological harm when employed in certain contexts should not be permitted. Some outcomes, such as those referred to in the Renewable Energy Directive that would result in the degradation of highly biodiverse areas or a significant net increase in greenhouse gas emissions as stored carbon is emitted, can be identified at the policy level as impermissible. The prohibition should also be extended to uses of land and of marine areas that are identified as being incompatible with the goal of supporting ecosystem functionality through the planning process.

Conflict between policy options that appear ecologically preferable to others on their face, but that can occasion ecological harm when deployed, could arise where their claims to be environmentally beneficial derive from their potential contribution to decarbonisation. The political imperative to mitigate risks of climate change may be used to justify actions that have adverse environmental effects because they could also reduce carbon emissions.[101] For example, the UK's national planning policy statement on energy infrastructure advises decision-makers that concerns over environmental harm should not automatically prevent the authorisation of projects where they will contribute to decarbonising

[99] A. Gillespie, 'The Precautionary Principle in the Twenty-first Century: A Case Study of Noise Pollution in the Ocean' (2007) 22 *The International Journal of Marine and Coastal Law*, 81–7.

[100] Chapter 5, Section 5.3.5.

[101] A. L. R. Jackson, 'Renewable Energy vs. Biodiversity: Policy Conflicts and the Future of Nature Conservation' (2011) 21 *Global Environmental Change*, 1195–208; K. Rietig, 'Sustainable Climate Policy Integration in the European Union' (2013) 23 *Environmental Policy and Governance*, 297–310; S. Owens and R. Cowell, *Land and Limits: Interpreting Sustainability in the Planning Process*, 2nd ed. (Abingdon: Routledge, 2011), pp. 13–15.

energy supplies.[102] It is difficult to understand the view that mitigating climate change risks should take precedence over the protection of ecosystems and biodiversity when a key plank of policies and measures for adapting to a changing climate is to bolster the resilience of ecosystems.[103] Similarly, mitigation measures are being taken in part to reduce risks that climate change will impair the provision of 'services' by ecosystems through causing changes in their state. With this in mind, actions that are likely in themselves to heighten risks of regime shifts occurring should be authorised, if at all, only as a last resort for reducing carbon emissions. In any event, it is not possible or appropriate to identify a general need to authorise ecologically harmful development in order to reduce risks of climate change at the project level of decision-making. This should be a policy-level decision made in light of knowledge that no alternative means are available of reducing dependence on carbon-emitting fuels.

The default position under ecological governance would be that development that would undermine ecosystem resilience should not be permitted irrespective of the possible environmental benefits that it may yield. The position will only be departed from if it becomes clear, through knowledge attained from the preparation of plans for policy implementation, that: (a) damaging activities must be authorised in order to displace the use of policy options that present greater threats of ecological harm, particularly those identified for sunsetting; and (b) that it is not possible to avoid their use through a stronger focus on less-stressful policy options, including reducing consumption and increasing the efficiency of resource use.

The same rationale should be applied to options that will cause serious harm in worst-case scenarios. Nuclear energy is heavily regulated because of the threats that it poses for human and ecological well-being.[104] The

[102] Department of Energy and Climate Change, 'Appraisal of Sustainability for the revised draft Overarching National Policy Statement for Energy (EN-1): Main Report' (HM Government, 2010), p. 22; Department of Energy and Climate Change, 'Overarching National Policy Statement for Energy (EN-1)' (HM Government, 2011), pp. 69–70, para. 5.3.6.

[103] Department for Environment, Food and Rural Affairs, 'Conserving Biodiversity: The UK Approach' (HM Government, 2007), pp. 9, 13; Department for Environment, Food and Rural Affairs, 'England Biodiversity Strategy: Climate Change Adaptation Principles' (HM Government, 2008), pp. 7–8; European Commission, 'Adapting to Climate Change: Towards a European framework for action', COM (2009) 147 final, pp. 10–12.

[104] L. Clarke, 'The Nuclear Option' in C. Lever-Tracy (ed.) *Routledge Handbook of Climate Change and Society* (Abingdon, Routledge: 2010), pp. 308–16.

debate over shale gas exploitation in Europe has considered whether regulations can reduce risks that this activity could damage human health and have negative environmental impacts (e.g., through the release of chemicals into the water table) sufficiently for its conduct to be authorised.[105] In both cases, regulatory regimes, however strictly enforced, cannot remove risks of environmental harm occurring due to human error, mechanical breakdown or unforeseen occurrences. Options of this nature would therefore be ranked by reference to the likely seriousness of impacts on ecosystem functionality if feared events occur. This would be likely to result in nuclear energy and shale gas being classified as means of energy production that should not be employed except where this is an absolute necessity to secure a rapid reduction of carbon emissions from present levels. Indeed, the clear threats that they could present if accidents occur may lead to them being identified as candidates for 'sunsetting'. Again, prior consideration should be given to possibilities for reducing consumption, improving energy efficiency and increasing the use of preferred options. Consideration of other impacts that an action may have, such as shale gas exploitation's need for land conversion over wide areas for drilling, the demands that this places on water supplies and its prolongation of carbon-emitting fuel sources (albeit with less intensity than coal and oil) will also determine how it is viewed as an option for progressing an ecological transition.

The second reason for considering the potential for options to have negative effects in certain contexts at the policy level is to formulate packages of measures that promote uses of them that are less likely to cause ecological harm. The Renewable Energy Directive does this by promoting the growth in production of 'second generation' biofuels produced from waste and from feedstocks with lower life cycle carbon emissions. Biofuels derived from these sources count twice towards achievement of a 10 per cent target for the consumption of renewables in energy consumed for transportation to be achieved by all Member States by 2020.[106] The multiplier will increase to four if proposed amendments to the Directive are adopted.[107] Similarly, financial support for

105 AEA Technology, 'Support to the identification of potential risks for the environment and human health arising from hydrocarbons operations involving hydraulic fracturing in Europe' (report produced for the European Commission, 2012), http://ec.europa.eu/environment/integration/energy/pdf/fracking%20study.pdf.

106 Renewable Energy Directive, Article 21(2).

107 European Commission, 'Proposal for a Directive of the European Parliament and of the Council amending Directive 98/70/EC relating to the quality of petrol and diesel fuels

research and development could be used to drive the development of less-harmful technological variants such as floating offshore wind farms to replace the pile driving of turbine foundations into sea beds.

3.3.4 *Forming strategic visions of desired futures*

Alternatives assessment would enable us to identify which options are most likely to be compatible with the maintenance of ecosystem functionality. However, it provides no guidance as to how they might be deployed so that the erosive effects of activities on resilience are reduced. Nor does it tell us how conflict with current economic and social practices that prioritising ecological protection would give rise to might be addressed. Four further steps are required in the policy-making process to answer these questions, and, thereby, to provide decision-makers with visions of feasible futures for use in forming policies that would meet the statutory obligation of reducing anthropogenic stresses on ecosystems. These are the envisioning of what a society that prioritises ecosystem health would look like, the identification of packages of measures that would move society towards that vision and for managing the consequences of change, the assessment of economic and social impacts that the implementation of 'ideal' strategies would have, and public discussion and debate of different possibilities for achieving ecologically desirable change.

In the following paragraphs proposals are set out for a strategic stage in policy-making which includes these steps, and whose outcome would be a package of information that decision-makers can use for deciding on policy contents. The process of strategy formation is central to a forward-looking precautionary approach in that it directs attention to how ecological risks might be reduced over different timescales and the societal and economic changes that would be necessary for this. It also represents a significant departure from traditional approaches to policy-making under which ways of meeting perceived needs are explored in the first instance and environmental effects assessed, if at all, as a secondary consideration. In contrast, the strategic process is concerned with identifying the policy solutions that would come closest to meeting the framework's statutory objectives.

and amending Directive 2009/28/EC on the promotion of the use of energy from renewable sources', COM (2012) 595 final, 7.

The proposals for strategy formation draw extensively from the practice in strategic planning of backcasting.[108] This technique has been developed as an alternative to forecasting and is promoted by its proponents as being better suited than forecasting to addressing the deep-seated problems that drive global decline in environmental quality.[109] Forecasting is widely used in policy-making to predict what future demands are likely to be and how policy options might be deployed to satisfy them.[110] Its principal concern is with meeting requirements rather than exploring how these might be changed if they or the options available for meeting them are not environmentally sustainable.[111] Backcasting takes a very different approach. Its starting point is the envisioning of a future in which objectives (for example, the significant reduction of stresses that energy generation places on ecosystems) *are* being realised.[112] Practitioners then work backwards from this endpoint to determine what policy measures might be taken to achieve it, the timescales over which it might be realised, and its feasibility in view of the economic and social impacts that its realisation would have.[113]

Backcasting is an iterative process which allows for different futures to be explored until possibilities are identified that advance objectives as far as possible given the challenges of achieving substantial change in

[108] The use of backcasting in decision-making on precautionary action is also advocated in Tickner, 'Precautionary Decision-making', pp. 167–8; and B. F. Noble, 'The Canadian Experience with SEA and Sustainability' (2002) 22 *Environmental Impact Assessment Review*, 7–8.

[109] P. Vergragt and J. Quist, 'Backcasting for Sustainability: Introduction to the Special Issue' (2011) 78 *Technological Forecasting and Social Change*, 748–9; A. Suwa, 'Soft Energy Paths in Japan: A Backcasting Approach to Energy Planning' (2009) 9 *Climate Policy*, 187; K. H. Dreborg, 'Essence of Backcasting', 814; J. Robinson, 'Future Subjunctive: Backcasting as Social Learning' (2003) 35 *Futures*, 841.

[110] Suwa, 'Soft Energy Paths', 187.

[111] Suwa, 'Soft Energy Paths', 188; J. Robinson, 'Futures under Glass: A Recipe for People who Hate to Predict' (1990) 22 *Futures*, 821; S. L. Mander et al., 'The Tyndall Decarbonisation Scenarios – Part I: Development of a Backcasting Methodology with Stakeholder Participation' (2008) 36 *Energy Policy*, 3756.

[112] Vergragt and Quist, 'Backcasting for Sustainability', 747–8; Suwa, 'Soft Energy Paths', 187–8; Robinson, 'Futures under Glass', 821–2; J. Robinson, 'Energy Backcasting: A Proposed Method of Policy Analysis' (1982) 10 *Energy Policy*, 337–8.

[113] Vergragt and Quist, 'Backcasting for Sustainability', 747; J. Quist and P. Vergragt, 'Past and Future of Backcasting: The Shift to Stakeholder Participation and a Proposal for a Methodological Framework' (2006) 38 *Futures*, 1031; Dreborg, 'Essence of Backcasting', 817; Robinson, 'Futures under Glass', 822; K. Geurs and B. van Wee, 'Backcasting as a Tool for Sustainable Transport Policy Making: The Environmentally Sustainable Transport Study in the Netherlands' (2004) 4 *European Journal of Transport and Infrastructure Research*, 48–9.

economic and social practices.[114] It is not intended to generate ready-made solutions for policy.[115] Rather, its role is to assist decision-makers with visualising desirable futures and with exploring how these could be achieved.[116] As such, it is well-suited for use within a legal framework that institutes normative precaution and ecological risk reduction as the new status quo in policy formation.

3.3.4.1 Picturing the future

The first and second steps of strategy formation require policy-makers to explore how anthropogenic stresses might be reduced over different timescales. I envisage three different strands to this exploration which, although they represent separate objectives, will necessarily influence and interact with each other. These are: the reduction of consumption; the deployment of preferred options; and the phasing out of options identified as presenting unacceptable threats to ecosystem health. Baselines are to be set representing futures in which levels of consumption and stress, and reliance on harmful options have been reduced as far as possible. It is for policy-makers to set these baselines and the timescales over which advances might be made. The statutory objective and principles act as guides for this exercise. A requirement for the independent review of policy proposals would also (as argued at Section 3.4.2.2) ensure that serious efforts are made to identify the most ecologically desirable outcomes that might be achieved.

The setting of baselines is followed by the backcasting process itself. The baseline is compared with the present position, and policy measures and actions identified that would promote movement from the latter towards the former. These may include measures that promote the use of preferred alternatives, that remove obstacles to their use, or that would make continued use of less ecologically desirable alternatives disadvantageous. Measures identified at this stage might also address potential economic and social impacts that realising a vision may give rise to (by, for instance, influencing the costs of domestic energy supply). Again, it is for policy-makers to establish programmes of measures and realistic lead-in times for their implementation with the objectives and principles

[114] Vergragt and Quist, 'Backcasting for Sustainability', 749; Robinson, 'Futures under Glass', 822.

[115] Vergragt and Quist, 'Backcasting for Sustainability', 749; Dreborg, 'Essence of Backcasting', 825.

[116] Dreborg, 'Essence of Backcasting', 825; Vergragt and Quist, 'Backcasting for Sustainability', 749; Quist and Vergragt, 'Past and Future of Backcasting', 1030–1.

acting as a beacon for, and the threat of review as a backdrop to the undertaking. The iterative nature of backcasting would allow for trial and error until feasible programmes of measures and endpoints for realising ecological goals can be matched.

3.3.4.2 Policy impact assessment

The purpose of the first two steps in the strategic stage is to identify endpoints and packages of policy measures for realising them that represent an ideal from an ecological perspective. This initial focus is necessary to ensure that information is available to support the formation of policies that are capable of driving reductions in anthropogenic stresses. However, it is also essential if effective policies for ecologically desirable change are to be developed that policy-making should take into account, and respond to, the economic and social impacts that their implementation would have.

Decision-makers with responsibility for policy formation should have available to them information concerning both the potentially negative effects that policies may give rise to and the steps that might be taken to avoid or mitigate them. They would also need to know how the public would be likely to react to the significant changes that an ecological focus in policy-making would bring, and to explore with them ways of introducing policies that would be publicly acceptable or, failing that, which reduce scope for active opposition. The third and final step of the strategic stage is therefore concerned with assessing the impacts that giving practical effect to the 'ideal' strategies identified under the first two steps would have and considering how these might be addressed without compromising achievement of the framework's statutory objectives.

Policy impact assessment is intended, as with strategic environmental assessment, to improve outcomes of decision-making although it is concerned with finding ways of reconciling the pursuit of ecological objectives with the social and economic changes that this would entail rather than with identifying the environmental consequences of development. In addition to this obvious difference, policy impact assessment would also depart from the current practice of strategic assessment in three respects. The first is that it would provide for participation by members of the public in the scoping stage that precedes assessment. The purpose of the exercise is to establish the full range of effects that ecologically oriented policies may have so that means of addressing them in ways that would allow the highest levels of risk reduction to be achieved can be identified. Early participation is required to ensure that the assessment process is comprehensive in its coverage of concerns that policy may give rise to.

Second, assessment involves the review of strategic possibilities for reducing risks of ecological harm rather than of formal policy proposals. Accordingly, it gives members of the public a role in shaping the future rather than reacting to the government's vision of what this should be. Third, alternatives assessment at this stage is concerned not with considering different options for action, but with exploring the effects that introducing policy over different timescales would have and how different packages of policy measures might be used to alleviate potential impacts. Backcasting has an important role to play in supporting this process as its iterative nature allows for the preparation of studies representing different pathways towards an endpoint and different timescales for reaching it that would provide a platform for public discussion and debate of how ecologically oriented policies should be introduced.[117]

Decision-makers should, at the completion of policy impact assessment, have sufficient information to form ecologically oriented policies. Their primary responsibility under the framework would remain to produce outcomes that satisfy the statutory objectives and principles. However, the wording I suggest for this objective recognises that the rate at which social and economic adaptation to an ecological transition can be achieved should be taken into account in decision-making on what can be done to advance the ecological agenda and how quickly. The intended output of this third stage in strategy formation is that policy-makers should have sufficient information to judge where these limits lie and, thereby, to establish programmes for reducing negative impacts on ecosystem functionality that would allow ecological ends to be achieved without destroying economic and social functionality.

3.3.5 *Public participation in policy-making*

Public participation is of central importance to the third stage of strategy formation and, more generally, for the effective conduct of ecologically oriented policy-making. It is vital if policy-makers are to produce policies that are capable of implementation that they should have knowledge of how measures for ecological risk reduction would affect the public, how different approaches to reducing risk would be viewed, and whether

[117] Dreborg, 'Essence of Backcasting', 815, 824; Robinson, 'Futures under Glass', 822; Quist and Vergragt, 'Past and Future of Backcasting', 1031–33.

proposals for mitigating economic and social impacts would allay concerns that policies would otherwise raise.

Organising meaningful participatory exercises in the formation of policy is recognised to present a number of practical problems.[118] The size of groups involved with discussing policy has to be limited for reasons of practicality, but this calls into question whether their views can be said to be representative of those held by all sections of governed populations and therefore whether they provide a reliable source for policy-making.[119] There are also questions over peoples' willingness to participate in debating strategic issues that may seem remote from their lives.[120] Even so, experience with small participating groups, collectively described by Goodin and Dryzek as 'mini-publics', in which members of the public are required to consider and deliberate issues placed before them reveals their potential value for improving the quality and effectiveness of public policy.[121] The suggested use in this context corresponds with Goodin and Dryzek's review of deliberation as a means of shaping policy by market testing.[122] Hoppe expresses concern that small-group participation in policy-making could end up being a 'mere symbolic ornament to the representative and neocorporatist modes of governance' if governments use it only to provide a veneer of legitimacy for policies that would have been pursued in any event. However, the meaningfulness of such exercises is context specific.[123] In this case, the purpose of the exercise is to explore possible impacts and reactions to

[118] M. Welp et al., 'Citizens' Voices in Environmental Policy: The Contribution of Integrated Assessment Focus Groups to Accountable Decision-making' in F. Coenen (ed.) *Public Participation and Better Environmental Decisions: The Promise and Limits of Participatory Processes for the Quality of Environmentally Related Decision-making* (Dordrecht: Springer, 2009), pp. 92–3; R. Hoppe, 'Institutional Constraints and Practical Problems in Deliberative and Participatory Policy Making' (2011) 39 *Policy and Politics*, 174–80.

[119] Welp et al., 'Citizens' Voices', p. 92; F. Coenen, 'Conclusions' in F. Coenen (ed.) *Public Participation and Better Environmental Decisions: The Promise and Limits of Participatory Processes for the Quality of Environmentally Related Decision-making* (Dordrecht: Springer, 2009), pp. 197–9; T. Dietz and P. C. Stern, *Public Participation in Environmental Assessment and Decision Making* (Washington, DC: National Academies Press, 2008), pp. 61–4.

[120] F. Coenen, 'Introduction' in F. Coenen (ed.) *Public Participation and Better Environmental Decisions: The Promise and Limits of Participatory Processes for the Quality of Environmentally Related Decision-making* (Dordrecht: Springer, 2009), pp. 11–12; Coenen, 'Conclusions', pp. 204–5.

[121] R. E. Goodin and J. S. Dryzek, 'Deliberative Impacts: The Macro-political Uptake of Mini-publics' (2006) 34 *Politics and Society*, 219–44.

[122] Ibid., 229–32. [123] Hoppe, 'Institutional Constraints', 180.

policies whose implementation is likely to disrupt peoples' accustomed ways of living, and, through this, to identify ways in which effects could be mitigated and measures made more palatable.

The process would provide an opportunity for participants to provide information as to how the implementation of 'ideal' strategies would affect them and to discuss and debate how policies for reducing risk should be put into practice. The involvement as witnesses of policy-makers and representatives from the independent body of experts on ecological protection (see Section 3.4.2.2), who would be able to explain why particular measures are under consideration when giving testimony, would be valuable for the conduct of this debate. Explanation of proposed actions may assist with overcoming a sense of abstraction from matters under consideration and enhance the understanding of participants so that they are better placed to participate meaningfully in the process. In addition, participants may come to the process with preferences that would conflict with the changes in economic and social behaviour that an ecological reorientation would require. Having an opportunity to question politicians and experts about why action to reduce risks of harm is necessary would enable them to reflect on their initial views in light of the ecological values that policy packages are designed to protect.[124]

I recognise, as Flynn argues, that the reaction of participants to possibilities that are discussed in a controlled forum will differ from how they are viewed when presented to the public at large.[125] However, a focused participatory process would be likely to reveal the dominant concerns that proposed policies may give rise to and allow consideration of how these might be addressed. In addition, the conduct of citizens' juries is not the only opportunity that the public would have to participate in shaping the transition to an ecologically desirable future. I argue in Chapters 4 and 6 in Chapters 4 and 6 that there should be substantial public involvement with exploring possibilities for policy implementation. Participation at this level would appear more meaningful for members of the public whose ways of life and values held in places may be challenged directly by proposals for

[124] The potential for people to modify or clarify their values through participation in deliberative processes is examined in further detail in Chapter 6, Section 6.2.

[125] B. Flynn, 'Planning Cells and Citizen Juries in Environmental Policy: Deliberation and its Limits' in F. Coenen (ed.) *Public Participation and Better Environmental Decisions: The Promise and Limits of Participatory Processes for the Quality of Environmentally Related Decision-making* (Dordrecht: Springer, 2009), pp. 60–1. See also S. Niemeyer, 'The Emancipatory Effect of Deliberation: Empirical Lessons from Mini-publics' (2011) 39 *Politics and Society*, 127–8.

development or for altering current practices (for instance in vehicle usage or energy generation and consumption) in regions and localities. From this perspective, participation in policy formation is the first stage of engagement in a system of governance that seeks to improve the quality and perceived legitimacy of policies and plans for their implementation by significantly enhancing opportunities for public involvement with political processes.

Knowledge provided and views expressed in the first stage of participation would, together with the strategies formed through the back-casting exercise, feed into the formation of draft policies. A second stage of participation would then follow with the outcomes of further debate informing the contents of final policy proposals. This could involve larger-scale participatory exercises such as the organisation of deliberative opinion polls to consider aspects of policy or of targeted consultations with a wider section of society being asked, perhaps through electronic media, to comment on and/or participate in discussion of policy proposals.[126] Although remote consultation does not provide an opportunity to discuss with respondees the reasons why particular proposals have been put forwards in person, it would have the virtue of reaching a much wider cross-section of the public. This would reduce scope for questioning the legitimacy of policies because their contents have been informed only by the views of the small groups of citizens that took part in deliberations.

One way of extending the influence of small-scale deliberative evaluations of alternative policy approaches would be to require both that records of the process be published and that policy-makers should issue a written statement advising how conclusions reached through deliberation have informed policy contents. These documents would be made available to participants or consultees in the larger-scale processes referred to above. Such an approach would enhance the meaningfulness of the smaller-scale deliberations by placing pressure on politicians to take views expressed in them seriously.[127] It could also assist with addressing the concern that they lack legitimacy by informing broader sections of society about conclusions reached by participants and affording them an

[126] G. Smith, *Democratic Innovations: Designing Institutions for Citizen Participation* (Cambridge: Cambridge University Press, 2009), pp. 78–9.

[127] The absence of formal requirements for decision-makers to consider and respond to the outcomes of innovative participatory processes is identified by Smith in 'Democratic Innovations', pp. 22–4, as a factor that can undermine their credibility.

opportunity to advise if they concur with conclusions reached through small-group deliberations. The government should also be obliged to advise how it has taken the wider range of views expressed in consultations or larger deliberative exercises into account in finalising policies. A legal requirement to respond to the outcomes of these processes would further assist with realising the potential value of participation for enhancing the perceived legitimacy of resulting decisions.

On completion of the strategic stage, I envisage that the outcomes of alternatives assessment, the 'ideal' strategies, potential packages of measures for addressing economic and social impacts of their implementation, and information generated during public participation would be used in the formation of policy. It would be for policy-makers to prepare policies that meet the statutory objective and principles of the framework although, as is suggested at Section 3.4.2.2, they should be able, and, on some matters, legally required, to consult independent experts on ecosystem protection. Policy proposals should be accompanied by a statement identifying how they depart from the ideal strategies and why movement away from them is considered necessary to allow for economic and social adaptation.

This is not an end to the policy-making process. It is likely, in view of the radical change in institutional behaviour that introduction of the proposed framework would require, that resistance would be encountered to an ecological orientation in policy-making. In addition, the process of adapting ideal strategies to take into account possible economic and social impacts and public views on them may leave scope for politicians to overstate the challenges involved with taking action to reduce ecological risks, and, thereby, to avoid making hard and potentially unpopular choices. I suggest therefore that proposed policies should be reviewed by an independent body. Proposals for this review are set out in the following section as part of a broader discussion of how the institutional challenges presented by the ad hoc nature of policy-making can be met.

3.4 Reforming the policy-making process

The environmental assessment of plans and programmes for policy implementation is increasingly regarded as a feature of good practice in decision-making,[128] but its extension to policy-making has been

[128] Tetlow and Hanusch, 'Strategic Environmental Assessment', 17–18.

limited.[129] International instruments for environmental assessment and public participation in decision-making have also, whilst making the assessment of plans and programmes mandatory, either omitted the assessment of policy[130] or included only a discretionary requirement for its conduct.[131] This lack of provision reflects a widely held belief that it would not be appropriate to impose legal structures on the processes by which policy decisions are reached. For example, the formal application of assessment to policy was opposed during the drafting of the Kiev Protocol on grounds that the character of policy-making differs from that of plan or programme development, and that it is therefore 'inherently unsuited to the application of strategic environmental assessment in legislated or prescriptive form'.[132]

The principal argument made against introducing legal requirements to prioritise or even reflect on environmental matters in policy-making has been that this would be incompatible with the complex nature of the process.[133] Politicians must adjudicate between conflicting values and take into account a wide array of considerations in forming policy. To try and constrain this dynamic process within a framework that seeks to give it a particular direction would be to ignore the complexities involved with attempting to establish what would be the best course of action for society's well-being. It has been suggested that this argument also conceals a general antipathy amongst politicians to measures that would limit political control over this level of decision-making. Sadler

129 Chapter 3, Section 3.3.

130 Council Directive 2001/42/EC of 27 June 2001 on the assessment of the effects of certain plans and programmes on the environment ('Strategic Environmental Assessment Directive') [2001] OJ L 197/30.

131 Protocol on Strategic Environmental Assessment to the Convention on Environmental Impact Assessment in a Transboundary Context ('Kiev Protocol'), Kiev, 21 May 2003, in force 11 July 2010, UN Doc. ECE/MP. EIA/2003/2, Article 13; Convention on Access to Information, Public Participation in Decision Making and Access to Justice in Environmental Matters ('Aarhus Convention'), Aarhus, 25 June 1998, in force 30 October 2001, 2161 UNTS 447, 38 ILM 517 (1999), Article 7.

132 Sadler, 'Strategic Environmental Assessment', p. 5; I. Lyhne, 'Between Policy-making and Planning: SEA and Strategic Decision-making in the Danish Energy Sector' (2011) 13 *Journal of Environmental Assessment, Policy and Management*, 322.

133 A. Brown and T. Nitz, 'Applying Strategic Environmental Assessment to Policy Making: the Policy Cycle Model and the Queensland Policy Handbook' in S. Marsden and S. Dovers (eds) *Strategic Environmental Assessment in Australasia* (Sydney: The Federation Press, 2002), pp. 86–7; W. R. Sheate et al., 'Integrating the Environment into Strategic Decision-making: Conceptualizing Policy SEA' (2003) 13 *European Environment*, 14.

anticipates resistance to the strategic environmental assessment of policy because it would intrude 'on territory and prerogatives that traditionally have been off limits to outside scrutiny'.[134] Similarly, Boothroyd argues that the formalisation of policy-making is likely to be opposed because it would be regarded as an encroachment on, and a threat to, long-standing preserves of political power.[135]

The strength with which this argument has been advanced is reflected in acceptance by some commentators on strategic environmental assessment that it must be tailored to the nature of policy-making if politicians are to accept any interference with this process.[136] They argue that assessment procedures that assume a linear approach to decision-making are ill-suited to the dynamic and informal reality of policy-making.[137] Instead, a more flexible model should be employed that seeks to take advantage of windows of opportunity during policy formation rather than imposing a structure on an inherently unstructured process.[138] However, others contend that the practices and procedures of governmental decision-making must change if the assessment of environmental effects is to have any influence on the contents of policy.[139] I join with them in arguing that the arcane processes by which policy is made must be reformed because the premises on which current approaches to policy-making are based are no longer valid. These are founded on historic assumptions that there are no significant environmental limits on the pursuit and promotion of economic and

[134] Sadler, 'Strategic Environmental Assessment', p. 7.

[135] Boothroyd, 'Policy Assessment', pp. 90, 101. See also Boothroyd, 'Integrating Economy, Society and Environment', p. 145.

[136] Brown and Nitz, 'Applying Strategic Environmental Assessment to Policy Making', pp. 87–8, 94; J. Bailey and S. Renton, 'Environmental Assessment of Policies' in A. L. Porter and J. J. Fittipaldi (eds) *Environmental Methods Review: Retooling Impact Assessment for the New Century* (Fargo: The Press Club, 1998), p. 110; Sadler, 'Strategic Environmental Assessment', p. 7; L. White and B. F. Noble, 'Strategic Environmental Assessment for Sustainability: A Review of a Decade of Academic Research' (2013) 42 *Environmental Impact Assessment Review*, 61 and 64.

[137] Hertin et al., 'Policy Appraisal', p. 117.

[138] Adelle and Weiland, 'Policy Assessment', 29.

[139] B. F. Noble and L. M. Christmas, 'Strategic Environmental Assessment of Greenhouse Gas Mitigation Options in the Canadian Agricultural Sector' (2008) 41 *Environmental Management*, 65, 77; R. Connor and S. Dovers, 'Strategic Environmental Assessment: Policy Integration as Practice or Possibility?' in R. Connor and S. Dovers (eds) *Institutional Change for Sustainable Development* (Cheltenham: Edward Elgar Publishing, 2004), p. 171; S. Dovers, *Environment and Sustainability Policy: Creation, Implementation, Evaluation* (Sydney: The Federation Press, 2001), p. 101; Hertin et al., 'Policy Appraisal', p. 130.

social objectives. Accordingly, it is not problematic for politicians to make decisions involving trade-offs between different interests without any transparency as to how the environment was considered in their deliberations or the basis on which decisions were made. These assumptions are not tenable in view of our growing awareness of the importance of ecosystem health for our own well-being and of the threats that our activities present for this.

The question we should be asking is not how law might be adapted to policy-making processes, but how we would design decision-making structures and what role law would play in them in light of current knowledge. I suggest that we would expect to see sufficient structure, systematisation and transparency in decision-making to ensure that judgments made in forming policy take into account, and seek not to impair, the functionality of ecosystems. We would not opt for an approach in which decisions are made through a secretive process of interest balancing for which there is no visibility as to how conclusions have been reached.

The design and enactment of a framework for policy-making would provide an opportunity to inject the necessary rigour into the process to ensure that ecological considerations are given priority in policy formation, that it is conducted transparently, and that policy-makers have some accountability for the choices they make. As part of this reform, new institutional structures should also be developed with a view to overcoming the likely resistance to constraints on political choice and, ultimately, to promote the cultural change that would lead to acceptance of ecological protection as a normative objective of policy formation. I consider in the following sections what reforms would need to be made to achieve these ends and how the legal framework might be used to introduce them.

3.4.1 A whole-of-government approach

Ecological policy-making would involve more than the assessment of policy proposals as they arise. It would require the government to conduct a periodic review of needs and demand in the different areas that its responsibilities encompass and of the options for satisfying them. This would be done with a view to identifying how policies might be put in place and existing policies revised to reduce the cumulative impacts of economic and social activity on ecosystem health. An all-embracing approach is necessary because the ad hoc review of proposed action would not be sufficient to drive a reduction in levels of ecological stress.

It is also required to ensure that the objectives of the framework can be advanced effectively. This contention is supported by three key considerations.

The first is that the direct causes of ecological degradation are themselves the products of policy decisions made in other governmental departments, and particularly those with overarching responsibility for macro-economic growth and societal well-being. There is little that would be achieved through seeking to improve policies in particular areas if decisions made externally to them (i.e., for economic growth driven by a major expansion in large-scale fixed infrastructure) would undermine efforts to reduce ecological risk. Accordingly, I envisage that reviews would be conducted on a 'whole of government' basis. This would be done with a view to engendering concerted and coordinated action by all governmental departments to reduce risks of harm to ecosystems. This cross-governmental approach is necessary if the links between different policy areas that entrench reliance on harmful activities are to be identified and broken.[140] It is also essential if the drivers of current patterns of consumption are to be identified and policy measures developed that might alter unsustainable trajectories of resource use.[141]

Second, a comprehensive approach is necessary to ensure that all of the choices made by the government in different policy areas are conducted within the framework and guided by its objectives and principles. A potential difficulty perceived by those who have called for policy assessment is that policies are not necessarily written down and may therefore evade formal review.[142] Buckley suggests that '[t]he most powerful policies are often unwritten, unspoken, unacknowledged, and hence not open to formal assessment'.[143] A further concern raised by these commentators is that government would seek to circumvent a mechanism for assessment by not labelling proposals as policy documents or presenting them within

[140] Connor and Dovers, 'Strategic Environmental Assessment', p. 166.

[141] S. Dovers, 'Too Deep a SEA? Strategic Environmental Assessment in the Era of Sustainability' in S. Marsden and S. Dovers (eds) *Strategic Environmental Assessment in Australasia* (Sydney: The Federation Press, 2002), pp. 25–6; Gibson et al., 'Sustainability Assessment', p. 97.

[142] Boothroyd, 'Integrating Economy, Society and Environment', p. 145; O. Bina, 'A Critical Review of the Dominant Lines of Argumentation on the Need for Strategic Environmental Assessment' (2007) 27 *Environmental Impact Assessment Review*, 589.

[143] R. Buckley, 'Strategic Environmental Assessment' in A. L. Porter and J. J. Fittipaldi (eds) *Environmental Methods Review: Retooling Impact Assessment for the New Century* (Fargo: The Press Club, 1998), p. 78.

bills or budgets.[144] The suggested approach addresses these issues to a large extent as it requires both the periodic review of all governmental action in different areas and the formation of policy that meets the framework's objectives.

Third, mechanisms for horizontal coordination are required to overcome difficulties with orienting governments towards the pursuit of cross-cutting environmental goals. These derive from the long-standing practice of giving responsibility for different sectors of public life to separate ministries.[145] The resulting fragmentation and tendency of ministries to concentrate on advancing their own policy agendas, irrespective of the environmental consequences, was identified in the Brundtland Report, and has been cited consistently in following international declarations, as a barrier to realising sustainable development.[146] The aim of a whole of government approach would be to replace division with a culture of collaboration on advancing ecological goals. As considered in the following sections, the establishment of joint ministerial bodies and of institutions for reviewing policy proposals have key roles to play in bridging gaps between ministerial power centres.

3.4.2 Promoting change in the culture of governmental decision-making

The reform of policy-making to introduce a structured approach is necessary to ensure that ecological considerations are given due weight in the formation of policies, and that this is seen to be done. However, more than the surface imposition of a structure on an existing process will be required to change the entrenched culture and conventions of governmental decision-making 'behind closed doors'. In particular, it may be difficult to accustom politicians to the notion that their authority to determine whether activities should be enabled or regulated should

[144] Gibson et al., 'Sustainability Assessment', p. 151; Noble, 'The Canadian Experience', 12–13; R. Buckley, 'Strategic Environmental Assessment of Policies and Plans: Legislation and Implementation' (2000) 18 *Impact Assessment and Project Appraisal*, 211; Lyhne, 'Between Policy-making and Planning', 335.

[145] Jordan and Lenschow, 'Environmental Policy Integration', 150–1; Ross, 'Sustainable Development', p. 102; R. Steurer, 'Sustainable Development as Governance Reform Agenda: An Aggregation of Distinguished Challenges for Policy-making', Discussion Paper 1-2009, Institute of Forest, Environmental and Natural Resource Policy, Universität für Bodenkultur Wien (2009).

[146] Steurer, 'Sustainable Development as Governance Reform Agenda', p. 5.

itself become the subject of regulation.[147] The reforms that I propose in this section are intended to promote adaptation of this culture to one in which, whilst flexibility remains over choosing which economic and social goals to pursue, it is recognised that the maintenance of ecosystem health places a ceiling on what can be achieved in these spheres of action.

The enactment of laws which require that the functionality of ecosystems be prioritised in decision-making would go some way to changing current practice. Entrenching legal obligations for government to review policy would, as has been argued in the context of strategic environmental assessment,[148] be an essential first step towards ensuring that ecological factors are taken into account in policy formation. Responsibility should be given for the 'whole of government' review and, as part of this, for assessing alternatives, creating strategies and developing policies based on them to a cross-governmental body.[149] This would help to create a new culture of ecological orientation in the way policy is formed as long as the initiative enjoys support at the highest levels of government and the body is involved from the earliest stages of policy development. Experience with the establishment of inter-ministerial groups in connection with attempts to 'mainstream' sustainability in political decision-making indicates that coordinating institutions must possess both of these attributes if their establishment is to result in outcomes that advance cross-cutting objectives.[150] Additional institutional reforms should also, as I argue in the following sections, be made to establish the new culture of decision-making as one which policy-makers, however alien it may seem to them, must adapt to, and to overcome any lingering hostility to the restriction of political powers.

3.4.2.1 The rolling review of policy

The first reform I propose is that the review of governmental action in different policy areas should be conducted at regular intervals. Establishing the 'whole of government' review as a recurring process would promote

[147] Connor and Dovers, 'Strategic Environmental Assessment', p. 167.

[148] Buckley, 'Strategic Environmental Assessment', p. 80; Sheate et al., 'Integrating the Environment', 14.

[149] Jordan and Lenschow, 'Environmental Policy Integration', 151; Ross, 'Sustainable Development', pp. 102–9, 113–4.

[150] Jordan and Lenschow, 'Environmental Policy Integration', 150–1; Ross, 'Sustainable Development', pp. 102–7.

adaptation to the prioritisation of ecosystem health in policy-making.[151] Repeat exposure to the conduct of reviews would also assist those involved in making policy with forming a clear understanding of what the statutory objectives and principles require and with tailoring policy-making processes to serve these requirements.[152]

A rolling review of policy is, in any event, essential under a legal framework for ecologically oriented policy-making in four respects. The first is that the regular reappraisal of policy options is important if the substitution principle is to be observed. New technologies whose commercial deployment was not feasible during previous review periods might be ready for ranking amongst other possibilities for meeting needs in different policy areas. The use of options for which further information has become available concerning their compatibility with maintaining the functionality of ecosystems might also be reassessed.

Second, an ability to adapt decisions to new information concerning ecosystem behaviour and the likely impacts of activities on ecosystem health is an essential feature of a legal system whose purpose is to protect natural systems of which our current knowledge and understanding is limited. For example, although we may have some difficulty with establishing the exact causes of ecological degradation, evidence that the rate of this is increasing may require an intensification of efforts to reduce anthropogenic stresses and the shortening of timescales for achieving reductions or for phasing out activities. The regular review of policies would go some way to establishing adaptive management as a standard practice at this level of decision-making.

The third is, as I argue in Chapter 7, that concerted research programmes should be put in place to improve knowledge and understanding of ecosystem behaviour, of what it is that makes ecosystems resilient, and of how human activities affect this property and trigger changes in ecological states. The regular review process would allow the improved understanding of ecosystems that this research would hopefully yield to be used both in the review of policy options and in improving the efficacy of the framework's mechanisms for producing ecologically desirable outcomes.

151 R. Connor and S. Dovers, 'Principles and Elements of Institutional Change for Sustainable Development' in R. Connor and S. Dovers (eds) *Institutional Change for Sustainable Development* (Cheltenham: Edward Elgar Publishing, 2004), pp. 221–2.

152 Connor and Dovers, 'Sustainable Management', p. 125; Ross, 'Sustainable Development', pp. 234–5.

Finally, the viability of policies would be informed by the exploration of how aspirations for reducing ecological stress can be realised under the arrangements for governance and for strategic planning that is proposed in Chapters 4 and 5. Policies would certainly need to be revised as the extent to which preferred options can be deployed becomes apparent through local, regional and national planning processes. An iterative approach is essential if packages of policies, once conditions on the ground have been taken into account fully, are to provide society with an effective normative steer in an ecological direction. Policy-making that is intended to serve a progressive objective of stress reduction cannot be conducted as a top-down process that produces expressions of desire and then expects them to be advanced come what may. It must be an ongoing undertaking that is sensitive to the challenges of implementation and allows for the adjustment of policies where difficulties are encountered with putting them into practice.

3.4.2.2 The independent review of policy proposals

Growing familiarity with ecological policy-making under the rolling review process would promote gradual change in the culture of governmental decision-making. The second institutional reform that I propose is the establishment of an independent advisory body on the protection of ecosystems to provide support for those involved with forming policy in a changing culture and to ensure that politicians take their responsibilities under the framework seriously. This body would act in an advisory capacity on the conduct of alternatives assessment, decision-making on sunsetting and the formation of strategies, with governments being required to consult the body on these matters, to take the advice given into account, and to produce written statements advising on the extent to which it has been accepted and reasons for departing from the body's guidance. It would be available to advise the government on the formation of policy itself although decisions on policy contents would remain the preserve of policy-makers. It would also take the lead role in forming and implementing research programmes into ecosystem behaviour.[153]

The body would carry out the duties referred to above as a provider of support for the effective conduct of policy-making under the framework. In addition, it would have a responsibility for reviewing the government's policy proposals and advising on whether they satisfy the

[153] Chapter 7, Section 7.2.

statutory objective and principles. The body would not have the authority to reject proposed policy if, in its view, it falls short of what might be achieved once the need to allow for economic and social adaptation has been taken into account. It would not be appropriate for an unelected organisation to have the final say over decisions that would be of great consequence for society as a whole.[154] Rather, its role would be to give the government advice on whether the statutory objective and principles have been observed and, if not, of the changes that should be made to draft policies so that they meet the requirements of the framework.

This advice and the government's response recording its acceptance of, or reasons for rejecting, recommendations would be published. This transparency would provide an incentive for the government to provide reasoned justification for the conclusions it reaches as to how ecological risks can be reduced over different timescales. It would also provide an incentive for the government to take its statutory duties seriously by providing a possible basis for judicial scrutiny of a decision to reject advice given by the independent agency. Analysis of the advisory role of the Committee on Climate Change under the UK's Climate Change Act 2008 casts doubt on whether the UK's courts would be willing to interfere with the government's decisions in complex policy areas such as identifying effective means for progressing the transition to a low carbon economy.[155] However, McHarg suggests that they may be more prepared to make mandatory orders compelling compliance by the government with its duties where a public advisory body has issued a clear recommendation that a course of action should or should not be pursued.[156] Clarity in the wording of the government's statutory duty to take into account and respond to guidance would further enhance the influence of the body's reviewing role by strengthening the grounds for judicial intervention. For example, a requirement that the government, if it rejects advice, should not only provide reasons for doing so, but also explain why its chosen approach would better advance the statutory objective than that which it rejects would concentrate governmental

[154] A. McHarg, 'Climate Change Constitutionalism? Lessons from the United Kingdom' (2011) 2 *Climate Law*, 483 makes a similar observation with regard to the acquisition of executive powers by the Committee on Climate Change under the UK's Climate Change Act 2008 in addition to its advisory remit.

[155] M. Stallworthy, 'Legislating against Climate Change: A UK Perspective on a Sisyphean Challenge' (2009) 72 *The Modern Law Review*, 423–7; McHarg, 'Climate Change Constitutionalism', 477–8.

[156] McHarg, 'Climate Change Constitutionalism', 479.

thinking on how stress reduction can be achieved rather than on identifying reasons for not observing its obligations.

In addition, a right of standing should be available for everyone to challenge decisions made by the government during the policy-making process, including its reaction to the independent body's advice on policy. This would add to the pressure placed on the government to produce policy that does contribute significantly to reducing levels of anthropogenic stress, and to produce a credible case for inaction where it concludes that economic and social conditions place limits on what can be achieved. Whilst I do not propose to explore here the many complex issues connected with the adequacy of access to justice, I suggest that provision for standing might offer an option to present arguments before an independent tribunal. This may provide a potentially less expensive and more accessible alternative for the public to mount challenges than bringing claims through formal legal processes before the courts.[157]

[157] Article 9(1) of the Aarhus Convention requires parties to offer an independent review process as an alternative to bringing a claim before the Courts concerning a request for environmental information.

4

Governing an ecological transition

4.1 Introduction

Ecologically oriented policies would provide normative guidance as to how levels of stress generated by human activities might be set on a downwards trajectory. However, structures for governing the conduct of human affairs that have been designed to support, facilitate and, where necessary, drive an ecological transition 'on the ground' would also be required if these visions of change are to be translated into real world outcomes. I consider in this and the two following chapters how a system of governance that is equipped to divert society away from its ecologically destructive course towards pathways which may allow for synergy between the functioning of socioeconomic and natural systems could be put in place.

I begin, in this chapter, by exploring what the basic parameters of such a system should be and how relations between different levels of government, and between governmental institutions and non-governmental actors, should be structured to enhance the state's capacity to deliver ecological objectives. In Chapter 5, I consider the form that a legal framework for planning should take if it is to foster the forward-looking, strategic and spatial approaches that would be needed to explore how policies for reducing levels of resource consumption, and meeting demands in less ecologically stressful ways, might be given effect. I also consider what powers decision-makers would need to steer proposed development away from places of importance for the healthy functioning of ecosystems. I conclude in Chapter 6 by giving thought to how institutions and institutional structures should be designed if these are to promote perception of governmental action to advance ecological policies as legitimate and to encourage, through public involvement with political debate, the popular reflection which would be required if people are to reassess their values and, based on this reassessment, to review their own behaviours.

It goes without saying that the introduction of constraints on economic practices and on peoples' lifestyles, which the framework for governance I present is intended to support, would encounter significant obstacles. There is a high degree of pessimism that state-based reform to improve the protection of ecosystems would be sufficient to 'counteract the (global) market approaches which currently dominate' or 'to formulate ways in which citizen-consumers can be successfully discouraged from market-based behaviour patterns'.[1] These anticipated difficulties have led some to argue that existing political arrangements must be discarded if sustainability is to be achieved. However, that would be to discount the ability of democratically organised political systems to engender, through open discussion and debate, a transformation in the public's perception of what is in individual and collective interests and a corresponding appreciation that these would be better served by enhanced environmental protection than by the continued provision of unrestricted access to opportunities for wealth accumulation.

The model of governance I propose is intended to encourage such a shift in the way people see themselves in relation to the environment. It makes provision for discourse, cooperation and collaboration between all levels of government and non-governmental actors. Crucially, it also allows for collaborative exploration of whether it would be possible for a modern society to pursue economic and social objectives in ways that would not result in ecological degradation. This process of experimentation may of course lead to the conclusion that such coexistence is not possible and that more fundamental reforms of the society/environment relationship are required. In these circumstances, a preceding process of deliberation would at least make it more likely that the need for stronger solutions would be recognised and accepted. In contrast, it is highly doubtful that the extreme proposals which have been made for an immediate scaling up or down of governance would be realisable without conclusive evidence that an environmental cataclysm would otherwise occur.

4.2 Designing a system of ecological governance

A framework for collective decision-making must empower actors possessing appropriate capacities to address the causes of ecological problems if it is

[1] M. Stallworthy, *Sustainability, Land Use and Environment* (London: Cavendish Publishing, 2002), p. 292. See also A. Giddens, *The Politics of Climate Change*, 2nd ed. (Cambridge: Polity Press, 2011), pp. 76–7.

to provide a platform for action to retard the deterioration of ecosystem health. The starting point for the design of such a framework should therefore be to ask some fundamental questions about the nature of the problems to be addressed. These include what their sources are, in what respects these are responsible for or heighten risks of ecological degradation, and over what spatial scales action would need to be taken to tackle them. Based on responses to these questions, the governmental and non-governmental actors who would be best placed to devise and implement solutions, the geographical areas over which they would need to exercise authority, and the extent to which different levels of governance would need to collaborate over the resolution of problems can be identified.

Analysing ecological problems in this way would provide a firm basis for considering how they can be dealt with. However, arguments have been advanced in the academic debate over how a system of ecological governance could be developed which do not start from this point. Instead, they display a lack of confidence in the ability of modern societies to evolve in suggesting that the best approach would be to begin again and design arrangements for governance that would, ab initio, usher in a new and harmonious relationship between humanity and the natural world. In particular, it has been argued that: units of governance should be constructed around ecological boundaries and concerned primarily with maintaining the functionality of ecosystems falling within them; and ecological problems would more likely be resolved if decision-making authority were handed down, in part or fully, to lower levels of government than if it were left with the state.

The validity of these arguments is considered in Section 4.3, and I agree to an extent with their call for the devolution of powers. The existence of institutions that can bring regional and local perspectives to bear in decision-making processes, and that provide a conduit through which public views and knowledge can influence their outcomes, is very important for determining how ecologically desirable changes might be introduced. However, I conclude that, in other respects, the proposals for governance they advance are not adequate to address the causes of harm to ecosystems. This is because they do not engage either with the multifaceted problem of ecological unsustainability as it presents itself to us now, or create bases for governing its principal sources which, ultimately, lie embedded in the DNA of our growth-obsessed society. Additionally, they call for a reduction in the state's role in responding to this problem although it is essential that it should be involved with formulating and then supporting the operation of a framework based on which an ecological transformation of society might occur. In this regard, I agree with Christoff's contention that '[t]he systematic realisation of strong ecological modernisation requires a proactive interventionist state to help undo the ecological ravages of two centuries of industrialization and to facilitate more ecologically rational modes of production and activity.'[2]

In the following sections, I argue that an ecologically coherent framework for governance must make provision for local, regional and national governmental institutions to collaborate in the effort to reduce levels of stress that human activities place on the environment. Whilst the state should take the lead in establishing the framework and overseeing its operation, it would need to work with lower governmental levels and non-governmental actors to achieve ecological objectives. Collaboration across scales is also necessary because the maintenance of ecosystem functionality and sufficient supplies of energy and other resources to meet national demands are not matters which could be dealt with effectively through regional and local action alone.

The relationship I envisage between the different levels of government remains hierarchical to the extent that central government would retain the authority to approve local and regional visions of ecologically desirable change and of how resources might be used in ways that carry less potential for ecological harm. The state should also have the power to intervene where decision-making is: procedurally unfair; results in substantive environmental injustice; or wilfully fails to contribute to prescribed goals. However, this hierarchy is far removed from the stereotypical 'top-down' model in which states command and lower governmental levels do as they are bidden. Rather, the governance framework should create a relationship between them in which the state empowers local and regional government to cooperate with members of the public in developing proposals for the implementation of national policy whilst using the power it derives from electorally conferred legitimacy to steer outcomes towards the realisation of nationally important objectives.

4.3 The limitations of devolution

The question of how political orders might be restructured with a view to stemming declines in ecosystem health has been the subject matter of

[2] P. Christoff, 'Green Governance and the Green State: Capacity Building as a Political Project' in R. Paehlke and D. Torgerson (eds) *Managing Leviathan: Environmental Politics and the Administrative State*, 2nd edn (Peterborough, ON: Broadview Press, 2005), p. 294.

extensive debate since the environmental crises of the early 1970s.[3] This debate has produced radical proposals under which existing structures for governance would be wholly or partly dismantled and new structures put in their place which, it is argued, would better provide for sustainable living and ecological protection than current arrangements. It has also generated more-moderate proposals for achieving these ends through the reform of existing structures and institutions. However, it is to the devolutionary arguments that I turn first as understanding why they are not adequate for tackling the causes of ecological degradation helps in designing a system of governance that would be adequate for this purpose.

Arguments for the deconstruction or reconstruction of governance to achieve ecological ends have been presented on a number of different grounds. The more anarchistically inclined amongst green political theorists have argued that the only way to stave off environmental catastrophe is to devolve authority completely to regional units whose extent would, as far as possible, be coterminous with those of ecosystems, and whose main objective in governance would be to control activities conducted within them so that these are capable of sustaining the region's population, but without damaging the functionality of ecosystems.[4] For example, bioregionalists have argued that the ideal unit of governance would be defined by reference to 'bioregional' boundaries, and that those subject to the governance regime would live only on what each unit's territories are able to provide.[5]

A less-dramatic response to environmental concerns, but one which would also require significant change in political structures, is that authority to regulate the exploitation of ecosystems and the natural resources they contain should be delegated to bodies typically comprised of local and regional actors, agencies with relevant responsibilities, and representatives of other interested parties who, collectively, would form decision-making

[3] L. J. Lundqvist, *Sweden and Ecological Governance* (Manchester: Manchester University Press, 2004), p. 2; A. Dobson, *Green Political Thought*, 4th edn (London: Routledge, 2007), pp. 62–4.

[4] Lundqvist, 'Ecological Governance', pp. 7–8; Dobson, 'Green Political Thought', p. 95; G. Smith, *Deliberative Democracy and the Environment* (London: Routledge, 2003), p. 78; A. Dobson, 'Trajectories of Green Political Theory' (2009) 8 *Contemporary Political Theory*, 321.

[5] Dobson, 'Green Political Thought', p. 91; M. V. McGinnis, 'A Rehearsal to Bioregionalism' in M. V. McGinnis (ed.) *Bioregionalism* (London: Routledge, 1999), pp. 1–9.

institutions for governing uses of the ecosystem concerned.[6] This approach has been argued for on grounds that those with an attachment to, and detailed knowledge of, particular ecosystems would be better placed to manage the impacts of activities on them, and thereby to restore or maintain their healthy functioning, than distant state authorities.[7] For example, Karkkainen contends that regimes which have been established for restoring damaged North American ecosystems (including the Everglades, Chesapeake Bay and the Great Lakes) provide a template for the governance of ecosystems and human uses of them.[8] A particular attraction of this model is, in his view, that it would result in management that is 'ecologically sound' (as opposed, say, to the remote setting of national standards) because it is 'local and/or regional in character' and 'tailored to the ecosystem context'.[9]

Finally, arguments for extending the influence of local levels of government and, through them, of members of the public in environmental decision-making enjoy widespread support amongst green political theorists.[10] This is seen as a development which, irrespective of how units of governance are structured, may lead to outcomes that would be better environmentally because they are 'context sensitive',[11] and that are more

[6] B. C. Karkkainen, 'Toward Ecologically Sustainable Democracy?' In A. Fung and E. O. Wright (eds) *Deepening Democracy: Institutional Innovations in Empowered Participatory Governance* (London: Verso, 2003), pp. 219–23; B. C. Karkkainen, 'Collaborative Ecosystem Governance: Scale, Complexity, and Dynamism' (2002–3) 21 *Virginia Environmental Law Journal*, 217–22. See also Lundqvist, 'Ecological Governance', pp. 25–9 on resource regimes and ecosystem management, the account of the development of ecosystem regimes given in R. O. Brooks, R. Jones and R. A. Virginia, *Law and Ecology: The Rise of the Ecosystem Regime* (Aldershot: Ashgate Publishing, 2002), Chapter 8 and pp. 382–3, and the argument for existing arrangements for environmental governance to be supplemented by commons-based regimes in B. H. Weston and D. Bollier, *Green Governance: Ecological Survival, Human Rights and the Law of the Commons* (New York: Cambridge University Press, 2013).

[7] Karkkainen, 'Collaborative Ecosystem Governance', 197–9; B. C. Karkkainen, 'Information-forcing Regulation and Environmental Governance' in G. de Búrca and J. Scott (eds) *Law and New Governance in the EU and the US* (Oxford: Hart Publishing, 2006), p. 294.

[8] Karkkainen, 'Collaborative Ecosystem Governance', 190, 194; Karkkainen, 'Information-forcing Regulation', pp. 294–5. See also the account of the Chesapeake Bay and Everglades regimes given in Brooks, Jones and Virginia, 'Law and Ecology', pp. 271–9.

[9] Karkkainen, 'Collaborative Ecosystem Governance', 206.

[10] Lundqvist, 'Ecological Governance', pp. 16–19; J. Barry, *Rethinking Green Politics* (London: Sage Publications, 1999), pp. 104–7, Chapter 7; Smith, 'Deliberative Democracy', p. 78.

[11] Karkkainen, 'Information-forcing Regulation', p. 293; N. Gunningham, 'The New Collaborative Environmental Governance: The Localization of Regulation' (2009) 36 *Journal of Law and Society*, 149.

likely to be accepted by those affected by them because the processes by which they are reached are considered to be legitimate.[12] This context sensitivity is, as I noted above, one of the arguments presented in favour of structuring governance around ecosystem boundaries. I agree in part, on grounds which I explore at Section 4.6, with the arguments that have been made for enhancing both the role of local governmental institutions and of the public in the development of solutions to ecological problems. However, the key questions are whether exclusive authority for decision-making is to be conferred and, if so, are the problems that local authorities are being asked to resolve ones which can sensibly be dealt with by them alone?

Elements of these devolutionary proposals would contribute to reducing the pressures we place on the natural world. The creation of institutions for regulating resource-extraction activities within a particular ecosystem would clearly be desirable where these pose a threat to its functionality. As the introduction of an ecological orientation would also require change at every level of society, it is essential that lower levels of government should be able, through planning processes, to shape the development of more sustainable communities and to control activities on an ecologically coherent basis. However, they do not offer a model for governance that would provide sufficient support for those involved with decision-making to take effective action against ecological problems. This is because they fail to recognise that their sources stem from a plethora of linkages in the highly complex society we have constructed which connect localities with other localities, localities with regions and, ultimately, localities with national and international currents. There are four particular respects in which deconstructing governance or reshaping structures along ecological lines would fail to provide actors with the powers they would need to act against these problems. These, as I discuss below, highlight the need for cooperative working between levels of government rather than the distribution of authority in a way which would denude devolved units of, or fail to provide them with, the ability to tackle issues that emanate from beyond their limited spheres of influence. They also point to the need for the state to take the lead in governing activities so that their impacts on ecosystem health are reduced.

The first is that the devolutionary arguments tend to wish away hundreds of years of economic growth and the organisation of societies around this goal instead of grappling with the ecological challenges that

[12] Lundqvist, 'Ecological Governance', pp. 10, 17.

complex socioeconomic systems give rise to. They present solutions that would be ideal if it were possible to start the design of a new system of governance from a blank slate, but which, in practice, are unrealisable or would address only the symptoms of ecological unsustainability in particular places rather than striking at its roots. As Lundqvist notes in arguing against a bioregional approach, 'natural regions and areas are today so interpenetrated and transgressed by linked human activities at different spatial scales' that it would be difficult to legitimise governance arrangements whose form is dictated by what would be appropriate from a purely ecological perspective.[13] Lipschutz also questions whether ecologically organised units in which 'history, economy, and nature would (again) be mismatched' would provide any better basis for governance than the arrangements we have in place already.[14] The clear conclusion is that we need a system of governance which, in its geographical scope, in the powers it confers on actors, and in the objectives it requires them to observe and collectively achieve, provides a better fit with the causes, both direct and indirect, of ecological harm.[15]

The second and related concern is that devolved units would be ill-equipped to address external sources of harm. Ecological degradation is driven by entrenched economic and social behaviours which can be changed, if at all, only through a concerted effort at all governmental levels and by non-governmental actors throughout society to reduce unsustainable levels of consumption. Similarly, threats to ecosystem health presented, for example, by carbon emissions, acid rain and fertiliser run-off are no respecters of jurisdictional boundaries and require collaboration between different governmental levels if they are to be alleviated. As Barry observes in questioning the effectiveness of 'anarchistic' arguments for devolution, the reality is that local units are unable to address most of the environmental problems that confront society because these are predominantly 'large-scale and interrelated and cannot be decomposed into smaller components'.[16]

[13] Lundqvist, 'Ecological Governance', p. 7.

[14] R. D. Lipschutz, 'Bioregionalism, Civil Society and Global Environmental Governance' in M. V. McGinnis (ed.) *Bioregionalism* (London: Routledge, 1999), pp. 102–3.

[15] V. Galaz et al., 'Environmental and Resource Regimes, and Broader Governance Systems: Insight and Emerging Challenges' in O. R. Young, L. A. King and H. Schroeder (eds) *Institutions and Environmental Change: Principal Findings, Applications and Research Frontiers* (Cambridge, MA: MIT Press, 2008), pp. 157–60.

[16] Barry, 'Rethinking Green Politics', p. 211. See also Dobson, 'Trajectories of Green Political Theory', 326; Galaz et al., 'The Problem of Fit', pp. 175–7; R. Cowell, 'The Greenest Government Ever? Planning and Sustainability in England after the May 2010 Elections' (2013) 28 *Planning Practice and Research*, 33–4.

This, as Dobson contends, leads to the conclusion that 'dealing with the environmental problems that the green movement has identified requires the kind of planning and coordination that can only be provided by a centralised political structure.'[17] That is not to say that devolved units of governance have no part to play in ecological governance. To the contrary, I have already noted that their involvement with developing solutions that are tailored to local conditions is essential for their effectiveness and for public acceptance of them. Rather, the issue of externalities highlights the importance of creating linkages between local and central government that would connect the important contribution of the former with the ability of the latter to coordinate responses to ecological problems and to take a big-picture view of how these can best be dealt with.[18]

Third, autonomous units of devolved governance may be as adept at creating externalities as they are incapable of managing sources of ecological harm that are external to them. For example, the refusal of one institution with responsibility for managing an ecosystem to permit activities may, if it is not supported by a holistic framework for controlling development, simply result in their being exported to places where controls are not in place or which are less able to resist the pressures of external economic drivers. Whilst the governed ecosystems may benefit, the net result may be that overall levels of ecological stress are not reduced and that the negative effects of activities become concentrated in other locations. There is also no guarantee where local institutions are given significant leeway to define what would be 'sustainable' for their area that ecologically desirable outcomes would result.[19] An obvious potential scenario is that local authorities would deem maintaining the character of a particular community as being a greater contribution to sustainability than making resources available for renewable energy when others might bear the burden of associated infrastructure construction. In this regard, Cowell and Owens question the wisdom of conferring a high degree of freedom on communities to make decisions without some provision for external supervision when these 'may have

[17] Dobson, 'Green Political Thought', p. 97. See also Galaz et al., 'The Problem of Fit', pp. 178–9.

[18] S. M. Wheeler, *Planning for Sustainability: Creating Liveable, Equitable, and Ecological Communities* (London: Routledge, 2004), p. 122; M. Baker and C. Wong, 'The Delusion of Strategic Spatial Planning: What's Left after the Labour Government's English Regional Experiment?' (2013) 28 *Planning Practice and Research*, 96–7.

[19] Wheeler, 'Planning for Sustainability', p. 46. See also Galaz et al., 'The Problem of Fit', pp. 172–3.

(sometimes unforeseeable) [or, in the case of infrastructure displacement, entirely foreseeable] consequences elsewhere'.[20]

Both of these considerations point again to the need for a framework for ecological governance that links higher and lower levels of government and places on them a responsibility for pursuing shared goals: in the first instance to coordinate action for reducing ecological stresses at all levels of governance; and, in the second, to allow central government to intervene where regional and local bodies fail, without justification, to engage with strategic initiatives that are intended to realise objectives of importance to the nation as a whole. Whilst it is important that lower levels of government should be given room to develop solutions, it is equally important that central government should have the power to take action where these make no effort to address matters of common concern.

A final difficulty is that a state comprised of localised units of governance, each one having a primary focus on controlling development within its own territory, would find it practically impossible to develop a capacity for strategic spatial planning. Knowledge of the possibilities for resource provision in the different localities and regions of the UK is required if ways of reducing the risks of ecological harm that the country generates as a whole are to be identified, and for the formation and implementation of strategic plans based on this information. Ensuring that energy needs throughout the country can be met is also a responsibility that can only be discharged by a body or bodies which are able to establish how this might be done in ways which lead to a reduction in the ecological stresses that this sector is responsible for, and then to carry their conclusions into effect.

Neither of the above are matters that can be dealt with sensibly by empowering localised units to do what they can independently and hoping that their separate contributions will amount to a sustainable whole.[21] Instead, they fall into the category of issues which Wheeler describes as lying within the national domain because lower levels of government, whilst they may be able to make important contributions to addressing these concerns, will not have 'the perspective, resources, jurisdiction or political will' to take effective action for their resolution in totality.[22] The need for a spatial overview of how goals of importance

[20] S. Owens and R. Cowell, *Land and Limits: Interpreting Sustainability in the Planning Process*, 1st edn (London: Routledge, 2002), p. 126.

[21] Ibid., p. 148. [22] Wheeler, 'Planning for Sustainability', p. 122.

to the nation can be met, and the ability to act upon outcomes of strategic planning processes if satisfactory solutions to these issues are to be found, requires that higher governmental levels should be involved with coordinating and, where necessary, directing action for their effective resolution.

It is clear from these concerns that the distribution of significant levels of authority to localised units would undermine rather than enhance our ability to act against problems that are endemic in society, and whose direct consequences are inextricably linked to socioeconomic forces operating at much broader scales than the local.[23] They also, through highlighting weaknesses with devolutionary arguments, point to two issues that we should focus on if we are to design an effective system of ecological governance.

The first is that ecological problems are rooted in the *cumulative impacts* of the political economies of places and the stresses that they place on ecosystems in order to maintain their own functionality.[24] In particular, they derive from the insatiable appetite for energy and resources of conurbations and industrial centres.[25] Accordingly, a sensible starting point would be to explore, working as far as possible through existing structures of governance, how the demands that places make on the natural world might be reduced and how their practices, where these are unsustainable, might be altered.[26] The second is that linkages should be created between local, regional and central governmental levels that would allow them to cooperate in identifying the least ecologically harmful means by which the needs of places might be satisfied. This is an objective which could only be achieved by local and regional bodies and individuals with knowledge of places working with the state to develop a national spatial overview of the different options available for meeting demands. An effective system of ecological governance would therefore be one in which different levels of government and non-governmental actors interact to develop solutions that are capable of advancing its objectives. I consider in the following sections what the

[23] Owens and Cowell, 'Land and Limits', 1st edn, p. 149.

[24] Lipschutz, 'Bioregionalism', p. 110.

[25] W. Rees, 'Scale, Complexity and the Conundrum of Sustainability' in M. Kenny and J. Meadowcroft (eds) *Planning Sustainability* (London: Routledge, 1999), p. 107; S. M. Wheeler, 'Regions, Megaregions and Sustainability' (2009) 43 *Regional Studies*, 864–6.

[26] Rees, 'Complexity and the Conundrum', p. 122.

roles of central, regional and local levels of government, and of members of the public, should be in this collaborative system and how relations between them should be structured to ensure that they contribute collectively to reaching overarching goals.

4.4 The state's role in ecological governance

Proposals for the devolution of authority have been closely associated with a critique of the role of nation states in addressing environmental problems, and with arguments either that they lack the strength in a globalised world to address the causes of harm to ecosystems or that they represent active obstacles to the realisation of sustainability. Doubts over the ability of states to bring about an improvement in ecological conditions is evidenced by the sheer range of prescriptions that have been advanced in green political thought as to how sustainable development might be achieved despite their perceived weaknesses, or even without their involvement.[27] Critics point to the failure of states to halt ecological degradation as evidence that environmental concerns would better be dealt with at higher or lower political levels.[28] States are also seen as institutions that are too bound up with the mechanisms of global capitalism (both as participants in and upholders of the international financial system) for them to take action that would undermine its hegemony.[29]

Others have recognised, although the deterioration of the global environment has happened, as it were, on their watch, that the involvement of states with reforming economic and social models remains essential if ecological challenges are to be met. Green political theorists who have explored possibilities for reforming current political structures rather than discarding them argue that the state alone possesses the authority, the legitimacy, the resources, and the powers of coordination and redistribution to initiate a transformation of the magnitude which the implementation of ecologically oriented policies would require, to impose associated environmental and resource constraints, and to manage the potential consequences of change where these may result in

[27] L. J. Lundqvist, 'A Green Fist in a Velvet Glove: The Ecological State and Sustainable Development' (2001) 10 *Environmental Values*, 456.

[28] Christoff, 'Green Governance and the Green State', pp. 290–4.

[29] M. Kenny and J. Meadowcroft, 'Introduction' in M. Kenny and J. Meadowcroft (eds) *Planning Sustainability* (London: Routledge, 1999), p. 2; Weston and Bollier, 'Green Governance', pp. 3–4, 20–3.

hardship or environmental injustice.[30] From their perspective, the state should not be seen as a barrier to sustainability, but, instead, as an institution which is 'part of the solution rather than part of the problem',[31] and one 'without which green proposals cannot be realised'.[32] A sensible approach to developing a new system of governance that is capable of addressing threats of ecological destruction would therefore be to 'contend with existing institutions' rather than to ignore them, and, where possible, to seek 'to rebuild the ship while still at sea'.[33]

Some authors also take issue with the claim that developed states have become too closely allied with corporate interests in the pursuit of economic growth to act against the environmental consequences of their behaviour.[34] Their accounts of the progressive acceptance by states of responsibilities for 'counteracting the effects of the market's externalisation of ecological costs', and of the adoption by them of large and growing bodies of environmental laws to that end does not sit well with the description of states as being hopelessly in thrall to markets.[35] They also draw parallels between the emergence of environmental protection as a fourth core responsibility of states and the gradual development of welfare states in response to growing evidence of the negative social effects of capitalist economies.[36] The latter has been, and remains, an episodic process, but the provision of welfare has become accepted by states, however unpalatable they may find it, as a necessary response to a phenomenon that may result in their destabilisation if it is not addressed.[37]

[30] Dobson, 'Green Political Thought', pp. 97–101; Barry, 'Rethinking Green Politics', pp. 111–3; A. Blowers, 'The Time for Change' in A. Blowers (ed.) *Planning for a Sustainable Environment* (London: Earthscan, 1993), pp. 8, 13–14; Kenny and Meadowcroft, 'Introduction', pp. 2–5; Christoff, 'Green Governance and the Green State', pp. 294–6; Lundqvist, 'A Green Fist', 457; R. Eckersley, *The Green State: Rethinking Democracy and Sovereignty* (Cambridge, MA: MIT Press, 2004), pp. 4–8; Giddens, 'The Politics of Climate Change', pp. 94–7.

[31] Dobson, 'Green Political Thought', p. 100.

[32] Barry, 'Rethinking Green Politics', p. 113. [33] Eckersley, 'The Green State', p. 5.

[34] J. Meadowcroft, 'Greening the State' in P. F. Steinberg and S. D. VanDeveer (eds) *Comparative Environmental Politics: Theory, Practice and Prospects* (Cambridge, MA: The MIT Press, 2012), pp. 66–76; A. Duit, 'Adaptive Capacity and the Ecostate' in E. Boyd and C. Folke (eds) *Adapting Institutions: Governance, Complexity and Social-Ecological Resilience* (Cambridge: Cambridge University Press, 2012), pp. 127–47.

[35] Duits, 'Adaptive Capacity', pp. 131–7; Meadowcroft, 'Greening the State', pp. 66–7.

[36] Duits, 'Adaptive capacity', pp. 131–3; Meadowcroft, 'Greening the State', pp. 73–6; A. While et al., 'From Sustainable Development to Carbon Control: Eco-state Restructuring and the Politics of Urban and Regional Development' (2010) 35 *Transactions of the Institute of British Geographers*, 80.

[37] Meadowcroft, 'Greening the State', pp. 71–2.

I concur with this pragmatic viewpoint in arguing that it would not be possible to challenge the drivers of ecological degradation without the involvement of a body possessing the necessary capacities to set in train societal initiatives for a more sustainable future and to direct them towards the realisation of this goal. However, I also recognise that there are limitations on the state's ability to secure desired change through its own efforts. In particular, the stimulation of public interest in, and support for, action to lessen threats of harm to ecosystems would be essential if the state's environmental policies are to be effected. In view of this, achieving an ecological transition would not, as some green theorists have argued, involve a reprise of the state's historic role as dictator of outcomes.[38] Rather, a system of ecological governance would need to establish a new relationship between lower levels of government and the state in which the former are given more scope to shape policy initiatives whilst the latter would retain the authority, through indirect and direct means, to influence and oversee the outcomes of decision-making processes. The state's direct involvement with deciding how policy should be implemented would be reduced under this relationship. However, its involvement with the government of governance (or metagovernance) as it is practised by others would see a corresponding increase.[39]

Accounts of the relations between central government and other actors involved with governance where aspects of state authority have been devolved have used analogies to games and game players to describe the different roles of participants in decision-making. This analogy could also be applied to the different respects in which the state would need to relate to other levels of government and non-governmental actors in a system of ecological governance. The state, through its authority to make legislative proposals, would retain 'a powerful role in setting the rules of the game' to be played by regional and local levels of government and by ad hoc institutions for deliberative public participation.[40] It would, at times, need to be a player itself in the game it has created, to carry out its own

[38] Dobson, 'Green Political Thought', refers at p. 105 to the arguments made by Heilbroner and Ophuls amongst others that only a strong (authoritarian) state would be capable of dealing with the environmental crises which confront the world. See also Giddens, 'The Politics of Climate Change', pp. 76–7.

[39] G. Haughton and D. Counsell, *Regions, Spatial Strategies and Sustainable Development* (London: Routledge, 2004), p. 35.

[40] G. Haughton, P. Allmendinger, D. Counsell and G. Vigar, *The New Spatial Planning: Territorial Management with Soft Spaces and Fuzzy Boundaries* (Abingdon: Routledge, 2010), p. 11.

responsibilities for meeting certain national needs. However, once the game is afoot, its principal role would be to act in a refereeing capacity. As overseer of decision-making activities, its responsibility would be to ensure that objectives of national importance are achieved or, at least, adhered to, and that standards of importance to the state as a democratic institution are observed by other participants in decision-making. In this respect, the state would not be 'just another actor in the game of resource 'governance''.[41] It would also be 'the umpire in that game, with a unique authority resting on regulations and enforceable sanctions'.[42] I consider the capacities that the state should possess and the different parts that it would need to play in a system of ecological governance if this is to function effectively in the following sections.

4.4.1 A guiding state

It is implicit in the concept of metagovernance that the state, whilst it devolves power to other governmental levels and non-governmental actors, would retain an ability to influence their deliberations in the hope that these will result in outcomes that advance nationally preferred objectives.[43] This presupposes that, although separate levels of authority have been established, they would operate within an overarching system of governance which lays down the ends that participants in decision-making processes should aim to accomplish, the criteria that should be observed in decision-making, and the relationships between levels of government including the circumstances in which it would be permissible for one to challenge the conclusions reached by another. Accordingly, the first way in which the state can employ its powers to promote ecologically desirable change is by seeking to put in place a framework which, whilst it confers a level of autonomy on regional and local bodies, also binds them to pursuing specified goals.[44]

The primary means by which the state can structure relations between itself and other actors in government to promote favoured outcomes is by using its executive authority to put forward and pilot through

[41] Lundqvist, 'A Green Fist', 459. [42] Ibid.

[43] Haughton et al., 'The New Spatial Planning', pp. 11–12; Haughton and Counsell, 'Regions, Spatial Strategies', p. 35; J. Meadowcroft, 'Planning, Democracy and the Challenge of Sustainable Development' (1997) 18 *International Political Science Review*, 184.

[44] Blowers, 'The Time for Change', p. 14; P. Hirst, 'Democracy and Governance' in J. Pierre (ed.) *Debating Governance: Authority, Steering and Democracy* (Oxford: Oxford University Press, 2000), p. 31.

legislation that would define the nature of the collaborative governance arrangement.[45] Legislation might be used, for example, to prescribe statutory objectives to be achieved, decision rules to be applied and 'red lines' to be observed by all those involved with decision-making. It can also provide a legal foundation for institutions and establish institutional structures that are specifically designed to promote the achievement of ecological end values. The re-creation of a regional layer of government provides an example, as I argue at Section 4.5.1, of how institutional design could be used to enhance a 'green' state's ability to further its ecological aims. Finally, the adequacy of provision made for public participation under legal frameworks that prescribe decision-making processes would, as I argue in the following section, have a significant influence on the way in which ecological policies would be perceived by the persons whom they affect. It is therefore through the development of appropriate legal structures at the outset that the state can create the conditions in which action to initiate and thereafter to entrench an ecological transformation of society can be taken.

The conscious manipulation of decision-making processes through, for example, specifying that decisions made and plans formed under the planning system should contribute to the realisation of ecological objectives may conflict with purists' views of planning as providing a neutral forum for discussing competing conceptions of the good.[46] It also departs from the ideal of communicative rationality that the outcomes of citizens' deliberations should be the product of free and unfettered debate.[47] However, it would clearly be desirable in a legal framework founded on ecological values that the state should use its steering capacities to manoeuvre actors towards decisions that would contribute to reducing levels of ecological stress.[48] After all, one of the key purposes of public participation in ecological governance would be to promote acceptance of, and involvement with, the delivery of governmental proposals for action to protect ecosystems. It is not to allow localities

[45] Gunningham, 'The New Collaborative Environmental Governance', 163.
[46] Owens and Cowell, 'Land and Limits', 1st edn, p. 7.
[47] Ibid.; M. Tewdwr-Jones and P. Allmendinger, 'Deconstructing Communicative Rationality: A Critique of Habermasian Collaborative Planning' (1998) 30 *Environment and Planning A*, 1976.
[48] M. Jacobs, 'Environmental Valuation, Deliberative Democracy and Public Decision-making Institutions' in J. Foster (ed.) *Valuing Nature? Ethics, Economics and the Environment* (London: Routledge, 1997), p. 229.

to pursue whatever courses of action they deem to be in their interests, irrespective of whether this contributes to the realisation of broader objectives.

4.4.2 A communicative state

The state cannot itself drive through solutions to matters of ecological concern. It must secure public support for the principles underlying its policies if these are not to be met with opposition. It must also encourage public participation with developing plans for their implementation. In view of this, an important means by which the state can use its executive authority to promote the achievement of ecological objectives is by proposing reforms to existing arrangements for governance so that these provide for more meaningful public involvement with shaping the outcomes of decision-making processes. Reforms that may achieve this end would include the provision of opportunities for participation in legal frameworks for planning that go beyond simple consultation on extant proposals, establishing channels of communication between institutions at different governmental levels by which information provided at lower levels can percolate upwards to and influence decision-making at higher levels, and requiring that public participation be conducted through deliberative fora in which members of the public debate issues raised by an ecological transition.

It is through the creation of decision-making structures that allow for interaction between different levels of government and non-governmental actors that the state can enhance its 'communicative capacity'. Christoff defines this as 'the state's ability to facilitate and participate in meaningfully discursive democritisation, and to weld effective and legitimate policy through the exchange'.[49] The extent to which a state possesses this capacity will determine its ability not only to 'foster ecological modernisation that is open and reflexive' as Christoff argues,[50] but also to put policy proposals for ecologically desirable change into practice when these are likely, because of the impacts that they would have on peoples' lifestyles, to give rise to significant levels of public concern. I consider in detail how the legal framework for planning might be structured and the form that institutions for public participation should take if this capacity is to be enhanced in Chapters 5 and 6.

[49] Christoff, 'Green Governance and the Green State', p. 297. [50] Ibid.

4.4.3 A coordinating state

The objective of ecological governance would be to reduce the stresses that human activities place cumulatively on the functionality of ecosystems. As these stresses stem both from disparate activities and, ultimately, from patterns of consumption distributed throughout society, the question of how they could be reduced can best be addressed by a coordinating body which is able to take an overview of: the demands that economic and social practices make on the natural world; the different options by which these demands can be met; and, based on this information, the most effective means by which ecological objectives might be advanced.

The state, with its position at the centre of government and its responsibility, on which its legitimacy rests, to act for the common good, is well placed to take on this role of coordinator and overseer.[51] It can, from its 'national' vantage point, work with regions and localities to explore how the ecological stresses that they generate can be set on a downwards trajectory over the timescales that ecologically oriented policies and plans for their implementation would cover. The state's role in this respect would be to act as the nerve centre of the governance system with responsibility for coordinating its disparate parts so that these are able to take collective action against the shared problem of ecological degradation.

There are two main respects in which a coordinating body would assist with identifying solutions to problems that extend beyond regional boundaries. The first would be to take a critical overview of the ability of regions to provide resources and meet demands using the ecologically preferred ways identified through the policy-making process. Regions are blessed with resources to differing extents. The potential ecological consequences of exploiting them will also vary. Some regions will be able to meet needs from their own resources whilst others, and particularly regions containing urban centres, will make demands that extend far beyond their borders. The state's task, in the first instance, is to work with regions and localities as necessary to identify whether resource needs can be met in ways which allow the progressive reduction of ecological stresses, and, if so, how this would best be achieved. This would involve drawing from possibilities for resource provision and reductions in resource consumption that are identified in local and regional plans.

[51] Hirst, 'Democracy and Governance', pp. 30–1; Eckersley, 'The Green State' (2004), p. 6.

This analysis would also provide a platform for the state's review of its own policies, and particularly of whether there needs to be a greater focus on structural change in the economy and society as a whole where possibilities for the spatial distribution of resource provision prove insufficient to alleviate threats of ecological harm. This process lies at the heart of the experimentation I refer to in the introduction to this chapter, in which the possibilities for a society to function without undermining ecosystem health and undergoing a complete change in political and economic structures and objectives are explored.

The relationship I envisage between the state and regional and local government in this exercise is far removed from the conventional top-down hierarchical approach that has been used in the UK for exploring how demand for resources can be satisfied. This, typically, has involved the placing of targets on regions to meet specified levels of demand and, where they have failed to achieve them, has resulted either in coercion, legal challenge or in the use of ad hoc spatial fixes to compensate for this.[52] Cowell and Owens' account of the proposed use of remote coastal 'superquarries' to provide aggregate for construction in English urban centres provides a good example both of a governmental attempt to compensate for the inability of certain regions (particularly the South East) to sustain their own demands, and also of a spatial fix which failed because of strong opposition to the proposed development.[53] This incoherent approach in the face of resource constraints can also be seen, to an extent, in the recent focus on offshore wind energy as a response to difficulties with creating a substantial capacity for renewable energy generation through onshore wind farm construction. Conversely, the relationship I propose involves the provision of information from the bottom up based on which all levels of government might participate in making a realistic assessment of prospects for reducing levels of ecological stress and producing strategic plans that capture the best available means of advancing this end.

The second aspect of the coordinating role involves avoidance of the environmental injustices which may result from the inability of regions to meet their own needs. There is, in view both of the uneven distribution

[52] See the analyses of top-down approaches to the implementation of resource policy in Owens and Cowell, 'Land and Limits', 1st edn, pp. 131–6 (aggregates) and H. Bulkeley, 'Planning and Governance of Climate Change' in S. Davoudi, J. Crawford and A. Mehmood (eds) *Planning for Climate Change: Strategies for Mitigation and Adaptation for Spatial Planners* (London: Earthscan, 2009), p. 284 (renewable energy).

[53] Owens and Cowell, 'Land and Limits', 1st edn, pp. 138–42.

of requirements for resources and the ability of different regions to meet them, a clear potential for disproportionate demands to be placed on resource-rich areas or on places which, because of an industrial past or poor economic conditions, may be seen as more amenable or less resistant to infrastructure development than affluent areas.[54] An over-viewing body would be in a position to recognise and address situations of this kind. It would also be able to explore how this potential might be avoided by exploring with resource-intensive regions whether there is greater scope for reducing consumption or meeting demand through their own resources, considering whether alternative spatial options to clustering resource provision are available that would be less ecologically consequential and more socially acceptable, and, failing this, to look again at whether the country's macro-economic structure is in need of revision to provide for a more sustainable and fairer society.

Action by the state to coordinate planning processes in the interests of environmental justice and in recognition that the reduction of stresses is a shared goal would also encourage perception of ecological governance as a fair system. In this regard, the ability of an overseeing body to consider with the major consumers of resources how they might contribute to the goal of ecological sustainability by reducing their levels of consumption and increasing their own capacity to meet them would promote acceptance of the system. As Barry observes with regard to national taxation, people do not object to the existence of a tax burden per se.[55] Opposition to taxation arises largely where the distribution of the burden is manifestly unequal.[56] In the same way, the significant changes in society that would result from the implementation of ecological policies would be more likely to be accepted as long as the costs of change are shared equitably throughout society and, of equal importance, if this can be seen to be the case.[57]

4.4.4 An enforcing state

A risk inherent in distributing authority amongst different governmental levels is that bodies with responsibility for decision-making will concentrate on, and prioritise, matters of immediate importance to the localities

[54] Ibid., pp. 128–31; J. Holder, 'Building Spatial Europe: An Environmental Justice Perspective' in J. Scott (ed.) *Environmental Protection: European Law and Governance* (Oxford: Oxford University Press, 2009), pp. 119–22.

[55] J. Barry, 'Rethinking Green Politics', p. 214. [56] Ibid. [57] Ibid., pp. 213–14.

and regions over which they have jurisdiction at the expense of objectives whose realisation are necessary for the well-being of broader communities, and, in the case of reducing threats of ecological harm, of the nation as a whole.[58] The potential result of this would be a fragmentation of authority and a reduced national ability to deal with environmental problems whose resolution would require all units of governance to 'pull in the same direction'.

To avoid this potential outcome it is necessary, as proponents of devolved decision-making power to localities have recognised, for the state to remain in place at the pinnacle of governance structures even where significant devolution has occurred, and to retain a capacity to challenge decisions where these fail to attain minimum performance objectives or where decision-making processes fail to observe standards of substantive and procedural fairness.[59] For example, Karkkainen advocates the use of regulatory penalty defaults in which the possibility of state intervention is intended to act as a stimulus for actors at lower decision-making levels to make a genuine attempt to produce solutions that advance national requirements as well as being adapted to local circumstances.[60] Dorf and Sabel also argue that an ability to intervene is necessary to protect citizens against abuses of power that 'may result from or be exacerbated by the pulverization of central authority'.[61] This capacity would be of particular importance if public participation is to be conducted through deliberative fora. A concern frequently expressed over deliberative processes is that debate will be dominated by the most powerful and well-educated deliberants, and, therefore, that the outcomes of deliberation will be skewed towards their interests.[62]

Advocates of democratic experimentalism argue that localised units of governance should be given significant levels of autonomy to make decisions on matters which, in line with the principle of subsidiarity,

[58] Owens and Cowell, 'Land and Limits', 1st edn, pp. 148–9; Wheeler, 'Planning for Sustainability', pp. 46–7; Galaz et al., 'The Problem of Fit', pp. 171–3.

[59] G. de Búrca and J. Scott, 'Introduction: New Governance, Law and Constitutionalism' in G. de Búrca and J. Scott (eds) *Law and New Governance in the EU and the US* (Oxford: Hart Publishing, 2006), pp. 7–8; M. C. Dorf and C. F. Sabel, 'A Constitution of Democratic Experimentalism' (1998) 98 *Columbia Law Review*, 283–4, 340; Karkkainen, 'Information-forcing Regulation', pp. 316–7; Galaz et al., 'The Problem of Fit', p. 179.

[60] Karkkainen, 'Information-forcing Regulation', p. 296, 305–310.

[61] Dorf and Sabel, 'Democratic Experimentalism', 340.

[62] Smith, 'Deliberative Democracy', p. 78; Tewdwr-Jones and Allmendinger, 'Deconstructing Communicative Rationality', 1981.

are best handled at the local level.[63] Their decisions would be left undisturbed unless there is some positive basis for intervention by central government. However, opportunities for devolution on this scale in a system of ecological governance would be limited because of the nature of the problems to be addressed and the objectives to be achieved. These, as I argued in the preceding section, would require that the state be involved as a coordinating body with identifying possibilities for reducing levels of ecological stress based on a nationwide knowledge of resource availability and demands placed on ecosystems by all of the country's communities. In circumstances where the state takes on this coordinating role, and, in association with it, the ultimate authority for the approval of strategic plans, a capacity for formal intervention in decisions made elsewhere would not be required.

The democratic renewal and the enhanced perception of governmental legitimacy which, in Dorf and Sabel's view, would result from adoption of a democratic experimentalist model of governance, would be provided in this system primarily by improved opportunities for local and regional levels of government to collaborate with national government in the formation of strategic plans. The latter should not have free rein to depart from their proposals. It would undermine the legitimacy of the system of governance if the state were to use its coordinating role to engage in the micromanagement of regional and local affairs.[64] Rather, it should work constructively with regions and localities to develop solutions which are conducive to alleviating threats of ecological harm. This need to cooperate could be reinforced by requiring the state to give reasons for departing from recommendations made to it by local and regional bodies, and to provide an explanation of how revisions it proposes to make to their proposals would advance the objectives of the system of governance.[65] The requirement to provide justification for its contrary views would provide a means of restricting the state's interventions to

[63] Dorf and Sabel, 'Democratic Experimentalism', 283–9; O. Gerstenberg and C. F. Sabel, 'Directly-deliberative Polyarchy: An Institutional Ideal for Europe?' in C. Joerges and R. Dehousse (eds) *Good Governance in Europe's Integrated Market* (Oxford: Oxford University Press, 2002), pp. 291–2.

[64] J. Meadowcroft, 'Deliberative Democracy' in R. F. Durant, D. J. Fiorino and R. O'Leary (eds) *Environmental Governance Reconsidered* (Cambridge, MA: The MIT Press, 2004), pp. 210–11.

[65] Jacobs, 'Environmental Valuation', p. 225. Jacobs argues that, for the creation of deliberative democracy, there would need to be in place a culture in which it is difficult for politicians to ignore recommendations unless 'overriding reasons can be given in terms of the public good'.

those which are necessary for the reduction of ecological stresses or to ensure that outcomes of decision-making would not result in procedural or environmental injustice.

4.5 Expanding the state's range

Whilst it is the state that must take the lead in and give direction to an ecological transition, it would not be able to effect this solely through its own efforts. It would also need to enhance its capacities to promote change by creating or working with existing regional and local bodies, and by conferring on them the powers for planning and decision-making that they would require to contribute to the achievement of ecological goals.[66] These bodies should not be ciphers of the state with a mandate restricted to policy delivery. To the contrary, they must have the independence to develop proposals which reflect the different capacities of localities and regions to implement policies if these are to be translated into practicable plans for action. It is also important for the perceived legitimacy of the system of governance that these bodies should carry sufficient weight in strategic decision-making to ensure that regional and local perspectives are taken into account and have an influence on national strategic planning.

4.5.1 Regional government

Legal and institutional frameworks for governing development in the UK have been reworked regularly since 1945 as part of the 'perennial search' by different governments 'for some combination of governance structures stretching from neighbourhood to national… which align with wider goals'.[67] Regional government has been perceived in these periodic reworkings, and depending on the ideological stance of the reforming administration, either as a governmental level that can assist the state with achieving its objectives or as an unnecessary bureaucratic layer which is more likely to stifle than facilitate economic growth.[68]

[66] Blowers, 'The Time for Change' p. 8; Christoff, 'Green Governance and the Green State', pp. 294–5; J. Meadowcroft, 'Planning for Sustainable Development: Insights from the Literatures of Political Science' (1997) 31 *European Journal of Political Research*, 441, 450.

[67] Haughton et al., 'The New Spatial Planning', p. 45.

[68] Haughton and Counsell, 'Regions, Spatial Strategies', pp. 6–7. This shifting attitude to regional government and planning is not confined to the UK. See the account of regionalism in the US in Wheeler, 'Regions, Megaregions, and Sustainability', 866–8.

In the UK, the Labour administrations that held power between 1997 and 2010 made reforms to the planning system that, on paper at least, gave regional bodies an important role in managing the spatial impacts of sectoral policies, and thereby with promoting sustainable development.[69] However, these reforms had little opportunity to bed in before the following Coalition Government abolished the regional tier of planning in entirety.[70]

There are two main reasons why a regional level of government would be desirable in a system of ecological governance. The first is, as noted at Section 4.4.3, that there are severe limits on the ability of local bodies with authority over comparatively small areas to achieve meaningful change in socioeconomic systems that operate at broader spatial scales. This is a difficulty which the Royal Commission on Environmental Pollution recognised in its report on environmental planning.[71] It concluded that areas for a system of planning which is capable of devising solutions to society's environmental problems would need to be 'sufficiently large and self-contained' to encompass 'interactions between environmental, economic and social factors within their boundaries',[72] and, consequently, that spatial planning should be conducted at the regional level because the areas covered by local planning authorities 'are not sufficiently large or self-contained to provide a satisfactory basis for strategic planning'.[73]

To overcome this spatial difficulty, local authorities would need, if they are to contribute to realising national objectives, to work with a coordinating body on the production of plans that, whilst they reflect local conditions (and therefore maintain the important link with public participation in the plan-making process) would also cover a sufficient scale to present strategic responses to problems that cross jurisdictional boundaries. Regional institutions would be well placed to provide this

[69] M. Tewdwr-Jones and P. Allmendinger, 'Regional Institutions, Governance and the Planning System' in H. Dimitriou and R. Thompson (eds) *Strategic Planning for Regional Development in the UK: A Review of Principles and Practices* (Abingdon: Routledge, 2007), pp. 34–6; M. Tewdwr-Jones, N. Gallent, and J. Morphet, 'An Anatomy of Spatial Planning: Coming to Terms with the Spatial Element in UK Planning' (2010) 18 *European Planning Studies*, 247–50.

[70] Secretary of State for Communities and Local Government, 'Revoking Regional Strategies', Ministerial Statement, 6 July 2010, http://www.communities.gov.uk/statements/newsroom/regionalstrategies. Baker and Wong, 'The Delusion of Strategic Spatial Planning', 91.

[71] Royal Commission on Environmental Pollution, 'Environmental Planning', 23rd Report, CM 5459, March 2002.

[72] Ibid., p. 147, para. 10.23. [73] Ibid., p. 159, para. 10.75.

coordination, and thereby to introduce national and regional perspectives to local planning processes because they operate at an interface between the national and the local. The regional level is seen to be closer and more sensitive to the local context than national government.[74] At the same time, its broader planning horizons would allow it to explore with local authorities how the organisation of identifiable social and economic regions, including, for example, those areas comprising cities and their hinterlands which Wheeler describes as 'commutesheds', might be restructured to reduce their ecological impacts, and the parts that individual communities might play in this restructuring.[75]

The second is that regional bodies which collaborate closely with local authorities, and through them with members of the public, will be able to assist central government with developing strategic plans that are more likely to be publicly acceptable because they rest on a firm foundation of local knowledge. Regional institutions have, in the past, tended to be 'national-facing' bodies with a primary responsibility for developing plans that advance policies of central government for economic growth.[76] However, their principal role in ecological governance would be to develop a spatial understanding of areas and knowledge of possibilities for, and constraints on, resource provision within them based on which they can then work with central government to develop plans that are genuinely strategic, in the sense that they capture what can be done to advance ecological objectives.[77] The legitimacy of a system of governance which incorporates regional bodies that are 'locality-facing' and that work predominantly with local authorities on the formation of regional plans would be enhanced as they would preserve a clear link with local governmental institutions and participatory fora in higher-level debates.

An important consideration and one which has dogged the efforts by the UK Government to introduce regional government during the

[74] H. Dimitriou and R. Thompson, 'Introduction' in H. Dimitriou and R. Thompson (eds) *Strategic Planning for Regional Development in the UK: A Review of Principles and Practices* (Abingdon: Routledge, 2007), p. 3.

[75] Wheeler, 'Planning for Sustainability', pp. 14, 151. See also Wheeler, 'Regions, Megaregions and Sustainability', 872–3.

[76] Dimitriou and Thompson, 'Introduction', p. 5.

[77] I refer to the classification of decision-making levels and their objectives in B. Mitchell, 'The Evolution of Integrated Resource Management' in R. Lang (ed.) *Integrated Approaches to Resource Planning and Management* (Calgary: The University of Calgary Press, 1986), p. 14.

preceding decade is the form that regional institutions should take.[78] A recurrent concern over proposals to place regional bodies in a top-down relationship with local government has been that the public, whose 'place loyalty is often strongest towards localities, counties and sub-regional levels of consciousness' have tended to view administratively defined regions as artificial political constructs rather than natural units of government.[79] The implication is that people would be reluctant to accept the legitimacy of regional governance in the same way that the authority of local government and the state are broadly accepted.[80] Haughton and Counsell suggest that, if this indifference is to be overcome, a programme of regionalisation would need to 'be directed to complex processes of place-making in the sense of trying to develop a wider acknowledgement and even ownership of particular definitions of what constitutes a region' by those who would be subject to its authority.[81] However, I question whether attempting to create a sense of attachment to regions where none exists or defining bodies as political representatives of geographical areas to which people feel no allegiance would provide an effective means of introducing a regional layer to a system of ecological governance.

A preferable approach would be to create regional institutions that function not as governors of localities, but as 'decision recommending institutions'. These would be responsible for determining, through debate involving representatives of localities, what the regional position on matters under consideration should be. Representatives of the regional body would then take part as advocates of regionally agreed positions in national strategic planning processes. Proponents of deliberative democracy see the creation of intermediate institutions of this kind as a way of providing channels through which public opinion can

[78] An account of the public's rejection of proposals for an elected body for the North-East which curtailed the administration's further pursuit of its plans for introducing an electoral dimension to regional governance can be found in A. Tickell, P. John and S. Musson, 'The North East Region Referendum Campaign of 2004: Issues and Turning Points' (2005) 76 *The Political Quarterly*, 488. See also Baker and Wong, 'The Delusion of Strategic Spatial Planning', 86–94; and Owens and Cowell, 'Land and Limits', 2nd edn, pp. 6–8.

[79] Haughton and Counsell, 'Regions, Spatial Strategies', p. 7. See also Wheeler, 'Regions, Megaregions, and Sustainability', 867–8.

[80] J. Glasson, 'Regional Planning and Sustainability Assessment' in H. Dimitriou and R. Thompson (eds) *Strategic Planning for Regional Development in the UK: A Review of Principles and Practices* (Abingdon: Routledge, 2007), p. 225.

[81] Haughton and Counsell, 'Regions, Spatial Strategies', p. 7.

directly influence decision-making at higher levels.[82] I agree that such an approach would assist with creating the linkages between local and national government that would enhance perception of the system of ecological governance as legitimate, but without interpolating a separate layer of governmental authority between them whose legitimacy may be questioned. There would still be a hierarchical relationship between regional and local institutions to the extent that local proposals would be modified in the development of draft regional plans, and then be expected to conform with regional plans after their revision and approval through the national planning process suggested above. However, the close collaboration I envisage between regional and local bodies would defuse potential tensions between them which have arisen, historically, from a perception of regional government as nothing more than a delivery vehicle for the state's initiatives.[83]

A concern with regional planning is that institutions established for this may, where they comprise representatives from disparate localities or conflicting interests, find it necessary to make decisions of limited ambition if they are to function at all.[84] This is, in part, because the need to reach positions that would be acceptable to all of the different localities involved in the planning process has tended to result in 'lowest common denominator' solutions.[85] I suggest that a system of ecological governance with a clearly defined statutory objective for reducing ecological risks and which is supported by policies providing clear statements of preferred options for satisfying requirements in different policy areas would leave less room for this conservatism. This is in contrast to the present planning system under which there is much more scope for arguing what the 'sustainable development' obligation requires of planning authorities.[86] In addition, the fact that the adequacy of regional positions would fall to be reviewed by the state in its coordinating role would provide an incentive for local authorities to reduce the scope for state intervention by presenting proposals that take the requirement to advance statutorily prescribed ecological objectives seriously.

[82] Jacobs, 'Environmental Valuation', pp. 223–5; Smith, 'Deliberative Democracy', pp. 73–5.
[83] Gunningham, 'The New Collaborative Environmental Governance', 162–3.
[84] Owens and Cowell, 'Land and Limits', 1st edn, pp. 58–9.
[85] Ibid., pp. 70–1. See also Baker and Wong, 'The Delusion of Strategic Spatial Planning', 99.
[86] Owens and Cowell, 'Land and Limits', 1st edn, pp. 28–30.

4.6 Local government

I have argued in this chapter that exclusive authority for decision-making should not be devolved to local institutions and that regional and national coordination is required because of the spatial shortcomings of local government. In doing so, I may have given the impression that a local political level would have no part to play in ecological governance other than as deliverer of national and regional policies. However, this is certainly not the case. It is only through the provision of information by bodies with a close connection to places and the people that inhabit them that regional and national strategic plans, which are capable both of implementation and of resolving ecological problems, can be developed. It would be more accurate therefore to regard local governmental units as the building blocks of a system of governance that is capable of forming strategic responses to ecological concerns rather than as passive recipients of decisions made at higher levels.

The organisation and coordination by local authorities of public involvement with decision-making is also essential if the state is to achieve its ecological objectives. The state's ability to advance policies that would affect significant areas of private and collective life would be limited if it were unable to secure public acceptance that proposed measures to reduce anthropogenic pressures on ecosystem health are legitimate.[87] It is unlikely either that acquiescence in, or involvement with, pursuing ecological goals could be achieved by coercion.[88] The likely result of such an attempt would be to stimulate levels of discontent that would preclude further attempts at reform. Instead, the best available means by which a positive attitude towards ecological change might be engendered is by creating opportunities for the public to get involved with shaping the future of their communities and contributing to the formation of plans at regional and national levels.[89]

The state can enhance its communicative capacity by creating possibilities for public involvement with decision-making at different points in a system of ecological governance.[90] However, local authorities are

[87] Lundqvist, 'Ecological Governance', pp. 148–9; Barry, 'Rethinking Green Politics', pp. 104–7, 199–200, p. 206; Lundqvist, 'A Green Fist', 457.

[88] Barry, 'Rethinking Green Politics', pp. 214, 226.

[89] Lundqvist, 'Ecological Governance', pp. 10, 17–18; Dobson, 'Green Political Thought', p. 110, Barry, 'Rethinking Green Politics', pp. 219–20; Stallworthy, 'Sustainability, Land Use', pp. 296–7.

[90] Chapter 4, Section 4.4.2.

much better placed than more-remote governmental levels to provide opportunities for participation in practice and to encourage engagement with decision-making and planning processes that may lead to public support for action to reduce levels of ecological stress.[91] I consider in the following sections why public participation would be of such importance for a state's ability to pursue ecological policies and why, in view of this, the ability of local levels of government to establish linkages between the public and higher governmental levels could make the difference between an ecological transition which is limited to the state's discouragement and promotion of certain activities and land uses and one in which people are fully engaged with bringing change to economic and social practices.

4.6.1 Legitimacy

There are three main respects in which public participation is needed if state initiatives for ecologically desirable change are to reach fruition. The first is to promote acceptance of actions required for implementing policy by encouraging public perception of them as legitimate. 'Legitimacy' is used as a term to characterise the appropriateness or the impropriety of governmental action in a number of different ways.[92] It can be employed objectively to suggest that a government would lack legitimacy if it failed to respond to particular circumstances including, for example, a material threat of environmental harm.[93] It is also used to indicate that a policy or decision is subjectively perceived to be legitimate by a sufficient proportion of the public for its acceptance as an appropriate action for the government to take.[94] This may be because there is public agreement with the substance of the policy or because the process by which a decision was reached is regarded as possessing the quality of legitimacy.[95] These different uses of

[91] Meadowcroft, 'Planning, Democracy and Sustainable Development', 181.

[92] F. Peter, 'Political Legitimacy' in E. N. Zalta (ed.) *The Stanford Encyclopedia of Philosophy* (2013), http://plato.stanford.edu/entries/legitimacy.

[93] Barry, 'Rethinking Green Politics', pp. 115, 213.

[94] C. Hilson, *Regulating Pollution: A UK and EC Perspective* (Oxford: Hart Publishing, 2000), p. 49; Ross, 'Sustainable Development', p. 234; J. Freeman, 'Private Parties, Public Functions, and the New Administrative Law' (2000) 52 *Administrative Law Review*, 815 and 818–9.

[95] Ibid.; A. Kronsell, 'Legitimacy for Climate Policies: Politics and Participation in the Green City of Freiburg' (2013) 18 *Local Environment*, 966–7. See also C. Gross, 'Community Perspectives of Wind Energy in Australia: The Application of a Justice and Community Fairness Framework to Increase Social Acceptance' (2007) 35 *Energy*

the term create a clear potential for conflict. For example, whilst acting to alleviate threats of ecological harm might be seen as something which a legitimate government should do in the national interest, taking positive steps to that end might be seen, if acceptance of their validity is not secured, as an illegitimate exercise of authority once the consequences of introducing an ecological orientation become apparent.

Irrespective of this conundrum, the reality for governments is that creating a perception that they are acting legitimately is something with which they must be concerned as, without it, their policies and programmes for their implementation may be opposed. Whilst it is inevitable that not everyone will accept the wisdom of governmental proposals, there is no shortage of examples in environmental and other policy areas where governments have been dissuaded by a critical mass of antipathetic public opinion from pursuing policies that, presumably, they perceived to be a legitimate exercise of power when they were first proposed.[96] In addition, significant opposition would present a tangible barrier to implementing ecological policies because, as I discuss in the following sections, active public involvement with introducing associated change would be required. The inescapable conclusion is that a government that wishes to effect ecological change would need to put in place a system of governance which engenders sufficient acceptance that it is acting legitimately to secure a mandate for proposed action in the places that policy implementation would affect. In this regard, making 'generous provisions for participation and influence in the planning process' would, as Lundqvist argues, provide perhaps the most effective means available to governments of reconciling the public to stringent measures for sustainability and enhancing possibilities that these will be viewed as an appropriate exercise of governmental authority.[97]

4.6.2 *Giving form to ecological sustainability*

The involvement of those with knowledge of places, of local environments, and of the connections between places that enable them to

Policy, 2727, in which the author argues that there is a close connection between perception of a decision-making process as fair and acceptance of the outcome.

[96] Cowell and Owens refer to infrastructure development programmes that had to be reconsidered by the UK Government because of the 'veto' effect of cumulative public opposition in R. Cowell and S. Owens, 'Governing Space: Planning Reform and the Politics of Sustainability' (2006) 24 *Environment and Planning C*, 404–6.

[97] Lundqvist, 'Ecological Governance', p. 10.

meet their respective needs is required if policy visions for ecological change are to be turned into plans for the future development of localities. Ecological sustainability embodies a prior value judgement which prioritises maintaining the health of ecosystems over the pursuit of social and economic objectives that may present a threat to this. Its determinism provides a basis for government to prohibit certain activities, to give clear policy guidance on preferred approaches to meeting needs, and to issue corresponding guidance on how spatial planning and decision-making on land use can contribute to reducing levels of ecological stress. However, it is not so well defined that professional planners would be able to form visions of sustainable communities without public assistance. To the contrary the involvement of those whom planned change would affect, and who have knowledge of local conditions and of how communities function with exploring what ecologically sustainable communities would look like, is essential if the generalised visions advanced in policy statements are to be converted into realistic proposals for how ecological objectives might be realised. It is also needed if the outcomes of planning to implement a concept that is lacking in precise definition are to be accepted as legitimate.[98]

Participation is also essential for the formation of regional and national strategies for ecological change. It is only through working with members of the public that strategic planners can gain access to the dispersed knowledge that they would need to present an accurate picture of what can be done to implement the government's policies for reducing levels of ecological stress.[99] Public involvement in open discussion of policy proposals can assist with the identification of means by which the objectives of policy can be advanced, and, conversely, of possibilities that should be discounted because of the negative effects that policy implementation may have.[100] In addition, engagement with the public in places where scope for development exist can assist with identifying whether there is a potential for conflict between the proposed land use and public values including those held in places.[101] Development in such circumstances

[98] Dobson, 'Green Political Thought', pp. 109–110; Barry, 'Rethinking Green Politics', pp. 203–4.

[99] R. Lang, 'Achieving Integration in Resource Planning' in R. Lang (ed.) *Integrated Approaches to Resource Planning and Management* (Calgary: The University of Calgary Press, 1986), pp. 35–7.

[100] O. Woolley, 'Trouble on the Horizon? Addressing Place-based Values in Planning for Offshore Wind Energy' (2010) 22 *Journal of Environmental Law*, 243–4.

[101] Ibid.

might simply be avoided if suitable alternatives are available. Alternatively, discussion of development proposals with those affected by them would allow for exploration of whether the potential for conflict is such that these should not be pursued or if the communities concerned would be willing to accept the validity of proposals having reflected on the public goods which they are intended to vouchsafe.[102]

An approach which sees citizens as a resource for problem solving rather than as likely objectors is needed to avoid the problems that successive governments have experienced as a result of attempts to use the planning system as a top-down vehicle for delivering policy.[103] Such approaches have often encountered difficulties due to a failure to recognise that people value places in quite different ways to the instrumental value that central government attaches to them.[104] Top-down decision-making is also prone to exacerbating whatever potential is present in a situation for opposition by providing limited opportunity for public participation in advance of particular development proposals being presented.[105] As Haggett notes, public protest in such circumstances may stem as much from a lack of meaningful involvement in the planning process and a resulting sense of powerlessness in the face of decisions made at higher levels than from an antipathy to the proposed development itself.[106]

The response by the UK's last Labour administration to problems that it encountered with pursuing infrastructure projects was to attribute these to the planning system and to impose an even-more centralised framework for infrastructure planning under the Planning Act 2008.[107] In doing so, it failed to appreciate that policy statements are not holy writ, and that treating them as such will almost inevitably result in situations where the aspirations they contain come into conflict with physical realities

[102] Ibid., 243.

[103] Stallworthy, 'Sustainability, Land Use', p. 311; Bulkeley, 'Planning and Governance of Climate Change', p. 287.

[104] For example, Woolley, 'Trouble on the Horizon?', 228–30, gives examples of conflicts that have arisen between the valuation by governments of the marine environment for its renewable energy generation potential and public values held in coastal places and seascapes.

[105] Woolley, 'Trouble on the Horizon?', 234–5.

[106] C. Haggett, 'Public Engagement in Planning for Renewable Energy' in S. Davoudi, J. Crawford and A. Mehmood (eds) *Planning for Climate Change: Strategies for Mitigation and Adaptation for Spatial Planners* (London: Earthscan, 2009), p. 300.

[107] Woolley, 'Trouble on the Horizon?', 235–240. The approach to infrastructure planning established under the Act has been adopted by the following coalition government with some modifications. See Cowell, 'The Greenest Government ever?', 37–9.

and public values held in places. The approach to policy implementation that I call for recognises that policies, whilst they provide vital sources of guidance and direction, are statements of what ought to be done rather than of what can be achieved. They must be tempered by knowledge of what is possible if they are to be turned into practicable strategic plans for infrastructure development.

4.6.3 *Promoting behavioural change*

A major concern over the extent to which ecologically desirable change to modern societies could be achieved is that people who have grown up in socioeconomic systems which encourage egregious consumption and under political systems whose primary objective has been to maximise the efficiency of economic growth may respond with bewilderment and hostility to rhetoric and measures that promote restraint and require whole populations to change their lifestyles.[108] This may, in turn, result in the opposition which, as we have seen in discussing acceptance of governmental policies above, may lead a government concerned with its democratic credibility and electoral prospects to abandon proposals that clearly go against the grain of an entrenched consumption culture.

Anticipation that action for greater environmental protection would inevitably meet with a negative response has led some green political theorists to view the realisation of ecological sustainability as an impossibility in a democratic political system, and to advocate authoritarian rule as the only means by which environmental degradation might be halted.[109] However, the majority of commentators, recognising both the impracticability and the unpalatability of this position, see the use of new structures for governance and institutional reform as the best means of engineering the type of cultural change through which the replacement of wealth accumulation with maintaining ecosystem health as society's guiding principle may come to be accepted.[110] Central to their views is the contention that people living in a society which encourages both their involvement with shaping the world they live in and a consciousness that they are part of a wider community with shared environmental

[108] Stallworthy, 'Sustainability, Land Use', p. 288.
[109] Dobson, 'Green Political Thought', p. 105; Barry, 'Rethinking Green Politics', pp. 196–200.
[110] Barry, 'Rethinking Green Politics', pp. 104–7, 110; Jacobs, 'Environmental Valuation', pp. 228–9; Smith, 'Deliberative Democracy', pp. 66–8; Stallworthy, 'Sustainability, Land Use', pp. 290–2.

interests will tend to see themselves as citizens who bear a common responsibility for maintaining the conditions that provide a foundation for the quality of everyone's lives rather than as consumers whose primary interest lies in the satisfaction of personal preferences.[111]

I agree that creating dialogical spaces in which people can debate and discuss how the places they live in might develop and also how they themselves might alter their lifestyles as part of this process provides one way in which governments can nurture a shared consciousness of the need for human activities to be conducted within ecological bounds. In particular, participation through deliberative fora has the potential to make participants aware of the impacts that unsustainable (or selfishly parochial) behaviours can have not only on their own communities and the quality of local environments, but also on others and on the environmental health of distant places.

The reform of structures for governance is also important for creating a sense amongst participants and non-participants alike that everyone has a role to play in the process of building a better society and with addressing matters that are 'national' not because they are the concern of central government alone, but because they have the potential to affect the different populations of the UK indiscriminately. The creation of decision-making structures in which there is a transparent and purposive provision of pathways by which public input can influence outcomes would promote acceptance of decisions as legitimate even amongst non-participants. Further consideration is given to the role of deliberative processes and institutional design in the cultivation of new environmental perspectives and a corresponding willingness by people to change their own behaviours in Chapter 6.

4.6.4 Constructing a sense of sustainable places

I have concentrated in this section on public participation which is organised by, and conducted through, the institutions of local government. In making participation at local levels my focus, I am not suggesting that direct participation in decision-making at higher governmental levels would be inappropriate. However, I do suggest that involvement with governance at a level where decisions would have a material effect both

[111] Barry, 'Rethinking Green Politics', pp. 106, 228–30; Jacobs, 'Environmental Valuation', pp. 217–22; Smith, 'Deliberative Democracy', p. 64; Stallworthy, 'Sustainability, Land Use', pp. 309–10.

on communities that participants are part of and the places they inhabit would stimulate the type of public engagement that is required if people are to become actively involved with an ecological transition, to develop an understanding of why this is necessary, and, ultimately, to review and revise their own values and behaviours towards the environment.

There are two main reasons for this. The first is that it is simply more practical than attempting to generate significant levels of public interest in, and reflection on, issues which seem far removed from peoples' everyday lives. People are more likely to give their time and to contribute meaningfully when decision-making concerns issues of direct relevance to them. Lipschutz recognises the importance of a close connection between the subject matter of deliberation and matters of tangible importance to participants in arguing that peoples' willingness to act collectively is greater 'when their personal experiences and surroundings are implicated in a process than when they are expected to respond to governmental directives from a distance or abstract predictions of future dislocations'.[112]

The second is that decision-making processes which invoke a sense of place are more likely to have an impact on how people see themselves in relation to the environment than those which are concerned with issues that are remote from participants. Studies of public reaction to changes in land use demonstrate that the sense people have of places significantly influences their attitudes towards proposed development of them.[113] People assign meanings to the places which they inhabit and experience, derive meaning in their own lives from a sense of belonging to and identifying with them, and develop emotional bonds with their environments.[114] In view of this, involvement with processes that raise participants' consciousness of the threats that ecological degradation may present to the environmental quality and the future viability of the places that they live in, work in and enjoy may encourage them to reflect on their own values and to take the importance of a healthy environment for their well-being and that of the communities they belong

112 Lipschutz, 'Bioregionalism', p. 106.

113 M. A. Davenport and D. H. Anderson, 'Getting from Sense of Place to Place-Based Management: An Interpretative Investigation of Place Meanings and Perceptions of Landscape Change' (2005) 18 *Society and Natural Resources*, 627; A. M. Brandenburg and M. S. Carroll, 'Your Place or Mine? The Effect of Place Creation on Environmental Values and Landscape Meanings' (1995) 8 *Society and Natural Resources*, 395; B. Norton and B. Hannon, 'Democracy and Sense of Place Values in Environmental Policy' in A. Light and J. M. Smith (eds) *Philosophy and Geography III: Philosophies of Place* (Lanham: Rowman and Littlefield Publishers, 1998).

114 Woolley, 'Trouble on the Horizon?', 230.

to into account in their own decision-making. This, in turn, may lead them to view governmental calls for more-sustainable ways of living in a positive light and to respond to them proactively.

A possible concern with the expectation that people would respond to perceived threats to the places they value is the 'free rider' problem.[115] The implication is that there would be a reluctance to alter personal behaviours and sanction changes to patterns of communal living for fear that others would not follow suit or that they may even take advantage of this public spiritedness. However, opportunities for 'freeriding' would be much reduced under a system of governance in which all communities are being asked to change their practices as part of a shared national endeavour. Indeed, the failure of individuals and communities to engage positively with this may, if the need for more sustainable ways of living has become widely accepted, lead to a perception of recalcitrance as socially unacceptable. As has been seen in many social contexts, a fear of the stigma that would attach to behaviour which is non-compliant with societal norms can provide a powerful incentive to conform.

In addition, it might be questioned whether a focus on the environments of particular places would promote any different attitude towards activities whose impacts would affect places far removed from them. Undoubtedly, it would be a challenge to extrapolate a broader concern for the global environment from a sense of responsibility for local environments. At the same time, awareness of the impacts that far-distant activities can have on valued places may lead to a general perception of them as negative, and, in a society where the need to alleviate threats of ecological harm has been accepted as a common concern, to the stigmatisation of those who reap the benefits from practices that export environmental harm. The promise that localised action offers of an altered perspective towards the global environment is that 'the experience of collective action on behalf of the local environment can serve to instil an ethic that will apply outside of that locality.'[116]

4.7 Marine governance

The discussion of governance in this chapter has, to this point, been concerned largely with arrangements for governing activities conducted

[115] Dobson, 'Green Political Thought', p. 104; Giddens, 'The Politics of Climate Change', p. 104.

[116] Lipschutz, 'Bioregionalism', p. 111.

on land. We also need to consider how the exploitation of resources in the seas would be controlled under a system of ecological governance. That I come to this subject latterly is fitting as the development of any regulatory structure for offshore activities, let alone one which offers effective ecological protection, has lagged far behind the evolution of controls over terrestrial development. This tardiness is a product of the perception of the marine environment as 'other' and the (still) prevailing 'out of sight out of mind' attitude towards its despoliation. However, the view of the seas as an inexhaustible source of resources has been challenged in recent years by a growing consciousness of: the rapid deterioration of marine ecosystem health; the increasing pressures that resource demands are placing on the seas despite evidence of their environmental vulnerability; and of the growth in stresses due to the introduction of new activities to the marine environment.[117] The seas are being turned to because land-based resources are no longer sufficient to meet demands or because the means by which they might be satisfied on land, including, for instance, through onshore wind farm construction, are regarded by some sections of society as unacceptable.

In view of the growing range of issues and concerns with uses of the seas, the adequacy of long-standing practices in marine regulation has been questioned.[118] The traditional method used by states to regulate sea uses has been to distribute responsibility for controlling activities amongst different agencies, but without the benefit of a coordinating body to address spatial conflicts between them or the cumulative environmental consequences of exploitation.[119] Overarching legal frameworks for the planning and control of the seas have also been lacking, an absence which is due in part to the jurisdictional range of states having expanded from coastal waters to encompass both the sea-bed and overlying waters of more distant marine areas only during the last thirty years.[120]

117 F. Douvere and C. N. Ehler, 'New Perspectives on Sea Use Management: Initial Findings from European Experience with Marine Spatial Planning' (2009) 90 *Journal of Environmental Management*, 77.

118 L. B. Crowder et al., 'Resolving Mismatches in US Ocean Governance' (2006) 313 *Science*, 617; O. R. Young et al., 'Solving the Crisis in Ocean Governance: Place-based Management of Marine Ecosystems' (2007) 49 *Environment*, 22.

119 A. A. Rosenberg and P. A. Sandifer, 'What Do Managers Need?' in K. McLeod and H. Leslie (eds) *Ecosystem-based Management for the Oceans* (Washington, DC: Island Press, 2009), pp. 18–19; L. B. Crowder et al., 'Resolving Mismatches', 617–8; S. A. Jay, *At the Margins of Planning: Offshore Wind Farms in the UK* (Aldershot: Ashgate Publishing, 2008), p. 109.

120 S. A. Jay, 'Built at Sea: Marine Management and the Construction of Marine Spatial Planning' (2010) 81 *Town Planning Review*, 175–6. The United Nations Convention on the Law of the Sea 1982 confirms that coastal states may exercise a limited jurisdiction

The response to historic failures of marine governance that commentators have called for, and that developed coastal states are now applying, is to give responsibility for controlling all activities within defined areas of the seas to a single body or, at least, to establish coherent decision-making structures in which different actors collaborate in pursuing set goals.[121] Many of these new governance arrangements have, on paper at least, espoused an 'ecosystem-based approach' to managing marine activities, and have adopted the restoration of marine ecosystem health as the principal objective of governance.[122] An ecosystem-based approach entails that different sectors should be regulated by reference to how, individually and collectively, they would affect ecosystem structure, functioning and key processes, and that the common goal of regulation would be to maintain these components of ecosystem health.[123]

Proponents of an ecosystem-based approach call for units of governance to correspond, as far as possible, with identifiable ecosystems. The aim is to minimise the 'number of factors outside the boundaries of the management system that need to be considered'.[124] This approach to establishing a framework for governance would be more easily applied than on land because large tracts of the seas fall under the jurisdiction of coastal states. However, it is recognised that '[d]elineating a finite number of regional ecosystems that can become the foci of management efforts will entail a compromise between our understanding of biological populations and oceanographic processes and the established structure of human institutions and political jurisdictions.'[125] An obvious constraint is that the jurisdiction of states, unless special circumstances apply, does not extend beyond 200 nautical miles from coastal baselines.[126]

in adjacent marine areas (the continental shelf and the exclusive economic zone) over which, to the extent laid down in the Convention, they have authority. See United Nations Convention of the Law of the Sea, Montego Bay, 10 December 1982, in force 16 November 1994, 1833 UNTS 3, 21 ILM 1245 (1982).

121 J. S. Jones and S. Ganey, 'Building the Legal and Institutional Framework' in K. McLeod and H. Leslie (eds) *Ecosystem-based Management for the Oceans* (Washington, DC: Island Press, 2009), pp. 174–7; see also in the same volume A. A. Rosenberg et al., 'Lessons from National-level Implementation Across the World' (2009), pp. 305–12 and K. McLeod and H. Leslie (2009) 'Ways Forward', pp. 349–50.

122 K. McLeod and H. Leslie, 'Why Ecosystem-based Management?' in K. McLeod and H. Leslie (eds) *Ecosystem-based Management for the Oceans* (Washington, DC: Island Press, 2009), pp. 3–11; Rosenberg et al., 'Lessons from Implementation', pp. 294–313.

123 McLeod and Leslie, 'Ecosystem-based Management', pp. 5–6.

124 Rosenberg and Sandifer, 'What do Managers Need?', p. 15. 125 Ibid.

126 R. R. Churchill and A. V. Lowe, *The Law of the Sea*, 3rd edn (Manchester: Manchester University Press, 1999), pp. 162–3.

In addition, it is difficult to draw boundaries between marine ecosystems or, indeed, to separate them from each other as the fluid medium allows the effects of activities to travel easily. This is not necessarily problematic for governance as ecosystem-based management is primarily concerned with 'managing people's influences on ecosystems, not ecosystems themselves'.[127] Regulation can be conducted by reference to consideration of the threats that activities may have on places and species that are understood to be of most importance to ecological functionality without the governed area necessarily encompassing the ecosystem(s) concerned in entirety.

The UK has, alongside many other developed coastal states, taken on board these views on the need for a new approach to marine governance. Statutory responsibility for the licensing of most activities in the waters off England[128] has been delegated by the Secretary of State for the Environment, Food and Rural Affairs to a new body, the Marine Management Organisation (MMO).[129] This body will also take the lead in developing marine spatial plans for the territorial sea and continental shelf areas lying off the coastline of England.[130] The development of plans that identify the ecological significance of marine places, the locations in which different marine activities are conducted, and, based on this knowledge, potential risks that combinations of marine activities will threaten ecosystem functionality is seen as a key supporting mechanism for an ecosystem-based approach to marine governance.[131]

I question whether the new regime for marine governance in the UK is appropriately endowed to improve ecological protection. The overarching duty of the MMO is to carry out its responsibilities 'with the objective of making a contribution to the achievement of sustainable development' rather than to pursue well-defined ecological goals.[132] As a result, much rides on the contents of the marine policy statement produced by central

[127] McLeod and Leslie, 'Ecosystem-based Management', p. 5.

[128] Marine and Coastal Access Act 2009, Part 4 Chapter 2.

[129] The Marine Licensing (Delegation of Functions) Order 2011 (SI 2011 No.627).

[130] Department for Environment, Food, and Rural Affairs, 'Marine and Coastal Access Bill – Policy Paper', (HM Government, October 2009), 'Part 1 – The Marine Management Organisation', Para.2, 1.

[131] Young et al., 'Place-based Management', 25–6; F. Douvere, 'The Importance of Marine Spatial Planning in Advancing Ecosystem-based Sea Use Management' (2008) 32 *Marine Policy*, 762; Douvere and Ehler, 'New perspectives', 78–9; Jay, 'Built at Sea', 178–84.

[132] Marine and Coastal Access Act 2009, section 2(1)(a).

government and approved by parliament.[133] Marine plans must be in conformity with this statement 'unless relevant considerations indicate otherwise'.[134] The distribution of authority for areas of the seas amongst the UK's devolved regimes also reintroduces the risk of fragmented governance to the new system. However, the fact that one body has been given responsibility for regulating many of the activities conducted in significant areas of the seas under the UK's jurisdiction, and that its central government and devolved administrations are subject to the common planning and regulatory regime established by the Act, at least creates the basic foundation of a system of governance for reducing the ecological impacts of sea uses. This arrangement would be retained in a system of ecological governance although the governing institutions would need to possess enhanced powers if they are to advance ecological objectives.

4.7.1 Bridging the land/sea divide

Whilst it is desirable that the seas should be subject to a governance regime in which institutions are given the authority to regulate the conduct of activities within defined areas, it is also important that they should not be treated as a separate realm from the terrestrial for the overarching purpose of reducing the levels of ecological stress that human activities are responsible for. As mentioned above, it is the tendency to regard the marine environment as somehow divided from, and not subject to, the same normative considerations as the familiar world of land-based activities and environments that has allowed its exploitation to the point where marine ecosystems are failing. Indeed, this attitude can still be seen in the view formed by the UK Government that it would be preferable to undertake an enormous programme of offshore wind farm construction and attempt to manage the environmental consequences of this rather than risk upsetting public sensibilities by significant further construction of onshore wind farms.[135]

If the seas are to be brought within an overarching framework for ecological governance, there are two main issues that would need to be addressed. The first is the question of what the relationship should be between governance for the seas and the wider system of ecological

[133] HM Government, 'UK Marine Policy Statement' (2011).
[134] Marine and Coastal Access Act 2009, section 51(6).
[135] Woolley, 'Trouble on the Horizon?', 227.

governance. The response to this is that, in most respects, marine institutions would interact in their plan-making activities with relevant local authorities and with central government in the same way as land-based regional bodies. It would be sensible for marine and local authorities that have responsibility for places whose economy is dependent on exploitation of the seas to explore collaboratively how the negative ecological consequences of this dependency might be reduced. In addition, the capacity of the seas to meet demand for resources should fall to be considered alongside those of terrestrial regions in strategic planning processes. The ecological benefits and potential impacts of offshore exploitation should be explored at the same time as those other options with possibilities for marine development and sea uses only being pursued if it is felt that these would contribute to reducing levels of ecological stress, and if preferred terrestrial alternatives are not available over the timescales for which plans are developed. This approach would, as I noted above, present a significant contrast with perception of the seas as an area in which activities that would be regarded as unpalatable if conducted on land can be pursued without consequence because there is no public to appease.

The second is how relations should be structured between units of marine governance and local authorities. I have already noted the need for interaction between them to mitigate the negative impacts of coastal economies and land-based activities on marine ecosystems. In addition, uses of the seas which have no immediate connection with coastal communities may be seen by them as incompatible with the character of coastal places or as a threat to their economic well-being. For example, early offshore wind farm developments have given rise to public concern, and, in some instances, opposition on grounds that this type of development would be inappropriate where it would be visible from coastlines that have previously enjoyed unencumbered views and from places which value, and sometimes trade on, the wilderness nature of coastal environments.[136] In view of this, collaboration between institutions for marine governance and local authorities and the participation of people who hold values in coastal places in any planning process under which possibilities for marine development are to be explored would be important if resulting plans and following proposals for development are to be seen as legitimate and accepted by the communities that they would affect.[137]

[136] Ibid., 228–30. [137] Ibid., 224–5, 230.

I envisage that this collaboration would follow the model I propose in this chapter for the formation of strategic plans. It would be sensible, rather than duplicating participatory processes, for marine bodies to take part in regional explorations of how relevant resource requirements might be met. This would allow for the identification of possible obstacles to offshore development or of any potential for value conflict that may exist at the outset of the planning process rather than when this is well advanced. Knowledge of public views expressed on possibilities for new sea uses would then be available to, and inform the preparation of, strategic plans. Finally, environmental assessment during strategic planning would provide a further opportunity for public involvement with discussing governmental proposals.

The hope is that provision for public engagement with policy implementation from an early stage and at other points in the chain of governance, when coupled with an institutional design which creates linkages between different governmental levels, would encourage acceptance of development that is intended to alleviate threats of harm to the UK's environment. In this regard, the context of decision-making processes is of great importance to the way people react to development proposals.[138] The goal here is to create a contextual backdrop of participation in a positive and shared endeavour to change current practices and utilise resources in pursuit of an objective whose realisation would be of broad societal benefit. This is in contrast to situations in which the public are asked to respond to individual projects, which, as noted at Section 4.6.2, tends to isolate communities and to focus attention on a negative critique of what is proposed rather than considering proposals on their merits.

[138] Ibid., 233–4.

5

Ecological planning

5.1 Introduction

Envisioning how the objectives of ecological governance might be advanced would, in itself, be a futile process if the visions formed are not shaped by an awareness of what can be achieved in practice and over what timescales. It would also be of limited value if the state is unable to enjoin non-governmental actors to participate in their realisation. Mechanisms are needed that require public bodies to identify possibilities for stress reduction, and to prepare plans that lay down how these are to be employed. They should also, to the fullest extent possible, promote the implementation of plans by requiring adherence to them, and by preventing spatial and natural resource uses that would be incompatible with ecological values.

In this chapter I propose a legal framework for planning that serves these purposes in two respects. First, it obliges actors in governance at all levels to form plans for implementing ecological policies that seek to reduce reliance on current practices and to replace them with less-stressful alternatives. The principal purpose of planning is to mirror the 'top-line approach' employed in policy-making (i.e., preferences for reducing consumption, increasing the efficiency of resource use and substitution)[1] by exploring how patterns of socioeconomic activity can be changed to alleviate the pressures that they place on the environment, and by examining scope for deploying preferred policy options. The resulting plans will lay down strategies for progressing an ecological transition nationally and in regions and localities. The plans would be given legal force by a presumption in decision-making that proposed development should be consistent with the pathways to sustainability that they present. Second, it establishes principles and rules that promote the avoidance of ecological harm (again in line with the 'top-line'

[1] Chapter 3, Sections 3.3.2.1, 3.3.2.2 and 3.3.2.3.

approach) through plan-making for land use, and that correspond with the bottom-line of policy-making (i.e., sunsetting)[2] by preventing development that could undermine the resilience of ecosystems.

The framework would not provide a simple top-down vehicle for giving effect to policy. An approach to governance in which policy-making is divorced from an analysis of the possible could in no sense be called strategic. Rather, the exploration of means by which an ecological transition might be pursued and the monitoring against plans of its progress would feed back into the rolling policy-making process. Accordingly, a third respect in which the legal framework would impart strategic direction is by generating information based on which the government can review its policies, refine strategies for their implementation, and give further consideration to how the ecological goals of the system of governance can be advanced. For example, information obtained through planning will enable assessment of whether the use of policy options that would otherwise not be employed because of their potentially negative effects should be considered in order to replace, or prevent recourse to, possibilities that present greater threats of harm.[3]

I am conscious that, in proposing comprehensive structures for strategic ecological planning, I am swimming against strong currents in planning and governance theory. The rational comprehensive approach to planning in which actors consider the full range of means of achieving a given end, evaluate the consequences of each alternative, and select one that provides the best result has come to be regarded as unrealistic, both in view of the complexity of dynamic socioeconomic systems and the many practical constraints on decision-makers' abilities to identify ideal outcomes.[4] Public planning processes are also seen as incapable of setting a course in the face of private sector domination of economic activity and the decline of public sector involvement with carrying out major development schemes.[5] The implication is that the decline of state

[2] Chapter 3, Section 3.3.2.4. [3] Chapter 3, Section 3.3.3.

[4] Lang, 'Achieving Integration', pp. 30–1; B. Cullingworth and V. Nadin, *Town and Country Planning in the United Kingdom*, 14th edn (London: Routledge, 2006), pp. 4–7; S. Davoudi, 'Sustainability: A New Vision for the British Planning System' (2000) 15 *Planning Perspectives*, 124–5; Jay, 'Built at Sea', 186; Wheeler, 'Planning for Sustainability', pp. 43–4; Giddens, 'The Politics of Climate Change', pp. 98–9.

[5] B. Evans, 'From Town Planning to Environmental Planning' in A. Blowers and B. Evans (eds) *Town Planning into the 21st Century* (London: Routledge, 1997), pp. 10–11; Stallworthy, 'Sustainability, Land Use', p. 102; Cullingworth and Nadin, 'Town and Country Planning', p. 12; Davoudi, 'Sustainability', 127; M. Gunder, 'Sustainability:

power over independent economic actors and institutions has reduced proactive planning to a largely notional paper exercise.

I agree that planning cannot encompass all aspects of society and the natural world with which it interacts and produce blueprints for the future conduct of human activities. Our incomprehension of how ecosystems behave and react to anthropogenic interference adds to other 'bounded rationalities' that compromise the ideal of rational comprehensive planning. At the same time, the fact that perfection cannot be achieved does not mean that the use of planning techniques to explore how undesirable situations might be avoided or moved away from when they are encountered should be abandoned. In this regard, opponents of rational comprehensive planning also criticise the inadequacy of incrementalism, a mode of planning that eschews a full analysis of available options in preference for making improvements to situations as opportunities arise, because of its inability to challenge the status quo or sustain a thorough review of whether changes in direction are needed.[6]

Lang argues that a happy medium must be found between these two poles of planning theory which allows strategies to be formed as per rational comprehensive planning whilst 'borrowing from incrementalism and observed common sense' to temper its theoretical abstractions.[7] I follow this approach in arguing that a move back towards a more progressive style of planning is necessary if strategies for reducing the threats of ecological harm are to be formed whilst recognising the impossibility of establishing a perfect balance between socioeconomic systems and the natural world in circumstances of profound uncertainty on both sides. The framework for planning that I propose does not aspire to produce an exact statement of society's future as the outcome of planning processes. Its purpose is to provide consistent guidance to planning and decision-making at all levels of governance and to create fora that enhance coordination with a view to ensuring that plans promote the pursuit of disparate sectoral, regional and local aims in a way which advances ecological objectives.

It is also an inevitable consequence of the diminution of its role in guiding socioeconomic systems that the influence of public planning on the private sector has been reduced. However, I suggest that this is more due to an ideological reluctance by governments to take action that could

Planning's Saving Grace or Road to Perdition?' (2006) 26 *Journal of Planning Education and Research*, 208.

6 Cullingworth and Nadin, 'Town and Country Planning', pp. 7–8; Lang, 'Achieving Integration', pp. 31–2.

7 Lang, 'Achieving Integration', p. 32.

impinge on the functioning of liberalised markets than that states lack the ability to give direction to non-governmental actors. The planning system I propose, when coupled with the framework for policy-making, employs the full range of legislative and regulatory authority available to the state by which market behaviour might be shaped. It represents a partial return to the state-led planning of the 1950s and the 1960s, but with the state's historic role of enactor of policies being replaced by that of choreographer of the actions of public and private bodies in the interests of promoting ecologically desirable outcomes.[8]

I refer to land use planning in England and Wales throughout this chapter as an example of a system whose capacities have been reduced by successive waves of reform. These have largely been driven by the perception of planning by UK governments since the late 1970s as a drag on economic growth rather than a potential force for the public good.[9] I also use analysis of its inadequacies for preventing environmentally damaging development to draw general conclusions as to the properties that a planning system should possess if it is to contribute effectively to a system of ecological governance.

The chapter focuses on terrestrial planning as long experience with this in England and Wales (stretching back to the first introduction of a comprehensive regime for land use planning in 1947) enables an informed critique of its effectiveness for protecting ecosystems. That does not mean that planning for the marine environment is unimportant in ecological governance. To the contrary, it is vital for the system's effectiveness that terrestrial and marine planning should be coordinated in the search for means of reducing pressures that human activities place on the environment.[10] It is more the case that I lack the time and space to do justice in this book to the features of marine spatial planning that distinguish it from its terrestrial equivalent. That said, the stress-reducing thrust of the statutory objective, and the principles and rules for planning that I propose in this chapter could equally be applied to allocating space for and authorising the conduct of activities offshore.

[8] Tewdwr-Jones, Gallent and Morphet, 'Anatomy of Spatial Planning', 254. My description of the state's role in an ecological planning system adapts the authors' portrayal of its relationship with other actors in spatial planning.

[9] Baker and Wong, 'The Delusion of Strategic Spatial Planning', 97–8; A. Lord and M. Tewdwr-Jones, 'Is Planning "under attack"? Chronicling the Deregulation of Urban and Environmental Planning in England' (2014) 22 *European Planning Studies*, 345–61; Owens and Cowell, 'Land and Limits', 2nd edn, pp. 3–4, 8–10.

[10] Chapter 4, Section 4.7.

5.1.1 *Reforming land use planning*

The land use planning system in England and Wales is widely regarded as being unable to promote desired ends beyond exercising some influence over patterns of development.[11] Stallworthy refers to widespread scepticism as to the ability of planning to contribute to societal or environmental progress or to deliver sustainability 'so long as it is construed and operated as a reactive tool to limit and redirect certain categories of private decision, and where every intervention in them has to be justified as an exceptional trespass on private rights'.[12] Davoudi also argues that changes made to the system since the 1970s have, in transforming planning from a proactive process to a regulatory rump, stripped the public realm of its capacity 'to think strategically'.[13] I argue in this chapter that planning's positive involvement with shaping developmental trends and the state's ability to prepare and act upon strategies would need to be restored under a system of governance whose principal purpose is to engender societal change.

In proposing reforms that are intended to recreate the state's strategic capacity, I draw from two bodies of literature in which it has been argued that change is necessary if the conception of planning as a process through which outcomes can be promoted, rather than one which simply responds to and manages events, is to be revived. The first explores how the system might be transformed from its narrow role of regulating land use into a fully fledged environmental planning system that would provide a 'holistic, integrated and strategic form of intervention' into social and economic activities founded on a purposive agenda for environmental protection.[14] The fullest statement of the form that such a system would take is provided in the Royal Commission on

[11] Stallworthy, 'Sustainability, Land Use', p. 105; Cullingworth and Nadin, 'Town and Country Planning', p. 252; Davoudi, 'Sustainability', 127; The Royal Commission on Environmental Pollution, 'Environmental Planning', p. 1, paras. 1–5.

[12] Stallworthy, 'Sustainability, Land Use', pp. 184–5.

[13] Davoudi, 'Sustainability', 127.

[14] A. Blowers, 'Society and Sustainability: The Context of Change for Planning' in A. Blowers and B. Evans (eds) *Town Planning into the 21st Century* (London: Routledge, 1997), p. 154. Literature on environmental planning that I refer to in this chapter also includes: Blowers, 'The Time for Change'; K. Bishop, 'Planning to Save the Planet? Planning's Green Paradigm' in M. Tewdwr-Jones (ed.) *British Planning Policy in Transition: Planning in the 1990s* (London: UCL Press, 1996), pp. 207–22; Evans, 'From Town Planning to Environmental Planning'; Owens and Cowell, 'Land and Limits', 1st edn; Stallworthy, 'Sustainability, Land Use'; Wheeler, 'Planning for Sustainability'.

Environmental Pollution's report on environmental planning.[15] The second explores more generally how spatial planning might contribute to the realisation of sustainable development, and thereby of improved environmental protection, by providing fora in which different sectors can visualise the impacts of their activities and coordinate them with a view to identifying patterns of development that balance economic, social and environmental concerns.[16]

My proposals share some common ground with arguments made in the relevant literatures concerning how planning's role in environmental protection might be strengthened, and with the visions of environmental and spatial planning systems advanced in them. They also depart from them in two important respects. First, some commentators on environmental planning have called for the positive identification of environmental limits as an essential first step if economic growth is to be kept within sustainable bounds.[17] It is argued that discovering where critical capacities to accommodate development arise in nature or establishing stocks of habitats and levels of biodiversity that must be preserved to maintain ecological functionality would provide objective justification for resisting demands for resources and arguments founded on economic or social need. The influence of this focus on identifying what is environmentally important remains apparent in academic

[15] The Royal Commission on Environmental Pollution, 'Environmental Planning'.

[16] Literature on spatial planning that I refer to in this chapter includes: Haughton and Counsell, 'Regions, Spatial Strategies'; Haughton et al., 'The New Spatial Planning'; V. Nadin, 'The Emergence of the Spatial Planning Approach in England' (2007) 22 *Planning, Practice and Research*, 43–62; Tewdwr Jones, Gallent and Morphet, 'An Anatomy of Spatial Planning'.

[17] The efficacy of this approach for constraining economic growth is analysed (although not necessarily supported) in the following: S. Owens, 'Land, Limits and Sustainability: A Conceptual Framework and some Dilemmas for the Planning System' (1994) 19 *Transactions of the Institute of British Geographers*, 445–7; R. Cowell and S. Owens, 'Sustainability: The New Challenge' in A. Blowers and B. Evans (eds) *Town Planning into the 21st* Century (London: Routledge, 1997), pp. 16–21; R. Cowell, 'Stretching the Limits: Environmental Compensation, Habitat Creation and Sustainable Development' (1997) 22 *Transactions of the Institute of British Geographers*, 297; Y. Rydin, 'Land Use Planning and Environmental Capacity: Reassessing the use of Regulatory Policy Tools to Achieve Sustainable Development' (1998) 41 *Journal of Environmental Planning and Management*, 749–51; Owens and Cowell, 'Land and Limits', 1st edn, pp. 30–3; Haughton and Counsell, 'Regions, Spatial Strategies', pp. 80–1; A. C. Flournoy, 'Protecting a Natural Resource Legacy While Promoting Resilience: Can It Be Done?' (2009) 87 *Nebraska Law Review*, 1008; Ross, 'Modern Interpretations', 45–7.

discussion of how an ecosystem-based approach to planning for the marine environment might be introduced.[18]

I have already taken issue with the utility of 'limits' as a foundational concept for ecological protection in Chapter 2,[19] and reiterate my concerns in Section 5.2 of this chapter. The suggestion that there may be some quantifiable point at which development becomes unacceptable or that decisions on proposed projects could be made by reference to it is not supported by scientific understanding of ecosystems as highly complex and dynamic entities. Regulation on this basis is not possible in view of the significant uncertainty concerning the impacts of human activities on systemic properties and the impossibility of knowing whether an ecosystem's resilience is sufficient to enable it to withstand disturbance. Even if it were feasible, it is questionable whether the knife-edge approach to balancing economic growth and environmental health that a focus on limits invites would be appropriate under a system of governance whose primary concern is with ensuring that what is ecologically valuable is preserved. Conversely, the first concern of an ecological planning system would be with promoting options for meeting demands and land uses that are judged to be least ecologically consequential amongst those available. The setting of absolute constraints on development where this may affect places of importance for ecosystem functionality is a key aspect of the regulatory framework. However, it provides a supporting bottom-line for more progressive 'top-line' mechanisms for reducing ecological stresses rather than bearing the exclusive responsibility for resisting developmental pressures.

Second, proposals made for spatial and environmental planning have tended to concentrate on bringing environmental considerations into the decision-making frame in the hope that giving them equal billing alongside economic and social matters will result in enhanced conservation. They offer little or no guidance on the circumstances in which conflict between the different concerns should be resolved in favour of preserving the environment. The influence of 'integrative' interpretations of sustainable development that promote a search for outcomes which advance environmental, economic and social goals simultaneously is apparent in this

[18] See, for example, M. M. Foley et al., 'Guiding Ecological Principles for Marine Spatial Planning' (2010) 34 *Marine Policy*, 955; L. B. Crowder and E. A. Norse, 'Essential Ecological Insights for Marine Ecosystem-based Management and Marine Spatial Planning' (2008) 32 *Marine Policy*, 772; Jay, 'Built at Sea', 173; Young et al., 'Solving the Crisis in Ocean Governance', 20.

[19] Chapter 2, Sections 2.2 and 2.3.

reluctance to give direction. However, the failure to provide clarity on what should be done when these goals clash has tended, in practice, to allow the continued dominance of short-term considerations of economic benefit over long-term strategic considerations of environmental health in decision-making.[20] Counsell and Haughton suggest that the emphasis on 'win-win' solutions has also had a chilling effect on the production of plans that advance environment-led or social equity-centred interpretations of sustainable development.[21]

In contrast, the legal framework I propose in Section 5.3 gives strong direction as to how plan-making should be conducted and decisions made on development proposals in the interests of maintaining ecosystem functionality and alleviating current threats to this. This is consistent with the progressive objectives of the system of governance and with its adoption of ecological sustainability as a guiding concept. It is also necessary in view of the clear inability of sustainable development, at least in the environmentally weak interpretations of it that the UK Government's policies have afforded,[22] to legitimise the imposition of constraints on economic growth. The provision made for a statutory statement of the purpose of planning, for guiding principles for planning and decision-making, and for decision rules that make it clear where development would not be ecologically acceptable are intended to rectify the long-standing imbalance between economic and environmental considerations in decision-making, and, indeed, to weight judgments in favour of preserving what is ecologically valuable.

5.2 Environmental limits and governance

Arguments that economic growth should be controlled and, if necessary, restricted in the interests of environmental protection must overcome a significant obstacle if they are to have any practical effect. This is the prevalent assumption that a constantly expanding economy is inherently desirable. The widespread acceptance of the need for development to be made sustainable has, to an extent, challenged this outlook with its message, expressed implicitly or more explicitly in recent interpretations of the concept, that the environment's capacity to absorb the negative effects of human activities is not boundless. However, its emphasis on

[20] Haughton and Counsell, 'Regions, Spatial Strategies', pp. 55–6, 60–3; Owens and Cowell, 'Land and Limits', 1st edn, pp. 40–3, 54–5.

[21] Haughton and Counsell, 'Regions, Spatial Strategies', pp. 56, 59.

[22] Ibid., pp. 55–6.

seeking outcomes that allow both economic and environmental objectives to be realised, but without advising how irreconcilable conflicts between them should be resolved has had two consequences. The first is that entrenched outlooks have gone largely unchallenged and, consequently, that economic concerns continue to predominate in decision-making.[23] The second is that the flexibility of the concept has allowed advocates of stronger environmental protection to advance interpretations of sustainability which encapsulate 'the idea that there are some absolute constraints to development... beyond which one cannot go without unacceptable change occurring'.[24] In view of this, the acceptability of economic growth should be determined and limited by reference to the carrying capacities of natural systems.

It is this notion of environmental limits as a basis for making judgments on proposed development, and the enthusiasm with which it has been adopted by those who call for a more environmentally oriented approach to planning, that I consider in the following section.

5.2.1 *Identifying environmental capacities*

The planning system in England and Wales provides, in theory, a neutral decision-making framework under which judgments are made through a process of balancing economic, social and environmental considerations as to whether proposed land uses would be in the public interest.[25] However, the widespread perception is that this balance is weighted in favour of development with the primary purpose of the system being to facilitate economic processes by making allocations of land to meet resource demands.[26] Environmental influence on planning is, at its highest, limited to making development 'benign' by seeking out locations

[23] S. Owens, 'Negotiated Environments: Needs, Demands and Values in the Age of Sustainability' (1997) 29 *Environment and Planning A*, 571; Owens and Cowell, 'Land and Limits', 1st edn, pp. 54–5.

[24] Rydin, 'Land Use Planning and Environmental Capacity' (1998), 749–50. See also Owens and Cowell, 'Land and Limits', 1st edn, pp. 30–3; Ross, 'Modern Interpretations'; Owens and Cowell, 'Land and Limits', 2nd edn, p. 3; Ross, 'Sustainable Development', pp. 287–310; Garver, 'Introducing the Rule of Ecological Law'; Bosselmann, 'From Reductionist Environmental Law'.

[25] Bishop, 'Planning to save the Planet?', pp. 211, 218; Stallworthy, 'Sustainability, Land Use', p. 100; Cullingworth and Nadin, 'Town and Country Planning', pp. 1–2.

[26] Owens, 'Negotiated Environments', 576; Owens and Cowell, 'Land and Limits', 1st edn, pp. 43–4; Cullingworth and Nadin, 'Town and Country Planning', p. 252.

'where environmental costs are lower or where the trade-off of environmental loss against economic gains is more acceptable'.[27]

The bias in favour of economic activity is apparent in the way that arguments made in favour of development proposals or against them on environmental grounds are viewed. Projections of demand and expected profit are regarded as possessing an objectivity in relation to which the environment is negotiable.[28] In addition, opposition to proposed projects on grounds of the value of places for environmental health or because of their aesthetic qualities tends to be viewed, unless the area concerned has a relevant statutory designation, as subjective and therefore as providing a less-valid basis for decision-making than statements of need or expected financial gain.[29] That is not to say that circumstances have not arisen in which proposals are rejected on environmental grounds. The concern is more that there is a manifest imbalance in that the benefits of environmental protection and conservation have to be demonstrated whilst 'the benefits of development are taken as axiomatic'.[30]

It is unsurprising that, faced with this strong systemic presumption in favour of development, planners and advocates of stronger environmental protection under the planning system have used concepts to support positions that offer potential to 'match the apparently objective status of other claims'.[31] In particular, notions that the environment's capacity to accommodate developmental pressures is not finite, and therefore that there is a need for humanity 'to operate within the ecological carrying capacity of the earth' have been readily adopted.[32] The UK Government has also, in its belated recognition that some basis for resolving conflicts between economic and environmental objectives must be found, included the importance of 'living within environmental limits' as one of the headline principles of its sustainable development strategy.[33] It defines 'environmental limits', albeit in a distinctly

[27] Cullingworth and Nadin, 'Town and Country Planning', p. 252.

[28] Owens, 'Negotiated Environments', 571.

[29] Owens, 'Negotiated Environments', 571; Owens and Cowell, 'Land and Limits', 1st edn, pp. 54–5, 123.

[30] Cowell and Owens, 'Sustainability', p. 18.

[31] Owens and Cowell, 'Land and Limits', 1st edn, p. 49.

[32] Ross, 'Modern Interpretations', 38. See also Owens, 'Land, Limits and Sustainability', pp. 445–6; Rydin, 'Land Use Planning and Environmental Capacity', 751; Owens and Cowell, 'Land and Limits', 2nd edn, p. 3.

[33] Department for Environment, Food, and Rural Affairs, 'Securing the Future', p. 16. The current government's sustainable development strategy (Department for Environment, Food, and Rural Affairs, 'Mainstreaming sustainable development: The Government's

anthropocentric manner, as 'the level at which the environment is unable to accommodate a particular activity or rate of activities without sustaining unacceptable or irreversible change'.[34]

The main focus in considering how limits-based concepts can be given effect in decision-making has been on developing an enhanced understanding of how ecosystems work and their resilience and vulnerabilities with a view to establishing, with as much precision as possible, where ecological limits lie. For example, Ross contends that ecological sustainability is highly dependent on science to establish what the carrying capacity of an ecosystem is, and, therefore, that our ability to strike a balance between maintaining 'baseline natural capital' and social and economic concerns will depend on 'first determining the ecological limits and then establishing what development is feasible' within them.[35] The constraints on the cumulative effects of human activities under the 'planetary boundaries' approach proposed by Rockström and his colleagues should be 'human-determined', but should be set by reference to knowledge of thresholds at continental and global scales.[36] They call for Earth System thresholds to be identified as a matter of urgency as the circumstances in which risks of crossing them would arise are not known with confidence (or at all in some cases).[37] In addition, the UK Government's sustainable development strategy places much emphasis on identifying 'where environmental limits exist' so that action can be taken 'to avoid breaching them'.[38] One of its initial objectives is to 'collate existing research and identify shortfalls in understanding about where environmental limits exist, and where they are being exceeded' so that 'future research needs in all policy areas' can be established.[39]

Theoretical literature on how the discipline of marine spatial planning should be conducted also focuses on identifying what components of ecosystems it would be important to preserve, and to what extent, as the principal means of striking a balance between maintaining

vision and what this means in practice' (HM Government, 2011)) advises that it builds on (and thereby implicitly endorses) the earlier strategy.

34 Department for Environment, Food and Rural Affairs, 'Securing the Future', p. 100.

35 Ross, 'Modern Interpretations', 47.

36 Rockström et al., 'Planetary Boundaries', under 'Introducing the Concept of Planetary Boundaries'.

37 Ibid.

38 Department for Environment, Food and Rural Affairs, 'Securing the Future', p. 99.

39 Ibid., p. 100.

ecosystem functionality and accommodating an ever-increasing range of sea uses.[40] Tolerable scales and patterns of exploitation are to be established by reference to a significantly enhanced understanding of how marine ecosystems function, of the habitats and species of particular importance for their functionality, and of the type, number, size and viable population levels that would be sufficient to support their resilience. Foley and her colleagues propose principles for the conduct of marine spatial planning that are largely concerned with identifying, enumerating and then preserving vital components of ecosystems.[41] Although these would require major advances in marine ecological science if they are to be given effect, the authors see no difficulty with proposing a decision-making framework under which the principles would be translated into 'operational decisions' by employing 'the best readily available science'.[42] Crowder and Norse also recommend an approach to planning that is founded on knowledge of what places are of importance for ecosystem functionality.[43] The aim is to conserve '*enough* well-chosen places, comprising *enough* cumulative area, so that populations in these places will be self-sustaining' and to protect 'unique places and representative examples of all ecosystem types to a degree *sufficient* to maintain the biodiversity and ecosystem services people value' [emphasis added].[44]

These passages display confidence that deficiencies in human comprehension of how marine ecosystems function can be rectified sufficiently to allow a knowledge-intensive approach to be adopted. The expectation is that, through research, it will be possible to secure 'the maximum sustainable benefits' from marine resources 'whilst ensuring appropriate environmental protection'.[45] This confidence is tempered by recognition that there are huge gaps in our understanding of marine ecosystem behaviour at present, and therefore of the need to take on a precautionary attitude in deciding which habitats and species to conserve. Precautionary measures are proposed that are intended to provide buffering for the scientific model of ecological protection by preserving habitats and species whose core importance to ecosystem functionality is

[40] For example see Foley et al., 'Guiding Ecological Principles', 955; Crowder and Norse, 'Essential Ecological Insights', 772; Jay, 'Built at Sea', 80–1; Young et al., 'Solving the Crisis in Ocean Governance', 22.

[41] Foley et al., 'Guiding Ecological Principles', 959–61. [42] Ibid., 962.

[43] Crowder and Norse, 'Essential Ecological Insights', 772 [44] Ibid., 774, 777.

[45] Department for Environment, Food and Rural Affairs, 'A Sea Change: A Marine Bill White Paper' (HM Government, 2007), p. 18.

not scientifically proven.[46] However, their utility must be in doubt in situations of high uncertainty as they presuppose some knowledge about what habitats and species *are* central to an ecosystem's well-being. There is no suggestion that an appropriately precautionary response under a planning system which is being developed, in part, to halt the degradation of marine ecosystems would be to concentrate on restricting either sea uses or the demands that drive them. Rather, the focus is on drawing a line to represent science's best guess as to what an ecosystem can tolerate and then seeking to hold it against developmental pressures.

5.2.2 The limitations of limits-based regulation

Uses of limits-based arguments to date have been dogged by difficulties with identifying actual points or thresholds at which development becomes unacceptable.[47] The resulting lack of clarity has allowed developmental interests 'to dismiss environmental objections and tools supporting them' as being subjective and motivated more by NIMBYism than any genuine environmental concern.[48] Despite this, as the discussion of marine spatial planning evidences, environmental capacity and analogous concepts are still seen, in principle, to offer a potentially valid basis for regulating development that science will flesh out in the fullness of time. The reasons for their continuing appeal to environmentalists are not difficult to identify. Means of operationalising them that define an irreducible core of natural assets as critical environmental capital ostensibly provide an economic basis for countering economically validated arguments in favour of development. The hope is that quantifying the environment will allow fire to be fought with fire. In a society in which economic values continue to predominate, a regulatory practice that can claim to be improving the efficient functioning of the economy by establishing bounds beyond which losses, because of the destruction of an identifiable ecological support base, would begin to outweigh gains may also appear to be the most effective means of advancing a case for environmental protection.

However, some commentators have suggested that the focus on fixed limits has proved a distraction from finding a sound basis for ecological

[46] Foley et al., 'Guiding Ecological Principles', 962; Crowder and Norse, 'Essential Ecological Insights', 776–7.

[47] Cowell and Owens, 'Sustainability', p. 25; Owens and Cowell, 'Land and Limits', 1st edn, p. 24; Haughton and Counsell, 'Regions, Spatial Strategies', pp. 77–8.

[48] Haughton and Counsell, 'Regions, Spatial Strategies', p. 81.

protection.[49] It has been argued that, even if it were possible to define environmental capacity, this would not provide a trump card against development.[50] To the contrary, consideration of whether activities that would yield tangible economic and social benefits should be restricted so that the intangible benefits of a functioning biosphere might be preserved, or the non-instrumental value of an environment recognised, leads us back inexorably to the ethical and political debate over what is valuable to us.[51] Scientific exploration of how ecosystems are affected by human activities certainly has a vital role to play in informing this debate, but it provides no more of a valid basis for dictating how society should proceed than that which economic arguments presented in favour of development lay claim to. Effective capacity constraints on economic growth will be established not 'by the properties of nature, as discovered by science, but by social judgements about the value of aspects of the environment'.[52]

I agree that there are serious difficulties with relying on the identification of objectively definable capacities to retard ecological degradation. Enormous weight has been placed on limits-based concepts which, for reasons explored in the following section, they cannot support. In any event, it will only be possible to establish ecologically appropriate constraints on human activities if the hegemony of economic values has first been challenged in ethically-informed political debate. I argued in Chapter 2 that such a debate and reflection on the true nature of our relationship with natural systems as the fortunate beneficiaries of their rapidly diminishing largesse rather than their masters should lead to acceptance of the supervening value of ecosystem health for human well-being.[53] The proposed objectives and structure of an ecological planning system that are set out in Sections 5.2.4 and 5.3 are informed by, and intended to effect, this re-evaluation.

5.2.3 *Ecological and ethical difficulties*

The obvious attraction of the capacity concept is that, if it could be made operational, it would provide a relatively simple basis for evaluating

[49] Owens and Cowell, 'Land and Limits', 1st edn, pp. 111–3; Haughton and Counsell, 'Regions, Spatial Strategies', pp. 80–1; Owens, 'Land, Limits and Sustainability', 443–4; Rydin, 'Land Use Planning and Environmental Capacity', 751–3.

[50] Owens and Cowell, 'Land and Limits', 1st edn, p. 111. [51] Ibid.

[52] Rydin, 'Land Use Planning and Environmental Capacity', 751.

[53] Chapter 2, Section 2.5.

proposed development. However, consideration of the current understanding of ecosystems, which I examine in Chapter 2, reveals that the goal of regulating human activities through precise knowledge of ecological conditions and of their vulnerabilities is not realistic. An obvious difficulty is that our comprehension of how ecosystems work is limited. We are only now beginning to explore what it is that enables them to function and to retain their structure in the face of negative impacts. This dearth of knowledge is at least recognised by the advocates of limits-based regulation, which is why a heavy emphasis is placed on research.[54] The question however is whether it would become feasible to control activities by reference to 'tipping-points' if our knowledge of ecological behaviour is vastly improved. I suggest, for the following reasons, that it would not.

The first is that the envisaged regulatory approach is based on an inaccurate oversimplification of an extremely complex reality. Resilience, the property which is central to the ability of ecosystems to maintain structure and functionality, is the product of myriad interactions between the living components of ecosystems, between biota and their surroundings, and between ecosystems, the climate and other Earth System processes.[55] The relative contribution of these interactions to resilience is barely known. The suggestion that this overarching systemic property and the innumerable processes that feed into it could be reduced to a few well-chosen indicators, or that fine judgments could be made about how activities undermine resilience as a basis for regulation, does not sit comfortably with the reality.

Second, resilience is not amenable to quantification.[56] Ecosystems are inherently dynamic. They evolve naturally. They also react to stimuli, including from natural influences, the effect of human activities on them and changes in climate. An obvious consequence of this dynamism is that the resilience of the system and factors that contribute to it are subject to constant change. It would not be meaningful to attempt to reduce what is a dynamic process to a set of static figures. In addition, judging activities to be appropriate against knowledge of ecological conditions at a particular point in time would not provide a satisfactory

[54] Ross, 'Modern Interpretations', 45; Jay, 'Built at Sea', 181.

[55] See my discussion of ecosystem complexity and resilience in Chapter 2 Sections 2.2 and 2.3.

[56] See my discussion of resilience in Chapter 2, Section 2.3.

regulatory approach when it is known that these will alter and that the magnitude of subsequent variance is unpredictable.[57]

Third, even if some indicators of resilience could be developed, decision-making over development would also require knowledge of the ecological impacts of proposed activities. In this regard, the non-linearity of ecosystems makes it particularly problematic to predict how activities and their effects on components of ecosystems will ultimately impact on the ecosystem and on systemic properties as a whole.[58] The extreme difficulty with predicting how stressors from different activities combine to undermine ecosystem functionality would also preclude a limits-based assessment of cumulative impacts.[59] The inescapable conclusion is that, on this and other counts, we are far from being able to control development by the accurate assessment of its propensity to move ecosystems closer to failure or to trigger tipping points.

The conception of environmental capacity as something that can be clearly defined or quantified is not compatible with the complexity of ecosystems and the properties that enable them to function. At its highest, environmental capacity is, as with resilience, a metaphor for the innumerable processes that contribute to ecosystem health as it is perceived by us.[60] Recognition of this and of our limited understanding of the natural world is not problematic. Rather, it provides a starting point for the design and adoption of regulatory practices that are appropriate for ecological protection. These, as they are founded on awareness of our ignorance, seek to preserve what is ecologically valuable by applying a due sense of caution in determining what activities are to be permitted and how, if approved, they should be conducted.

There is another good reason for rejecting a capacity-based approach to ecological protection. The implication that the natural world is ours to exploit up to a defined point represents a strongly instrumental evaluation and one which, because it leaves the presumption in favour of economic goods intact, would provide a flimsy defence against developmental pressures. This knife-edge approach to environmental management would also place enormous weight on measures for economic

[57] S. R. Carpenter et al., 'From Metaphor to Measurement: Resilience of What to What?' (2001) 4 *Ecosystems*, 779.

[58] See my discussion of non-linearity in Chapter 2, Section 2.2.2.

[59] Foley et al., 'Guiding Ecological Principles', 962 and B. S. Halpern et al., 'Managing for Cumulative Impacts in Ecosystem-based Management through Ocean Zoning' (2008) 51 *Ocean and Coastal Management*, 208.

[60] Haughton and Counsell, 'Regions, Spatial Strategies', pp. 80–1.

efficiency to prevent levels of activities and of demand made by growing populations for more affluent lifestyles from overwhelming ecological bounds. However, the hope that economic and environmental goals can be reconciled by these means is, as Cullingworth and Nadin observe, 'fanciful to the point of irresponsibility'.[61] I suggest that it would be no less irresponsible to employ a regulatory approach that makes no allowance for the unpredictability of future increases in the demands made on the environment by socioeconomic systems, and which rests on a bland assumption that technological advances will bail us out, than it would be to seek to control activities by reference to a notion of environmental capacities that has no demonstrable congruence with how the natural world actually functions.

5.2.4 Ecological planning

It is clear from the above that waiting on science to establish exact boundaries between economic and social practices that are acceptable or intolerable from an ecological perspective cannot currently, and, in all probability, will not provide an effective basis for protecting ecosystems. In any event, an exclusive reliance on 'objective' scientific and economic disciplines to provide defences would not retard ecological degradation as this, despite surface appearances, is not the product of evidentially impeccable cases for development having been made during the last 250 years, but of the uncontested prioritisation of economic growth and the design of systems of governance to support this objective.

Effective ecological protection would, as I argue in Chapter 2, be best achieved by adopting a holistic approach to governing human activities with a view to reducing their collective impacts on systemic resilience.[62] The principal purpose of a system of ecological planning would be to continue the exploration begun in policy-making of how ecological stresses can be reduced and, through it, to furnish policies for risk reduction with strategies for their implementation. To support this purpose, a legal framework should be put in place that employs both positive and negative approaches for devising strategies that will lead to desired end states. On the positive side, mechanisms for plan formation would require that localities, regions and sectoral ministries should develop proposals for actively reducing stresses by identifying the most

61 Cullingworth and Nadin, 'Town and Country Planning', p. 256.
62 Chapter 2, Section 2.4.

ecologically desirable means available to them of meeting their responsibilities and preparing long-term strategies for using them in a movement towards a future that places fewer demands on the natural world. The proposals should also identify aspects of social-economic functioning at the different levels that are incompatible with the system of governance's goal of maintaining ecosystem functionality, and explore pathways that would lead to more sustainable ways of living. The intention is that the mechanisms for planning will correspond closely to, be guided by and inform the policy-making processes I propose in Chapter 3 so that policies can be grounded in, and moulded by, knowledge of the resources available for an ecological transition, of situations that must be transformed if such a transition is to be achieved, and of possibilities available for transforming them at different scales.

The allocation of land and resources under the preparation of transitional plans should also be guided by a preference for solutions that are judged least likely to undermine the resilience of ecosystems. Strategic environmental assessment, with its objects of enquiry suitably altered to explore the risks of ecological harm that spatial and natural resource uses and combinations of them pose, would support this search for ways of reducing stresses that do not themselves exacerbate ecological deterioration.[63] This would correlate to an extent with Stallworthy's description of land use planning's role at its most proactive as being to divert 'resources into preferred land uses and facilities'.[64] However, the analysis of available spatial resources and the selection of ecologically preferable options would, in contrast to the flexibility afforded to planners in exercising judgment over how the environment should be protected, be positively required by the introduction of a statutory objective to be observed in plan formation and implementation.[65] This process may of course lead to a preference for activities that, whilst they may not be regarded as the least consequential amongst alternatives in policy-making, would be seen as such when the ecological conditions of areas under consideration are taken into account. Decision-making concerning an appropriate balance between different activities and land and sea uses would fall to the state in conjunction with regional and local institutions under its coordinating role.[66]

I argued in Chapter 3 that the principle of substitution should be underpinned by a practice of phasing out options that are deemed too

[63] Chapter 5, Section 5.4. [64] Stallworthy, 'Sustainability, Land Use', p. 102.
[65] Chapter 5, Section 5.3.3. [66] Chapter 4, Section 4.4.3.

hazardous for their continued use.[67] Similarly, decision rules on proposed development would add force to the stress-reducing mechanisms by setting absolute constraints on growth. The rules would prevent land uses that could impact negatively on ecosystems, including by affecting places identified as being of importance for their functionality during the environmental analysis stage of plan-making.[68] Their use emphasises the need for a prioritisation of structural over spatial fixes by making it clear that there are ultimate restrictions on the availability of spatial resources, and that these will be encountered if difficult choices are not made in advance concerning the societal need for actions to be taken or resources appropriated.

5.3 A national framework for ecological planning

It will be apparent from the references I have made to it in the preceding sections that the planning system in England and Wales is ill-equipped to promote the pursuit of environmental goals. Its sectoral role as the mechanism through which the government's land use policies are applied limits its influence to allocating spatial resources rather than questioning the need or environmental desirability of proposed activities.[69] Its objective of advancing sustainable development and the vulnerability of plans to being bypassed if other material considerations sway decision-makers provide an inadequate, and, as we have seen, easily challengeable mandate for advancing and implementing environmentally progressive or socially equitable visions of development in regions and localities.[70] The legal separation of regional and local planning from planning for infrastructure undermines the system's ability to coordinate development or to deliver coherent accounts of how the nation's resources might be used to serve specific ends.[71] Finally, the system's

[67] Chapter 3, Section 3.3.2.4. [68] Chapter 5, Section 5.3.5.

[69] Owens, 'Negotiated Environments', 576; Blowers, 'Society and Sustainability', pp. 158–9; Owens and Cowell, 'Land and Limits', 1st edn, pp. 43–4; Stallworthy, 'Sustainability, Land Use', p. 102.

[70] Owens and Cowell, 'Land and Limits', 1st edn, pp. 24–5; Haughton and Counsell, 'Regions, Spatial Strategies', pp. 56, 59.

[71] Chapter 4, Section 4.6.2. The Royal Commission on Environmental Pollution, 'Environmental Planning', p. 144 para 10.7 cites the separation of infrastructure planning from regional and local planning and the resulting 'lack of coherence' as a 'serious deficiency' of the planning system. The critical analysis of national planning initiatives pursued by the UK's Coalition Government in C. Wong et al., 'A Map for England: Spatial Expression of Government Policies and Programmes' (2012) The Town

top-down legal structure, which reflects governmental perception of it as a delivery vehicle for policies, is inimical to a genuinely strategic planning approach built up from knowledge of regional and local circumstances.[72] In view of these weaknesses, the land use planning system would need to be replaced if a system of ecological governance is to be introduced by a legal framework that possesses the five capacities I discuss in the following sections, and which, by virtue of them, would enhance the state's ability to marshal resources, to coordinate actors in governance, to engage non-governmental actors in plan-making, and thereby to implement its policies for an ecological transition.

The proposed framework is 'national' in two senses. The first is that it would establish common principles and parameters for the conduct of local and regional planning processes. In part, this enables the state to perform its guiding role in ecological governance.[73] The second is that the state would work with local and regional planning bodies to develop a nationwide strategy for stress reduction.[74] In this regard, the purpose of its involvement would be to address drivers of ecological degradation that cannot be dealt with by local and regional institutions acting in isolation, and to consider how measures could be used to mitigate or redistribute the environmental, economic and social effects of an ecological transition where these fall disproportionately on certain regions and localities. The development of a national perspective through interaction with local and regional planning would also enable the state to conduct planning processes for which it is responsible, such as for the development of nationally important infrastructure, on an informed and collaborative basis.

5.3.1 Comprehensive planning

A planning system and the legal framework that gives it form should be comprehensive if it is to provide adequate support for ecologically progressive planning. By comprehensive, I mean that all sectoral

Planning Institute: London, pp. 10–17, reveals that they fail to provide 'understanding of how these sectoral issues might complement or conflict with each other'. This is attributed to a failure to integrate infrastructure planning with other planning processes and the limited spatial content of the documents concerned.

72 See my argument that planning, if it is to be strategic, should be based on the provision of information from the bottom up at Chapter 4, Section 4.4.3.

73 Chapter 4, Section 4.4.1.

74 This is in line with the state's coordinating role in ecological governance. See Chapter 4, Section 4.4.3.

planning and governmental decision-making would take place within, and be assessed for its compliance with, an overarching framework that requires observance of common goals, principles and rules. This all-embracing approach would best be provided by the establishment of a national planning framework. A formal capacity for national planning has been absent from the planning system for England and Wales since its inception, although devolved administrations have introduced strategic planning for the whole of their territories.[75] However, it has been argued that a framework which engenders a shared sense of purpose and broader spatial perspectives amongst governmental bodies, and between central government and regional and local authorities, would significantly enhance the state's ability to pursue its policy goals.[76]

The system would need to be comprehensive in four respects. The first is that the legal framework should encompass all governmental ministries and agencies in a horizontally comprehensive process that provides, from the outset, for a commonality of approach between the disparate bodies. For consistency with the policy-making process I proposed in Chapter 5.3, a whole of government approach to preparing and reviewing strategic plans should be employed and coordinated, as far as possible, with policy formation.[77] This is necessary to reduce scope for the fragmentation in governance which, if unaddressed, would impair the state's ability to pursue goals of national importance. Ministries should be required to prepare plans for policy implementation that are designed to advance ecological objectives and which respect ecological constraints in their formation. I envisage that these would feed into a central institution for reviewing and coordinating plan proposals of the type that, in any event, would be required to take an overview of local and regional planning processes. In this regard, Cullingworth and Nadin refer to the need for 'a forum where national spatial development issues can be discussed and their consequences understood' as a key reason for introducing a national spatial planning capacity.[78] To promote cohesion

[75] Cullingworth and Nadin, 'Town and Country Planning', pp. 96–9.

[76] Blowers, 'The Time for Change', p. 16; Cullingworth and Nadin, 'Town and Country Planning', pp. 96–9; J. Alden, 'Scenarios for the Future of the British Planning System: The Need for a National Spatial Planning Framework' (1999) 70 *Town Planning Review*, 385; C. Wong, 'Is There a Need for a Fully Integrated Spatial Planning Framework for the United Kingdom?' (2002) 3 *Planning Theory and Practice*, 277; D. Stead and V. Nadin, 'Environmental resources and energy in the United Kingdom: The potential role of a national spatial planning framework' (1999) 70 *Town Planning Review*, 339.

[77] Chapter 3, Section 3.4.1.

[78] Cullingworth and Nadin, 'Town and Country Planning', p. 99.

plans should also be built, as far as possible, on a common foundation of spatial and socioeconomic knowledge, including of resource availability and of the ecological significance of places. The creation of a national spatial support base for plan-making is, as I consider at Section 5.3.2, central to developing a capacity for strategic ecological planning.

Second, ecological planning should be vertically comprehensive. It is essential in a multi-level system of governance that the separate decision-making levels should operate under the same framework, and that their activities should be coordinated to ensure that they contribute to the achievement of common goals.[79] A national planning framework could provide this coordination by setting out clear objectives, principles and rules to be observed by all participants in governance. It should also empower the state to review regional and local plans with the planning bodies responsible for them and to produce nationally coordinated plans based on them, or challenge them where needed to advance ecological objectives. The desirability of the state's involvement with planning in an overseeing capacity was recognised in the Barlow Report of 1940 that preceded the development of the first land use planning system for England and Wales.[80] The report concluded that an overarching plan comprised of 'a patchwork of schemes of varying size, and varying merits, which had not been coordinated and moulded to form a coherent whole' would not constitute a national plan in a true sense, and recommended, in view of this, that provision should be made for a central authority with 'effective responsibilities for national planning and with the duty of watching, stimulating and guiding local and regional planning'.[81] Successive governments have preferred not to get involved with coordinating regional and local planning beyond issuing planning policy statements. However, an important aspect of the state's role in ecological governance would, for reasons I consider in Chapter 4, be the coordination of planning processes at lower levels with a view to ensuring that best use is made of national resources to advance the system's objectives.[82]

Third, the planning system should be ecologically comprehensive in that preferred activities should be selected and particular projects evaluated according to the full range of their ecological impacts and benefits. The argument that planning's limited focus on the potential effects of

[79] See Chapter 4, Sections 4.4.1, 4.4.3 and 4.4.4. [80] Wong, 'Is There a Need?', 278.

[81] Report of the *Royal Commission on the Distribution of the Industrial Population* (Cmd. 6153, 1940) quoted in Wong, 'Is There a Need?', 278, 294.

[82] See Chapter 4, Section 4.4.3.

activities on places where development is proposed should be combined with broader consideration of waste management, water resource management, pollution control, and energy and resource consumption is a common theme in the literature on environmental planning.[83] Assessment of ecological impacts should also extend to the effects of associated development that new infrastructure may require including, for example, the construction of electricity transmission lines to convey energy generated by offshore installations or from the remote areas that are often most suitable for onshore wind farms.[84]

Finally, an ecological planning system should be spatially comprehensive. The creation through local and regional planning processes of a national consciousness of available resources and of concentrations of activities is necessary if the state is to fulfil its coordinating role, and thereby to secure ecologically progressive outcomes of planning processes. This would also assist with identifying an equitable distribution of the impacts, including those resulting from the construction of new infrastructure, that would be associated with an ecological transition. The need for a spatial overview to overcome the limitations of local and regional planning and to support compliance with objectives and with promoting the equitable distribution of development is widely cited as a reason for developing a national planning capacity.[85] Wong argues that the 'differential spatial contours' created by the movement of investment, pollutants, traffic and people give rise to inter-regional issues and that these pose 'the need to examine inter-sectoral linkages over a broader spatial framework at national or even supranational levels'.[86]

Surprisingly little is said in the literature concerning a national spatial planning framework on the form that this should take. Wong suggests that this could be established through an overarching planning policy statement of the type provided by the European Spatial Development Perspective.[87] She prefers this to the more directional approach of establishing a clear hierarchy of plan-making in law with the state at

[83] Blowers, 'The Time for Change', p. 15; Evans, 'From Town Planning', pp. 5–6; The Royal Commission on Environmental Pollution, 'Environmental Planning', p. 146, paras 10.17 and 10.18; Wheeler, 'Planning for Sustainability', pp. 36–8.

[84] The Royal Commission on Environmental Pollution, 'Environmental Planning', p. 145, para 10.8.

[85] Alden, 'Scenarios for the Future', 397; Stead and Nadin, 'Environmental Resources', 359–60; Stallworthy, 'Sustainability, Land Use', p. 106; Wong, 'Is There a Need?', 279, 281; Baker and Wong, 'The Delusion of Strategic Spatial Planning', 94–7.

[86] Wong, 'Is There a Need?', 283. [87] Ibid., 297.

its apex. However, I find this conclusion difficult to understand when reasons given for a national planning framework, including the spatial limitations of lower-level planning processes and the need to coordinate them in the interests of advancing nationally important goals, would depend on the active involvement of the state in planning. In addition, a concern with relying exclusively on policy statements to set a lead is, as Klein notes in discussing problems with implementing New Zealand's Resource Management Act, that the lack of statutory status or parliamentary scrutiny provides governments with the opportunity to make grand rhetorical statements but without exercising rigour in preparing policy contents or providing specific guidance as to how these should be put into practice.[88] Policy statements are also more easily cast aside than legislation as an incoming government's ideological perspective replaces that of its predecessor. The better approach where there is a recognised need to alter society's course would be to provide a clear statement of what it is that planning should aim to achieve and a set of legally enshrined principles and rules that bind decision-makers to, and support them in, advancing ecological objectives.

5.3.2 *Analytical planning*

An ecological planning process would complement policy-making by exploring how the endpoints envisaged in policies might be realised in ways that respect ecological principles of resource and land use. In view of this, it is essential that the planning system is supported by a solid informational foundation that would allow the sources of existing levels of ecological stresses and the means of reducing them to be identified and employed in the formation of strategies for policy implementation. There is a significant crossover in this respect with spatial and environmental planning theories which also stress the importance of a robust evidence base for determining how sustainable development might be promoted through the more rational territorial organisation of land uses.[89] For example, the Royal Commission on Environmental Pollution argues that 'high quality information... on the structure and

[88] U. Klein, 'Integrated Resource Management in New Zealand: A Juridical Analysis of Policy, Plan and Rule Making under the RMA' (2001) 5 *New Zealand Journal of Environmental Law*, 36.

[89] Nadin, 'Emergence of Spatial Planning', 57; The Royal Commission on Environmental Pollution, 'Environmental Planning', pp. 116–7, paras 8.65 - 8.69, p. 147, para 10.19, p. 150, para 10.41.

dynamics of environmental systems, the current state of the environment, the pressures on it and its likely response should be an integral part of a modern planning system'.[90] It proposes that 'state of the environment' reports should be produced at the outset of planning processes.[91] The mapping of marine space that literature on marine spatial planning calls for would also provide a sensible platform for ecologically oriented planning.[92] Crowder and Norse argue that an essential precursor to preparing plans that are intended to strike a balance between sea uses and marine conservation would be, through biophysical, socioeconomic and jurisdictional mapping, to 'produce meaningful mosaics of places suitable for the practice of place-based management of marine ecosystems'.[93]

Information on a variety of matters would be required to support strategic thinking on how ecological stresses might be reduced. First, given the prioritisation of alleviating developmental pressures through reducing consumption or finding means of obviating development, local and regional planning should be founded on analysis of the demands generated by resource-intensive places and how these are met.[94] This would create a necessary backdrop for the consideration and selection of options that would provide a realistic means of moving away from current behaviours and the timescales over which these might be deployed. Second, regions and localities should identify both the availability of resources and possibilities for adopting options that are identified as ecologically preferable in policy and the extent to which these might replace less-ecologically desirable options including those earmarked for 'sunsetting'. These analyses will operate together to allow

[90] The Royal Commission on Environmental Pollution, 'Environmental Planning', p. 75, para 6.1.

[91] Ibid., p. 5, para 23.

[92] Young et al., 'Solving the Crisis', 23–4; Crowder and Norse, 'Essential Ecological Insights', 772–3; Douvere, 'The Importance of Marine Spatial Planning', 766; Halpern et al., 'Managing for Cumulative Impacts', 208; D. A. Sivas and M. R. Caldwell, 'A New Vision for California Ocean Governance: Comprehensive Ecosystem-based Marine Zoning' (2008) 27 *Stanford Environmental Law Journal*, 247, 257.

[93] Crowder and Norse, 'Essential Ecological Insights', 773.

[94] Wong and her colleagues argue in their reports for the Royal Town Planning Institute that an understanding of relationships within and between 'large polycentric regions' and of their links with rural areas and national significance is essential if planning processes are to identify issues resulting from these relationships and to devise policies and programmes that address them. See C. Wong et al., 'Uniting Britain: The Evidence Base – Spatial Structure and Key Drivers' (London: Royal Town Planning Institute, 2006), pp. 8–12; Wong et al., 'A Map for England', pp. 18–25.

the formation of proactive strategies for stress reduction. Third, knowledge of existing economic and social activities and their location is required to enable consideration of the cumulative impacts that subsequent development proposals may have.

Finally, knowledge of ecosystems and the places that, on our current understanding, seem likely to be of importance for their functionality, should be gathered. This information would serve two purposes. The first is to identify current practices that should be discontinued because they represent a threat to places of ecological value. This analysis, which links in with the gathering of data on existing economic activities, would provide an equivalent process to that of sunsetting in policy-making. Even those practices which would be judged ecologically preferable in the abstract should be discontinued where their conduct in particular circumstances would be ecologically harmful. The second is to provide for ecologically rational planning both in the allocation of space in planning processes and in decision-making on development consent applications. In this regard, the ecological analysis would support a genuinely strategic planning process in that knowledge of environmental conditions would feed into consideration of how, and the extent to which, preferred resources can be exploited without causing harm.[95]

In emphasising the importance of gathering information in several spheres for the effective conduct of ecological planning, I am conscious that I may appear to be calling for a knowledge-intensive approach of the type that I criticise in Section 5.2. However, my intention in making this criticism is not to denigrate efforts to advance scientific comprehension of ecological behaviour. A concerted effort to increase our understanding of ecosystem behaviour, of the importance of places and species to ecosystem functionality, and the effects of activities on ecosystems, is, as I argue in Chapter 7, important for our ability to regulate activities effectively including by directing them to places where their ecological impact would be minimal. It is the weight placed on that information and the expectation that clear dividing lines can be established between human activities and the natural world which some of the limits-based concepts convey that is of concern. In contrast, the acquisition and analysis of information I propose is intended to serve precautionary decision-making frameworks whose structures reflect an appreciation of the extreme difficulty of establishing, with any exactitude, the present

[95] I consider the role of environmental analysis in the planning system further at Chapter 5, Section 5.3.4.

and future effects of human activities on ecosystem functionality. This is why the system of ecological governance's focus is on reducing the pressures that human activities place on the environment rather than on carving out sufficient space for nature. It is also why the categories of knowledge I refer to above are largely concerned with improving understanding of socioeconomic systems, of the demands they make on natural resources, and of the availability of possibilities for reducing those demands or replacing ways of meeting them with less ecologically consequential alternatives.

The production of these analyses and the mapping of activities and of ecosystems should be legally required as part of the preparation of plans for locations and for terrestrial and marine regions. This is not a formal requirement under the UK planning system, although legal provision for strategic environmental assessment has made it mandatory that plan-making is informed by consideration of environmental conditions. However, the German federal planning system provides a precedent with its requirement for the production by municipalities of landscape plans that capture the current state of the environment.[96] These must be considered in the preparation of regional development plans.[97] The information generated should also feed into the institutional structures for enhancing knowledge and understanding of ecosystem behaviour which, as I argue in Chapter 7, are needed to ensure that a flow of information to support the system of governance is maintained, and to enable the adaptation of decisions to changes in ecological conditions.

5.3.3 *Strategic planning*

The planning system has the potential to have a broad influence on society's trajectory because, even in its limited regulatory form, it interacts with the majority of sectoral activities. Key questions for advocates of environmental planning have therefore been how this potential might be used to improve environmental protection and what obstacles lie in the way of environmentally proactive planning. It has been suggested that the traditional perception of planning as a 'neutral' process, and the

[96] S. Wilding and J. Raemaekers, 'Environmental Compensation for Greenfield Development: Is the Devil in the Detail?' (2000) 15 *Planning Practice and Research*, 213. Bundesamt für Naturschutz, 'Landscape Planning: The Basis of Sustainable Landscape Development' (2008).

[97] Ibid.

corresponding emphasis on identifying justifiable compromises between competing concerns, conflicts with its use to promote outcomes, and that this must be overcome if the system is to have a part in setting an environmentally desirable course.[98] The reality, however, is that the lack of a clear statement of the system's purpose in the legal framework for planning at any stage in its history has allowed successive governments to use it as a blank canvas on which to paint ideological visions of how economic and social activities should be conducted.[99] For example, Haughton and Counsell argue that sustainable development policies, in combination with the introduction of sustainability assessment as a tool for shaping regional and local plans, have been used to tie planning strategies at all scales 'into a single form of rationality based on Central Government's own integrated definition of what sustainable development means'.[100] The current UK Government seeks to promote a preference for development in local planning, save where its adverse impacts 'would significantly and demonstrably outweigh the benefits', through its adoption of a National Planning Policy Framework that equates sustainability with sustained economic growth.[101]

The Royal Commission on Environmental Pollution questions the wisdom of maintaining legal structures for planning that are liable to 'oscillate between... the competing 'ideologies' of planning law...' because they are 'infused with such a degree of discretion'.[102] Whilst I agree that the system's vaunted flexibility hampers its use to impart a strategic direction that promotes stronger environmental protection, the fundamental difficulty is not with the legal framework itself, but with long-standing governmental preferences for facilitating a strong economy and, in line with this, for a weak understanding of sustainability that presents no challenge to the status quo. The focus on the absence of statutorily entrenched objectives for planning is misplaced when the problem stems ultimately from a failure to reconsider what is societally valuable, and to reform legal frameworks that lay down parameters for

[98] Owens and Cowell, 'Land and Limits', 1st edn, pp. 7–8; Bishop, 'Planning to Save the Planet?', pp. 218–9.

[99] Cullingworth and Nadin, 'Town and Country Planning', pp. 11–12; Stallworthy, 'Sustainability, Land Use', pp. 102–3.

[100] Haughton and Counsell, 'Regions, Spatial Strategies', p. 63.

[101] Department for Communities and Local Government, 'National Planning Policy Framework' (HM Government, 2012), p. 4. Cowell, 'The Greenest Government ever?', 34–7.

[102] The Royal Commission on Environmental Pollution, 'Environmental Planning', p. 107, para 8.28.

decision-making in light of that re-evaluation so that they accord the preservation of ecosystem health its proper place amongst factors of importance for society's well-being.

I consider in this chapter how the planning system should be restructured to reflect a prior choice in favour of maintaining ecosystem functionality where this objective is in conflict with economic and social goals. Accordingly, my concern here is with exploring how the system could be used to provide strategic support for the objectives of ecological governance. I suggest that the legal framework should mirror that which I propose for policy-making in combining an equivalent statutory statement of the purpose of planning with principles that lay down how plan-making should be conducted if it is to advance this end.[103] The statutory objective would again make the reduction of anthropogenic stresses on ecosystems as far as possible and within the quickest feasible timescales for social and economic adaptation, planning's principal purpose. The principles should also correspond with the hierarchy of reducing consumption, obviating development and substitution used in policy formation so that plan making is primarily concerned with establishing how the reductions in ecological stresses envisaged in policies might be achieved through modifying practices and replacing current means of meeting local, regional and sectoral needs with less ecologically demanding alternatives. The assessment of plans with a view to identifying the most effective means available of securing reductions in environmental pressures will assist with observance of the planning system's statutory objective.[104]

Giving strong direction in this way, and, as I discuss below, through setting rules for decision-making on development proposals, would be necessary if planning is to support the significant change in direction that an ecological transition entails. In this regard, my proposals go beyond those of the Royal Commission on Environmental Pollution which concludes, in its report on environmental planning, that a statement of purpose for the planning system and a requirement that certain environmental matters be considered in decision-making would 'be sufficient to influence the general direction of planning'.[105] This reflects a difference in emphasis on what the envisaged planning systems are intended to achieve. The Royal Commission's recommendations seek to

[103] Chapter 3, Section 3.3.1. [104] Chapter 5, Section 5.4.

[105] The Royal Commission on Environmental Pollution, 'Environmental Planning', p. 109, para 8.37.

ensure that environmental considerations are given equal weight to, and sometimes greater weight than, other matters and that proposed development should be refused or modified where, in a decision-maker's judgment, 'the quality of the environment' would be jeopardised.[106] The generality of this objective, potentially embracing as it does ecological impacts, conflicts with values held in the environment's aesthetic qualities, social considerations and the quality of built as well as natural environments necessitates that flexibility in decision-making be preserved. In contrast, the system of ecological governance is founded on a much clearer understanding of what it is that should be protected, of why ecological protection is necessary, and of the best means available of going about this in view of the significant uncertainties surrounding ecosystem behaviour. It provides support for a legal framework that gives strong statutory direction as to how activities are to be regulated in the interests of reducing ecological stresses.

As with the policy-making process,[107] governmental observance of the statutory obligation should be promoted by legal requirements for the independent review of plans before their adoption under the national planning process. These should establish an equivalent process to that which policies are subjected to, with the independent advisory body giving guidance on the consistency of plans with the statutory objective, the government accepting its guidance or giving reasons for not following it, and the provision of standing for parties (including the independent advisory body itself) to challenge the legality of adopted plans.

5.3.4 *Ecological land use planning*

Ecological planning seeks to advance the system of governance's objective of reducing anthropogenic environmental pressures in two respects. The first, as we have considered in the preceding sections, is by formulating strategies for the transformation of socioeconomic systems at local, regional and national levels. The second, as I explain in this and the following section, is by minimising the cumulative environmental effects of land use. As with the assessment of alternatives in policy-making, planners should aim to further the planning system's statutory objective[108] by seeking to identify combinations of land and resource uses that are assessed to present the least threat to ecosystem

[106] Ibid., p. 108, paras 8.33 and 8.34. [107] See Chapter 3, Section 3.4.2.2.
[108] Chapter 5, Section 5.3.3.

functionality and resilience when compared with other possibilities. The development of national planning policies may assist with this process by identifying types of land that would be regarded as generally preferable and those which should not be used for particular development types, and by requiring planners to conduct a search for the former and avoid the latter in plan-making.

This 'top-line' approach should be backed up by the identification in plan development of areas that should be protected because of their contribution to sustaining ecological resilience. The identification and designation of certain habitat types and habitats of certain species is already the core legal method used by the EU and in the UK for protecting environmentally valuable places.[109] A legal framework for ecological planning would build on this by extending protection to all areas identified as being or likely to become of importance for the functioning of ecosystems. These should be identified through the assessment of landscapes at ecoregional levels (e.g., watersheds).[110] The spatial breadth of analysis is necessary to understand how separate sites interact with each other and how they contribute to ecological processes operating at larger scales.[111] For example, sites that are not themselves biodiversity hotspots may still be of importance for the resilience of protected areas. They may be able to offer them support in the event of disturbance (e.g., by fire) by accommodating biotic communities that can repopulate damaged areas.[112] Conversely, an isolated site situated in otherwise unprotected areas may not survive in the long term because it has no reserves to draw on if it suffers harm.[113] The term modularity is used in general resilience literature to capture the desirability of having multiple loosely connected units in ecosystems so that the demise of one module may not undermine the functioning of the ecosystem as a whole.[114]

[109] Council Directive 92/43/EEC of 7 May 1992 on the conservation of natural habitats and of wild fauna and flora [1992] OJ L 206/7 ('Habitats Directive') is the EU's main legal instrument for protecting habitats and species. C. P. Rodgers, *The Law of Nature Conservation: Property, Environment, and the Limits of Law* (Oxford: Oxford University Press, 2013) provides a full account and analysis of the legal framework for protecting habitats and species in the UK (including the influence of EU law on this).

[110] R. G. Bailey, *Ecoregion-based Design for Sustainability* (Seacus, NJ: Springer, 2002), pp. 99–101.

[111] Ibid.

[112] J. Bengtsson et al., 'Reserves, Resilience and Dynamic Landscapes' (2003) 32 *Ambio*, 389–96.

[113] Ibid. [114] Chapter 2, Section 2.3.2.

Corridors between separate units should be provided for in plans that allow species to move between sites.[115] Communities that have become isolated lose their resilience to external events.[116] The ability of species to relocate is also important for the adaptation of biodiversity to a changing climate. Species are expected to migrate as changes in temperature, patterns of precipitation, and the biota that systems support alters their 'climate space'.[117] The identification and protection of areas should be extended for this reason to sites that may be suitable for migrating species to colonise in the future even if they are not viewed as being of ecological significance in the present.[118]

Plans should state the level of protection to be applied to areas identified in them as being of importance for ecosystem functionality. Should activities that may disturb them be forbidden? Alternatively, should certain uses of the land be prevented or made subject to prior notification and approval before they can be conducted? They should also specify any positive requirements for maintaining and enhancing the condition of sites that landowners should be required to observe. Controls on particular activities and orders requiring that action be taken to restore the condition of protected areas are used in the UK under its legal regime for designating and maintaining sites of special scientific interest,[119] although a report of 2010 commissioned by the Secretary of State for the Environment, Food and Rural Affairs on the UK's network of protected sites identifies several respects in which this regime could be improved upon.[120]

5.3.5 Decision rules

As the discussion of arguments for limits-based regulation in this chapter reveals, the holy grail for environmental planning has been, and remains, the establishment of grounds on which the relentless drive of economic growth

[115] Bailey, 'Ecoregion-based Design', pp. 90–3. J. Lawton et al., *Making Space for Nature: A Review of England's Wildlife Sites and Ecological Network* (2010), a report commissioned by and submitted to the UK's Secretary of State for the Environment, Farming and Rural Affairs, also calls for the use of spatial planning to identify and establish protections for corridors alongside other measures for transforming the UK's fragmented catalogue of protected sites into a functioning ecological network.

[116] Walker and Salt, 'Resilience Practice', p. 94.

[117] E. Wilson and J. Piper, *Spatial Planning and Climate Change* (Abingdon: Routledge, 2010), pp. 334–6.

[118] Ibid. [119] Rodgers, 'The Law of Nature Conservation', pp. 68–99.

[120] Lawton et al., 'Making Space for Nature'.

can be reined in. I have questioned the viability of identifying a hard core of places and species whose conservation can be objectively justified on grounds of environmental need as the sole basis for ecological protection. The significant uncertainty over how our activities affect ecosystems requires that the focus should be on the progressive reduction of their collective impacts. At the same time, the setting of firm constraints on the development and exploitation of ecosystems where this may undermine their functionality is an essential feature of ecological planning. It is clearly consistent with a system of governance whose objective is to support ecosystem health that proposed uses should be assessed and approved or refused according to their anticipated effects on the components of ecosystems with which they may interact. It also supports the prioritisation in ecological governance of reducing consumption by making it clear that capacities for exploiting spatial and natural resources are finite, and by doing so not through setting numerical limits that the economy will inevitably expand towards, but by raising the potential that any proposal may be refused if it is judged to be incompatible with the systemic goal of supporting ecosystem functionality in itself or with the conditions in which it is to be conducted. Employing regulatory approaches that are sufficiently restrictive to deny 'easy access to a ready supply' is, in Rydin's view, essential if attention is to be shifted away from spatial fixes and towards managing demand.[121] Cowell and Owens also suggest, in the context of minerals exploitation, that establishing strategic constraints on development by reference to environmental conditions would provide a means of forcing the state-driven extraction programme to concentrate more on managing demand and on the careful management of existing sites.[122]

A requirement for proposed actions that fall under a statutory definition of 'development' to secure prior authorisation for their lawful conduct would create an opportunity for assessing and, if necessary, preventing ecologically harmful uses of spatial and natural resources. Environmental assessment should be mandatory for development proposals. Its conduct would not be limited, as is the case under the EU's Environmental Impact Assessment Directive, to circumstances in which a likelihood of significant effects on the environment is anticipated.[123]

121 Rydin, 'Land Use Planning and Environmental Capacity', 755.

122 Owens and Cowell, 'Land and Limits', 1st edn, p. 130.

123 Council Directive 2011/92/EU of 13 December 2011 on the assessment of the effects of certain public and private projects on the environment [2012] OJ L 26/1, Article 2.

As with the first paradox of the precautionary principle,[124] a precondition whose operation depends to an extent on knowledge of possible outcomes would not be appropriate in an ecological context. A precautionary approach that subjects all proposed development to assessment in the first instance should be employed because of the impossibility of knowing how individual interferences will combine with others to affect the system as a whole. Observance of this requirement should not be unduly onerous in cases where impacts are genuinely likely to be insignificant.

The control of development has provided the main means of preventing harmful land uses under the planning system in England and Wales since its inception.[125] However, the exclusion of agriculture and forestry from that system's definition of development has allowed the industrialisation and intensification of agriculture to proceed without the legal oversight that it provides in urban areas.[126] As a result, the use of ecologically valuable land for agriculture has been one of the main causes of significant deterioration in the UK's biodiversity during the last sixty years.[127] In contrast, the definition of development under the legal framework for ecological planning would cover all land uses. It would also encompass material change in use including the conversion of uncultivated or semi-natural land for agricultural purposes. Bringing previously unexploited land into cultivation has contributed significantly to the loss of habitats in England and Wales because of the lack of development control and the belated introduction of restrictions on conversion to align UK law on agricultural land use with EU law on environmental impact assessment.[128]

Activities that fall under the definition of 'development' should be scrutinised under decision rules that are designed to encourage ecologically benign development and to weed out proposals that present threats of ecological harm. The former aim would be supported by a presumption in favour of development proposals that are consistent with the

124 Chapter 3, Section 3.2.1.

125 Holder and Lee, 'Environmental Protection, Law and Policy', p. 510; S. Bell and D. McGillivray, *Environmental Law*, 7th edn (Oxford: Oxford University Press, 2008), pp. 393–4.

126 Holder and Lee, 'Environmental Protection, Law and Policy', pp. 513–14, 680–1; Bell and McGillivray, 'Environmental Law', pp. 734–6.

127 UK National Ecosystem Assessment, 'The UK National Ecosystem Assessment', pp. 26–7.

128 Holder and Lee, 'Environmental Protection, Law and Policy', pp. 681–2.

provisions of sectoral, regional or local plans following their finalisation and adoption under the national planning framework. Proposals that are not in accordance with plans should not be permitted unless they can be justified on grounds that they would make a greater contribution to reducing ecological stresses than solutions identified through the planning process. This presumption is intended to address the concern that plan-making has little influence over markets by requiring that market actors present proposals that are compatible with recommendations contained in plans on preferred development types and on preferred locations for development. The intention is to encourage developers to explore with public bodies where a project would be likely to be acceptable before seeking development consent.

Provisions of this nature cannot force market actors to provide the services that would be required to implement policies if they choose not to do so. However, the presumption in favour of development that is consistent with plans, operating in conjunction with measures identified and adopted during policy-making for promoting preferred options, are designed to steer markets towards ecologically desirable behaviours by indicating (e.g., through taxation and subsidies) what types of activities are regarded as preferable, and by closing off access to activities that are judged to be incompatible with the goal of maintaining ecosystem health. The presumption is also intended to encourage the participation of business in plan formation. Whilst this has become common practice in England and Wales since plan-led development was reintroduced in the 1990s,[129] the hope is that participation under a framework that closes down options where these would be ecologically incompatible will have a positive influence on the preparedness of market actors to engage with the search for stress-reducing outcomes.

Second, decision rules would make it clear when the pursuit of economic and social goals will be restricted in the interests of ecological protection. The provision of guidance on when environmental considerations should take precedence is recognised by Cowell and Owens as essential if a regulatory system is to exercise any real influence over demand projections and markets.[130] The issue, in their view, is that 'environmentally favourable outcomes cannot be guaranteed' in view of the long-standing dominance of economic concerns in decision-making unless formal provision is made for a priori consideration of

[129] Davoudi, 'Sustainability', 125–6.
[130] Owens and Cowell, 'Land and Limits', 1st edn, p. 112.

what is important for environmental health.[131] The clearest basis for setting a bottom line in ecological planning would be to use areas identified in plans as being of importance for ecosystem functionality as a reference point.[132] Activities that would disturb these areas would either not be permitted or would be allowed subject to prior notification and approval as identified in the relevant plan.

In addition, decision rules should be applied to all development proposals, whether or not they affect protected areas, to determine their compatibility with the system of governance's ecological objectives. Application of these rules will, as noted above, be informed by the prior environmental assessment of proposals. I suggest that a staged approach, similar to that already used in the UK in decision-making on projects that would harm biodiversity and under EU law for projects and plans that present threats of harm to protected sites, should be employed.[133] Development that could undermine resilience should not be permitted if alternative possibilities that present no threat of harm to ecosystems, including different locations, scales of development and means of realising the same benefits that the proposal pursues, are available. As I argue throughout this book, a search for alternatives that pose less of a threat of harm than those under consideration is of the essence in a system of governance that aims to improve the protection of ecosystems despite the impossibility of knowing the extent to which our activities heighten risks of their degradation and failure. The identification in plans of preferred areas for development would significantly assist with this search whilst the presumption in favour of consistency with plans would hopefully limit the number of conflicting proposals coming forwards. If no alternatives to the proposal are available, then measures to mitigate the perceived threat of harm to ecosystem functionality should be taken. These should only enable the award of development consent where they engender complete confidence that the feared harm can be avoided.

The decision rules to be applied in ecological planning would depart from those used in the EU and UK[134] by advising that a project whose features of concern cannot be removed through ex ante mitigation should not be permitted. The policy statement and the Habitats Directive permit damaging development respectively where this can be

[131] Ibid., p. 57. [132] Chapter 5, Section 5.3.4.

[133] Department of Communities and Local Government, 'National Planning Policy Framework', p. 27, para.118; Habitats Directive, Article 6(4).

[134] Ibid.

'compensated for' or where 'all compensatory measures necessary to ensure that the overall coherence of Natura 2000 is protected' have been taken. It is not possible in practice, because of the complexity of ecosystems and of their interactions with each other and with the Earth System, either to determine exactly how the resilience of an ecosystem may be affected by disturbance or to assess the adequacy of measures that seek to compensate for the harm concerned. A bottom line that legitimises potentially damaging activity without any basis beyond hope for making that damage good has no place in a legal framework that seeks to preserve ecosystem functionality.

Proposals should be assessed purely by reference to their potential impacts on places where deployment is proposed. It would be inconsistent, for reasons I explore in Chapter 3,[135] to permit ecologically damaging development on grounds that it may contribute to minimising some greater risk of ecological harm (e.g., climate change). Judgments on the permissibility of such development should be made, in the first instance, at the policy level in light of information reaped through planning processes, rather than on a case by case basis.[136] Ecological harm should only be legitimised under a system whose purpose is to improve the protection of ecosystems where it is clear that this has become necessary to replace more damaging options, and particularly those earmarked for sunsetting, with alternatives.

An important consideration is how development proposals should be dealt with in the event that there is insufficient information, even when applying broad qualitative criteria, to determine whether they would or would not be ecologically compatible. This is a question which I explore in Chapter 7 in considering how law can be used to generate the information on ecosystem behaviour that would be required to support and enhance the operation of ecological governance.[137] I note here that in circumstances where progress in deploying preferred options identified in policies is not feasible, a sensible response would be to allow trials of the development type where the issue is that there is insufficient understanding of how it would interact with ecosystem components in general. An alternative solution would be to authorise staged development if this is possible where the difficulty lies with knowledge of a development's effect in specific ecological conditions. In both cases, the trials can be monitored and informed decisions made if they yield sufficient evidence for conclusions on compatibility to be drawn.

[135] Chapter 3, Section 3.3.3. [136] Ibid. [137] Chapter 7, Section 7.4.2.

Finally, a potential restriction on the effectiveness of decision rules to steer attention towards demand management is the need in environmental regulatory systems to make some provision for derogation. I accept that circumstances may arise in which it would be ethically necessary to permit environmentally damaging development.[138] However, the danger with defining the circumstances in which derogation would be allowed is that scope may be provided for the developmental pressures that the statutory scheme is designed to resist to reassert themselves if derogations are drafted too loosely. For example, Ludwig Krämer, in his analysis of Article 6(4) of the Habitats Directive,[139] reveals how a concession for the conduct of development that would harm priority natural habitat types and species, where this is supported by an opinion of the European Commission, has allowed a range of projects to proceed on economic grounds without the proper scrutiny of whether alternative solutions are available which is a precondition to the Article's application.[140]

I suggest that a stronger version of Article 6(4) which allows derogation only on the limited grounds it refers to of threats to 'human health or public safety', and only in circumstances where the applicant has demonstrated a genuine absence of alternative solutions for addressing the problems concerned, would be appropriate under a system of governance whose purpose is to provide impetus for significant social change. This, in contrast to Article 6(4), which contains no mechanism for challenging the Commission's opinion, should allow for judicial scrutiny of decisions by the government to permit environmentally harmful development.

5.4 Environmental assessment

At present, legal requirements for environmental assessment provide the principal means of ensuring that environmental information is before public bodies during plan-making and in decision-making on development consent applications. It is therefore unsurprising that attention has been given to how relevant laws might be reformed to enhance environmental protection alongside arguments for revisions to the planning system itself. In particular, it has been considered whether the cause of

138 Owens and Cowell, 'Land and Limits', 1st edn, pp. 123–4.

139 Habitats Directive, Article 6(4).

140 L. Krämer, 'The European Commission's Opinions under Article 6(4) of the Habitats Directive' (2009) 21 *Journal of Environmental Law*, 59–85.

environmental protection would be better served if they were to require that plans and projects be assessed against, and approved or rejected by, reference to statutorily prescribed environmental standards.[141] The concern with environmental assessment in its purely procedural form is that it may have no effect on decision-making. This is because decision-makers, whilst they must take environmental information provided into account, are not obliged to accord it any specific weight as against other matters.[142] The sole requirement is that it is considered, although this may have substantive implications if clear grounds for refusing development or rejecting proposals are ignored. However, an important consideration is whether giving environmental assessment substantive content would exchange its potential to promote the identification and adoption of alternatives that represent the best option from an environmental perspective for a focus on identifying those that would satisfy specific standards.[143]

The weak influence of environmental considerations in decision-making cannot be attributed solely to weaknesses in legal requirements for environmental assessment. It is more a consequence of a systemic failure at European and national levels to hold an ethical debate of the type I call for in Chapter 2, to make the ecological value judgment that I argue would flow from this, and to make corresponding reforms to laws that lay down decision-making procedures. That said, both sides of the above debate are relevant to an exploration of the role of environmental assessment in ecological governance. The evaluation of alternatives is central to the search for ways in which ecological stresses can be reduced.[144] Environmental assessment would remain valuable as an independent mechanism for feeding information into decision-making

[141] C. Jones et al., 'Environmental Assessment: dominant or dormant?' in J. Holder and D. McGillivray (eds) *Taking Stock of Environmental Assessment: Law, Policy and Practice* (Abingdon: Routledge, 2008), p. 41; W. Howarth, 'Substance and Procedure under the Strategic Environmental Assessment Directive and the Water Framework Directive' in J. Holder and D. McGillivray (eds) *Taking Stock of Environmental Assessment: Law, Policy and Practice* (Abingdon: Routledge, 2008), p. 188.

[142] Jones et al., 'Environmental Assessment', pp. 32–3; J. F. Benson, 'What is the Alternative? Impact Assessment Tools and Sustainable Planning' (2003) 21 *Impact Assessment and Project Appraisal*, 261.

[143] D. McGillivray and J. Holder, 'Taking Stock' in J. Holder and D. McGillivray (eds) *Taking Stock of Environmental Assessment: Law, Policy and Practice* (Abingdon: Routledge, 2008), pp. 11–12.

[144] See my discussion of alternatives assessment at Chapter 3, Section 3.3.

processes on the available possibilities and the ecological concerns they may raise. With regard to the coupling of environmental protection with substantive requirements, the influence of environmental assessment is certain to be enhanced under a legal framework in which the information it generates feeds into planning processes that positively require adoption of the least ecologically consequential means of meeting demand that can be identified in both plan-making and authorising development. The Royal Commission on Environmental Pollution describes the combination of strategic environmental assessment with 'strong and specific environmental objectives' as an 'ideal outcome' from an environmental perspective and one that would 'adjust public decision-making towards an objectives-led proactive process of strategic environmental management'.[145] Cowell and Owens, whilst they express concern that environmental assessment could be used to legitimate dominance in patterns of growth and development, also accept that it could assist with constraining growth 'if coupled with mechanisms for judging serious and irreversible impacts unacceptable'.[146]

I illustrate these points by providing examples of the important part that assessment procedures would play under a planning system in which a value judgment in favour of ecological protection has been made. Strategic environmental assessment would be able to fulfil its potential as a tool intended to aid decision-makers with reviewing and identifying alternatives that would realise progressive objectives.[147] It would enable the formation of coherent strategies rather than providing ad hoc judgments on extant proposals. Strategic assessment would be conducted under ecological planning simultaneously with the development of local, regional and sectoral plans. Its role would be to aid exploration of the different means of effecting an ecological transition and assessment of them with a view to identifying outcomes that would contribute most to reducing ecological stresses. With this in mind, its objects of enquiry should be expanded beyond those set out in Annex I to the EU's Strategic Environmental Assessment Directive.[148] Assessment

[145] The Royal Commission on Environmental Pollution, 'Environmental Planning', p. 97, para 7.42.
[146] Owens and Cowell, 'Land and Limits', 1st edn, p. 53.
[147] See my discussion of alternatives assessment at Chapter 3, Section 3.3.3.
[148] Council Directive 2001/42/EC of 27 June 2001 on the assessment of the effects of certain plans and programmes on the environment ('Strategic Environmental Assessment Directive') [2001] OJ L 197/30.

would still include the subject matter set out in the Annex as information on likely environmental effects is required to assess the relative merits of different land use configurations. It should also advance the progressive goals of the system by requiring analysis of alternative possibilities for reducing consumption, for enhancing the efficiency of resource use and for employing preferred policy options.

Environmental impact assessment, whose value has tended to be downplayed as the use of strategic environmental assessment has increased, would also be revitalised in two respects: first, as a tool for reviewing and actively influencing locational decisions in view of the ecological importance of certain places and of decision rules on preferring alternatives that present no ostensible threat to the environment; and, second, as a means of giving plan-making teeth by ensuring, again in combination with decision rules, that the type of development proposals that come forwards from the market fall to be reviewed against the indications of favoured development given in ecologically oriented policies and strategic plans. In both respects, environmental impact assessment would have a more proactive role in forming operational decisions rather than reacting to them as they are presented.

6

Public participation in ecological governance

6.1 Introduction

I have already noted the importance of nurturing positive public attitudes towards ecological governance if its objectives are to be advanced.[1] On a basic level, it is vital that individual decisions and the project for ecological stress reduction as a whole should be seen as a legitimate action of government if the significant intrusions that this would have on most aspects of economic and social life are to be accepted. On a deeper level, a cultural shift is needed from a society in which citizens consistently prioritise their own interests whether or not this would be at the expense of the environment, and participate sporadically in politics through voting, to one in which they have a defined role in political decision-making and make positive choices themselves to live in ways that place less stress on ecosystems.

Reforms to governance and the creation, for example, of new environmental taxes would have some influence on how people behave by limiting options available to them or steering their strategic choices.[2] Public education might also be used to persuade individuals to abandon or modify harmful practices.[3] However, there is strong doubt that extraneous governmental action would result in the widespread internalisation of environmental considerations and acceptance of the moral rightness of protecting ecosystems that would be necessary if an ecological transition is to be pursued as a long-term objective.[4] In view of this, attention has been given in green political thought to whether

[1] Chapter 4, Section 4.6.

[2] G. Smith, 'Liberal Democracy and the Shaping of Environmentally Enlightened Citizens' in M. Wissenburg and Y. Levy (eds) *Liberal Democracy and Environmentalism: The End of Environmentalism?* (London: Routledge, 2004), pp. 141–2.

[3] Ibid.

[4] Smith, 'Liberal democracy', pp. 141–4; S. Owens, ''Engaging' the Public: Information and Deliberation in Environmental Policy' (2000) 32 *Environment and Planning A*, 1141.

greater public involvement with, and influence on, decision-making would increase the acceptability of environmental policies. In particular, the use of deliberative democratic approaches in which people are actively involved with debating political issues and determining what should be done in the best interests of society as a whole has been called for.[5] It is argued that this would promote a sense of civic unity and, as a result, a heightened consciousness of how individual preferences impact on shared public goods.[6] This is in contrast to liberal democratic models that treat citizens (as they are characterised in the literature on environmental politics) as isolated individuals possessing the right to consume with impunity, but with few responsibilities to their fellow citizens other than those laid down in law.[7]

I consider in the following section of this chapter the arguments that have been made in favour of deliberation as a process that would further the goals of environmental politics. I agree that a deliberative style of democracy, at least as its advantages are portrayed in the supportive theoretical literature, would provide strong backing for the effective operation of ecological governance. Participation in discussion and debate of environmental questions is claimed to promote preferences amongst participants for ecologically benign outcomes in public contexts, and perhaps also in their private decision-making.[8] It may result in an increased likelihood that participants will view decisions reached as legitimate; and in a restored confidence in politics that may enhance the acceptability of decisions even amongst non-participants because these have been made or, at least, shaped by members of the public rather than being formed exclusively by a remote political elite.[9] Deliberation involving those who would be affected by plans to apply ecological policies would also, as I note in Chapter 4, allow for the identification, discussion and, where possible, avoidance of conflict between ecological and other values, including those held in places for reasons other than their contribution to ecosystem health (e.g., their aesthetic qualities).[10] In view of

[5] Jacobs, 'Environmental Valuation', p. 211; Barry, 'Rethinking Green Politics', pp. 118–23, 214–36; Smith, 'Deliberative Democracy', pp. 61–73; Lundqvist, 'Ecological Governance', pp. 17, 148–51; Meadowcroft, 'Deliberative Democracy', p. 183.

[6] For example see Jacobs, 'Environmental Valuation', pp. 217–21; Barry, 'Rethinking Green Politics', pp. 228–36; Smith, 'Liberal Democracy', pp. 145–8.

[7] M. Sagoff, 'Values and Preferences' (1986) 96 *Ethics*, 301; Barry, 'Green Political Thought', pp. 206–9; M. de Geus, 'The Environment versus Individual Freedom and Convenience' in M. Wissenburg and Y. Levy (eds) *Liberal Democracy and Environmentalism: The End of Environmentalism?* (London: Routledge, 2004), p. 87.

[8] Chapter 6, Section 6.2.3. [9] Chapter 6, Section 6.2.4. [10] Chapter 4, Section 4.6.2.

these potential benefits, I conclude that the use of deliberative institutions for public participation in the new structures for governance I propose should at least be explored. If the claims made for it are realised, deliberation would clearly have an important part to play in promoting a societal embrace of ecological values.

Whilst the appeal of deliberation in the abstract is widely recognised, it has been questioned whether its putative advantages can be realised in practice. In Section 6.3. I consider the different aspects of the gulf that some commentators argue exists between deliberation as a theoretical construct and the realities of political decision-making.[11] I agree that results may well fall short of the ideal when this is confronted with the 'messiness' of everyday life, including existing power imbalances and unequal capacities to participate in debate. Even so, I argue that the use of deliberative participation for considering how ecological policies might be implemented should not be discounted. There are responses to concerns raised over deliberation, the efficacy of which can only be tested through their application. Indeed, a problem with the debate is the limited availability of empirical evidence against which to test the positions of competing schools of thought.[12] In addition, it would be far preferable to see if deliberation can be made to work than to fall back on more limited forms of public engagement through remote consultation. As I argue in Section 6.3.4., these, whilst they may have a greater reach, possess none of the potential positives of deliberation and would not therefore provide adequate support for an ecological transition.

[11] For example see Tewdwr-Jones and Allmendinger, 'Deconstructing Communicative Rationality', 1975; Owens, 'Engaging the Public', 1141; D. Chalmers, 'The Reconstitution of European Public Spheres' (2003) 9 *European Law Journal*, 127; S. C. Stokes, 'Pathologies of Deliberation' in J. Elster (ed.) *Deliberative Democracy* (Cambridge: Cambridge University Press, 1998), p. 123; K. Bäckstrand et al., 'The Promise of New Modes of Environmental Governance' in K. Bäckstrand, J. Khan, A. Kronsell and E. Lövbrand (eds) *Environmental Politics and Deliberative Democracy: Examining the Promise of New Modes of Governance* (Cheltenham: Edward Elgar, 2010), pp. 16–18. See also Smith, 'Democratic Innovations', pp. 11, 13–20. Smith's summary of arguments presented by 'sceptics and critics of citizen participation' captures the main points that have been made to support the claim that the deliberative ideal cannot be realised in practice.

[12] W. F. Baber and R. V. Bartlett, *Deliberative Environmental Politics: Democracy and Ecological Rationality* (Cambridge, MA: The MIT Press, 2005), pp. 121,128; Smith, 'Liberal Democracy', pp. 149–50. See also Bäckstrand et al., 'New Modes of Environmental Governance', p. 4 and Smith, 'Democratic Innovations', pp. 8–9 although both works contribute significantly to academic study of whether the theoretically perceived benefits of deliberative democracy can be realised in practice.

6.2 The promise of deliberation

6.2.1 Transforming preferences

Green political theorists argue that the primary concern of politics 'should be the transformation of preferences rather than their aggregation'.[13] The reference to 'preferences' relates to the thought processes by which people rank possible outcomes. Brown contends that people possess 'held values' representing an 'enduring conception of the preferable' based on which they assign value to different possibilities.[14] Elster uses the terminology of 'fundamental preferences' and 'derived preferences' to describe this evaluation with factual beliefs about the means that would be most likely to deliver preferred ends providing the link between them.[15] Both Brown and Elster argue that the assignation of values and the derivation of preferences are affected by the context in which these thought processes are conducted and the range of information available to those making a choice.[16] Challenges to habitual modes of preference ordering may also prompt reflection on the validity of a person's scheme of held values.

The transformation of preferences is regarded as essential if change in society's relationship with the environment is to occur.[17] The concern is that people, unless they revise the way in which they attribute value, will continue to place what is in their personal self-interest ahead of outcomes that would be of value to society as a whole. An individualistic approach both to personal decision-making and under a system of government that aims to maximise welfare by identifying solutions that match the desires of the largest number is unlikely to prioritise the long-term benefits of environmental protection over

[13] J. Elster, *Sour Grapes: Studies in the Subversion of Rationality* (Cambridge: Cambridge University Press, 1983), p. 35, quoted in Barry, 'Rethinking Green Politics', p. 226; J. Barry, 'Sustainability, Political Judgement and Citizenship: Connecting Green Politics and Democracy' in B. Doherty and M. de Geus (eds) *Democracy and Green Political Thought: Sustainability, Rights and Citizenship* (London: Routledge, 1996), pp. 122–3.

[14] T. C. Brown, 'The Concept of Value in Resource Allocation' (1984) 60 *Land Economics*, 232–4.

[15] J. Elster, 'Introduction' in J. Elster (ed.) *Deliberative Democracy* (Cambridge: Cambridge University Press, 1998), pp. 6–8.

[16] Elster, 'Introduction', pp. 6–8; Brown, 'The Concept of Value', 234–7.

[17] Barry, 'Rethinking Green Politics', pp. 121, 226; Meadowcroft, 'Deliberative Democracy', p. 184; Jacobs, 'Environmental Valuation', pp. 211–12; Barry, 'Sustainability', pp. 122–3.

short-term gain.[18] Decision-making based on the aggregation of peoples' inchoate wants is also seen as inappropriate where judgments would affect public goods including the environment.[19] Barry argues that, to the contrary, the character of environmental issues 'requires a decision-making procedure in which individuals make judgements about the public good in question and not just private calculations'.[20] Jacobs also suggests that, where choices may impact on public goods, personal preferences necessarily become other peoples' business and should be justified in a public context.[21]

The transformation sought is a metamorphosis of consumer preferences and the selfish materialism they embody into 'public good values' that encapsulate what is of importance for the well-being not only of the individual, but also of broader communities with which he or she is connected.[22] Barry describes the altered attitude that it is hoped will result from preference transformation as 'a willingness to accommodate the interests of others within an expanded conception of the ecological common good, a common good within which one's own good is located'.[23]

6.2.2 *Internalising environmental considerations*

The key to developing a 'public good' outlook both in public and private decision-making lies in the internalisation by individuals of others' interests and values, and reflection, in light of this, on personal preferences and the underlying values that inform them.[24] It is important if this outlook is to be ecological that the broadening of perspectives should engender consciousness of shared interests in the healthy functioning of natural systems. Analysis of how people review their preferences and modify them in light of new information and changing situations indicates that values are malleable.[25] However, alternative viewpoints must be accepted as credible and legitimate by receiving

[18] de Geus, 'The Environment versus Individual Freedom', p. 93; Barry, 'Sustainability', pp. 124–5.

[19] Barry, 'Rethinking Green Politics', pp. 121–2; Jacobs, 'Environmental Valuation', pp. 211–12.

[20] Barry, 'Rethinking Green Politics', p. 121.

[21] Jacobs, 'Environmental Valuation', p. 212.

[22] Ibid., pp. 212, 217–21.

[23] Barry, 'Rethinking Green Politics', p. 231–2.

[24] Lundqvist, 'Ecological Governance', p. 17; Smith, 'Deliberative Democracy', p. 64; Barry, 'Rethinking Green Politics', pp. 226–9.

[25] Woolley, 'Trouble on the Horizon?', 233–4.

parties if a willingness to review their own positions is to follow. The exploration of how political arrangements with an environmental focus should be structured to encourage the internalisation of ecological considerations, public acceptance of the need for ecologically protective action, and a related sense amongst non-governmental actors that they are valued partners alongside the state in environmental management has therefore provided a common theme in green political literature.[26]

Realisation of the latter aspiration would require that people should cease to regard their own interests as paramount in every case and begin to see themselves as citizens. Citizenship as a concept encompasses the formation of connections between individuals and institutional levels of society, and of 'a common identity which links otherwise disparate individuals together as a collectivity with common interests'.[27] Reviving citizenship in liberal democracies is viewed as a necessary precursor to the cultivation of ecologically virtuous patterns of behaviour.[28] Accordingly, green political theorists have also sought to identify the means by which individuals can be made to recognise that they are part of wider social networks and to accept that they bear responsibilities and duties towards each other.[29] The ideal outcome from an environmental perspective would be to create a sense of ecological citizenship based on awareness of increased interdependence between people and resulting recognition of the relations that exist between otherwise unconnected populations by virtue of the negative impacts of human activities on the functionality of natural systems.[30] Ultimately, this new self-perception may lead, because ecological citizenship is based on notions of interconnectedness and reciprocality, to the formation of 'transnational allegiances ranging from the bioregional through to the global, as well as to other species and the survival of ecosystems'.[31]

[26] For example see Barry, 'Sustainability', pp. 121–6; Barry, 'Rethinking Green Politics', pp. 206–26; Baber and Bartlett, 'Deliberative Environmental Politics', pp. 119–42; Dobson, 'Green Political Thought', pp. 103–14.

[27] Barry, 'Sustainability', p. 123. [28] Barry, 'Rethinking Green Politics', p. 103–6.

[29] Smith, 'Liberal Democracy', pp. 139–40; Barry, 'Sustainability', pp. 126–8; Baber and Bartlett, 'Deliberative Environmental Politics', pp. 165–82; Barry, 'Rethinking Green Politics', pp. 226–36; P. Christoff, 'Ecological Citizens and Ecologically Guided Democracy' in B. Doherty and M. de Geus (eds) *Democracy and Green Political Thought: Sustainability, Rights and Citizenship* (London: Routledge, 1996), 149–66.

[30] Barry, 'Rethinking Green Politics', pp. 106–7, 228–9; Smith, 'Deliberative Democracy', pp. 64–5.

[31] Christoff, 'Ecological Citizens', p. 154.

6.2.3 *Catalysing value formation*

Public engagement with deliberative processes in which equal participants provide relevant knowledge, make known their views and values, and have opportunities to persuade each other with a view to identifying outcomes that would address matters under consideration, is regarded as the mechanism through which the goals of internalisation and citizenship are most likely to be realised.[32] A cornerstone of arguments made in favour of deliberative participation is that having an understanding of the positions held by others and the values underpinning them may help people to examine their own values and preferences and make judgments with the benefit of an 'enlarged mentality'.[33] In this regard, commentators on deliberation have noted the scope it creates for participants to alter their views on hearing those held by others.[34] Steele refers to the belief that 'citizens have the capacity, through deliberating, to amend their views and expectations'.[35] Barton concurs that involvement in deliberation can result in personal preferences being 'shaped and modified by the processes to which they are subjected'.[36]

Deliberation is thought to be particularly effective for transforming preferences because participants are encouraged to identify outcomes that command common support through reasoned argument about what would be in the public interest. In Jacobs' view, the process of reasoning about interests other than one's own is fundamental to developing public good values.[37] These 'do not come fully formed into the world from within the breast of each individual' but are 'articulated through the public processes of debate and argument'.[38] Other commentators agree that public disputation

[32] For example see Jacobs, 'Environmental Valuation', pp. 219–21; Barry, 'Rethinking Green Politics', pp. 214–21; Smith, 'Deliberative Democracy', pp. 61–6; Lundqvist, 'Ecological Governance', p. 17; Meadowcroft, 'Deliberative Democracy', pp. 184–9.

[33] Smith, 'Deliberative Democracy', pp. 25–6, 59–60; S. Benhabib, 'Toward a Deliberative Model of Democratic Legitimacy' in S. Benhabib (ed.) *Democracy and Difference: Contesting the Boundaries of the Political* (Princeton, NJ: Princeton University Press, 1996), pp. 71–2; M. Cooke, 'Five Arguments for Deliberative Democracy' (2000) 48 *Political Studies*, 950–2; Smith, 'Democratic Innovations', pp. 24–5.

[34] Jacobs, 'Environmental Valuation', pp. 220–1; Smith, 'Deliberative Democracy', pp. 63–5.

[35] J. Steele, 'Participation and Deliberation in Environmental Law: Exploring a Problem-solving Approach' (2001) 21 *Oxford Journal of Legal Studies*, 428.

[36] B. Barton, 'Underlying Concepts and Theoretical Issues in Public Participation on Resources Development' in D. N. Zillman, A. R. Lucas and G. Pring (eds) Human Rights in Natural Resource Development: Public Participation in Sustainable Development of Mining and Energy Resources' (Oxford: Oxford University Press, 2001), p. 97.

[37] Jacobs, 'Environmental Valuation', p. 219. [38] Ibid. p. 221.

and mutual reflection on different viewpoints is more likely than private contemplation to result in a shared perception of what is genuinely valuable for peoples' well-being. Harrison, Burgess and Clark contend that 'it is often through open and sustained debate that 'values', whose relative stability distinguishes them from more subjective and labile personal preferences are revealed'.[39] Barton also notes the value of deliberative processes for helping participants formulate an understanding of where their true interests lie.[40]

In addition to influencing citizens in participative processes, deliberation may be effective in three respects for instilling the consciousness of human dependence on healthy ecosystems and of their vulnerability in the face of mass exploitation that may lead to more far-reaching change in patterns of living and in societal perception of what constitutes acceptable or unacceptable behaviour. The first is that deliberation has an educational effect because it exposes people to alternative conceptions of issues that they would not otherwise come across in their everyday lives or would dismiss if they were presented with them independently. Hearing and internalising information about ecological conditions and the causes of ecological degradation may lead to a longer-lasting awareness of the impact of current practices on ecosystems and therefore on everyone who depends on their functionality. Smith suggests that 'democratic deliberation offers conditions under which citizens will encounter and reflect upon ecological knowledge and values', and that they 'are more likely to internalise these in their judgments and practices' because they have been required to consider them in a context that places them in the role of problem solver rather than powerless critic of executive action.[41]

Second, the formation of values possessing a permanence that volatile preferences based on pure self-interest lack is likely to influence personal choices made outside of public contexts. Promoting value formation and the development of public good attitudes are viewed as part of deliberation's educative function. For example, Barry describes democratic deliberation as 'a process of mutual learning' that promotes self-reflexivity because it encourages participants to think on interests other than their own.[42] Jacobs uses similar language in arguing that deliberative processes provide 'a form of education which is constitutive of human flourishing'.[43]

[39] C. Harrison, J. Burgess and J. Clark, 'Capturing Values for Nature: Economic, Ecological and Cultural Perspectives' in J. Holder and D. McGillivray (eds) *Locality and Identity: Environmental Issues in Law and Society* (Aldershot: Ashgate, 1999), p. 87.

[40] Barton, 'Underlying Concepts', p. 114. [41] Smith, 'Liberal Democracy', pp. 145–6.

[42] Barry, 'Rethinking Green Politics', pp. 228–9.

[43] Jacobs, 'Environmental Valuation', p. 229.

Third, listening to and analysing others' perspectives and re-evaluating personal views in light of them may encourage the development of a critical attitude towards received wisdom and entrenched practices that is absent in a passive state–citizen relationship. Unpalatable as it may be for politicians, a citizenry that asks how particular states of affairs have come to pass and whether it is desirable that they should continue would be more conducive to an ecological transition than one which suffers in silence until an opportunity to vote arises. Dryzek argues that the creation of competences that would enable citizens themselves to recognise and oppose ideologies and structural forces that perpetuate distorted views of the political world would be a positive consequence of deliberative democracy, even if it does not lead to consensus over appropriate courses of action.[44] Baber and Bartlett also suggest that the most important contribution of deliberation to the social evolution that would be required if a collective ecological consciousness is to arise may be that it enhances 'the critical capacities of the citizens themselves'.[45]

The empirical evidence of deliberation's long-term impacts has been described as being 'no more than suggestive', although Smith concludes that 'backing is beginning to emerge for the theoretical claims made for the transformative and educative powers of democratic deliberation'.[46] However, a case can be made, based on the strong conclusions concerning its merits in the theoretical literature, that the use of deliberation as a means by which the active and willing participation of citizens in realising ecological goals can be encouraged should be explored. As Baber and Bartlett argue, 'societies must take positive steps to encourage the give and take of argument about controversial political issues' despite the absence of precedent for this if they are serious about encouraging democratic citizens 'to value political liberty as more than a means of pursuing self-interest'.[47]

6.2.4 *Enhancing the acceptability of ecological governance*

An argument made in support of public involvement with decision-making in general is that this will tend to promote acceptance of decisions because they are perceived to be more legitimate by those who have

[44] J. Dryzek, *Deliberative Democracy and Beyond: Liberals, Critics, Contestations* (Oxford: Oxford University Press, 2000), p. 21.

[45] Baber and Bartlett, 'Deliberative Environmental Politics', p. 171.

[46] Smith, 'Liberal Democracy', p. 150.

[47] Baber and Bartlett, 'Deliberative Environmental Politics', p. 125.

participated in the process.[48] However, the extent to which this effect is realised and the type of participatory processes that would be needed to bring the public on board will of course depend on the nature of the decision concerned and whether it is relatively clear cut or raises matters over which prior debate is required, if a consensus position is to be identified. Ecological policies and decisions about how they should be implemented, because they will almost certainly require citizens to make some personal sacrifices in the public interest, fall into the category of decisions for which extensive involvement with political decision-making would be necessary if the chances of their acceptance are to be increased.

Situations in which the public have an open opportunity to present their views and values and to challenge those advanced in support of other perspectives are more likely to result in acceptance of the outcome than those which simply allow individuals to make their views known. The key factor in this is, as Smith argues, that participants, because of their personal involvement, are able to understand the validity of the process by which it was reached even if they disagree with its substance. Whilst there is no guarantee that acceptance will follow from involvement in deliberation, its inclusive and open nature is more capable of providing a defensible justification for decisions (to those bound by them) where controversial issues are raised than a remote process in which no tangible opportunity has been provided for influencing its result.[49]

Public participation in deliberative fora would, as I note in Chapter 4, be needed to flesh out what ecological sustainability entails when regional and local circumstances are taken into account, and, in general, to obtain support for a governmental position that immediate and on-going action to reduce ecological stresses must be taken.[50] The decision-making frameworks I propose lay down ecological objectives and provide guidance on how these might be advanced. However, it is for regional and local authorities, working in conjunction with the public, to explore how ecological values, and the limitations that their supervening status places on conflicting economic and social goods, are to be reflected in the future development of the areas that they are responsible for governing and inhabit. Structures for ecological governance may set the desired course, but central and lower levels of government must make the case through deliberation and other media that this is an

[48] Barton, 'Underlying Concepts', p. 105. [49] Smith, 'Deliberative Democracy', p. 58.
[50] Chapter 4, Section 4.6.2.

appropriate initiative for a responsible administration to pursue. Their success in presenting the argument will become apparent from the extent that citizen participants in plan-making processes are willing to accept the validity of the government's position, from their own willingness to take an active part in identifying ecologically desirable solutions rather than limiting themselves to a critique of proposals placed before them, and by how radical the resulting strategies are. It would also doubtless be revealed in subsequent voting patterns.

Two question marks hang over the claim that participation in deliberative democratic practices would significantly enhance the acceptability of ecological governance. The first is that deliberation, because it allows for open-ended debate of issues, may not result in outcomes that favour ecological protection.[51] This would not be problematic in circumstances where the government's position is not accepted by a minority of participants. Barton expresses confidence that gains in the credibility and legitimacy of decision-making stemming from public participation in general would 'produce a greater level of satisfaction even amongst parties who have not got what they want'.[52] The absence of unanimity is also not regarded as fatal to the successful conduct of deliberation.[53] What is important is that conclusions have the support of those involved whether because the processes by which they were reached are seen as fair or because the reasoning behind the majority view is understood and accepted by opponents as a valid position even though their view differs.[54] In this regard, an additional educative effect that deliberation may have is that it provides participants with 'an insight into the moral and practical complexity of political judgment'.[55] Of greater concern would be a situation in which there is widespread rejection of the argument that steps should be taken to reduce ecological stresses. I consider further at Section 6.3.1. the perceived difficulty that deliberative participation is not certain to yield environmentally positive outcomes

[51] E. Lövbrand and J. Khan, 'The Deliberative Turn in Green Political Theory' in K. Bäckstrand, J. Khan, A. Kronsell and E. Lövbrand (eds) *Environmental Politics and Deliberative Democracy: Examining the Promise of New Modes of Governance* (Cheltenham: Edward Elgar, 2010), pp. 52–4.

[52] Barton, 'Underlying Concepts', p. 105.

[53] Jacobs, 'Environmental Valuation', p. 221; Baber and Bartlett, 'Deliberative Environmental Politics', pp. 127–9.

[54] Smith, 'Deliberative Democracy', p. 58; Jacobs, 'Environmental Valuation', p. 221; J. Petts, 'Evaluating the Effectiveness of Deliberative Processes: Waste Management Case-studies' (2001) 44 *Journal of Environmental Planning and Management*, 219–20.

[55] Meadowcroft, 'Deliberative Democracy', p. 186.

and whether this provides grounds for questioning its potential efficacy in ecological governance.

The second is the suggestion that deliberation will only influence those who take part in the process itself. The preferences of persons who have not been involved will therefore remain unchanged, and, consequently, are unlikely to be positively inclined towards policies that may impinge significantly on their personal freedoms. A response to this is that the introduction of a more deliberative approach to democracy would improve confidence in the political system and therefore incline the public in general to accept decisions emanating from it. Smith argues that the development of a politics in which there is better provision for meaningful citizen participation may provide a means of overcoming alienation and restoring trust and legitimacy in political institutions.[56] The fact that members of the public have been involved with making decisions and have had a transparent influence on them may also increase the likelihood that their fellow citizens will receive them and the values they espouse as founded on publicly agreed norms.[57] That said, the representativeness of deliberation and whether positions reached through it can provide a reliable platform for binding decision-making has also been raised as a potential problem with deliberative democracy. I consider this issue and the question of how fora for public participation can be designed to promote the positive aspects of the process whilst addressing practical difficulties with its conduct in Section 6.3.3.

6.3 Putting deliberation into practice: challenges and responses

Arguments for deliberative democracy are closely related to the theory of communicative rationality.[58] This posits that if political debate is conducted through impartial institutions in which those affected by a proposed decision or their representatives are included, and which allow for undistorted communication as a basis for reaching a consensus, then the public good will out.[59] The value of this theory as a critique of

56 Smith, 'Liberal Democracy', pp. 145–6.

57 Barry, 'Sustainability', p. 125; Smith, 'Liberal Democracy', p. 145.

58 See the account of Habermas' theory of communicative rationality at Tewdwr-Jones and Allmendinger, 'Deconstructing Communicative Rationality', 1975–7.

59 Tewdwr-Jones and Allmendinger, 'Deconstructing Communicative Rationality', 1976; A. Dobson, 'Democratising Green Theory: Preconditions and Principles' in B. Doherty and M. de Geus (eds) *Democracy and Green Political Thought: Sustainability, Rights and Citizenship* (London: Routledge, 1996), pp. 140–1.

political decision-making in liberal democracies is recognised even by those who question its practicability.[60] However, its perceived weakness (with which proposals for deliberation are tarred by association) lies in its 'utopian' disdain for the realities of power politics and its resulting failure to offer guidance as to how current practices can be improved upon.[61] As Dobson notes, it is an inconvenient reality that the idealised conditions which communicative rationality requires 'do not obtain in actually existing democracies', and therefore that 'the green-sounding outcomes that seem guaranteed by the procedures of discursive democracies are not at all guaranteed in real ones'.[62] The obvious concern for green political theorists for whom deliberation appears so attractive in principle is whether the potential it seemingly offers to promote both positive outcomes for the environment in decision-making and the adoption of ecological values are, in fact, realisable.

In this section, I consider the potential difficulties that have been identified with translating the theory underpinning calls for deliberation into deliberative practice. Of the possible responses that Dobson suggests for bridging the gap between the hypothesis and democratic societies as they are currently constructed, I prefer the option of exploring how institutions can be developed that would 'push real democracies in a discursive direction' rather than rejecting reform because the ideal and the actuality are too far apart.[63] I adopt this approach as some means must be found of altering popular attitudes if ecological governance is to take hold. In addition, I am not convinced that the obstacles which critics of deliberative theory have raised are insuperable. I accept that the ideal is out of reach. Indeed, its full implementation, because of its emphasis on undistorted debate, would not be desirable under a system of governance that seeks to give society a deliberate steer in an ecologically responsible direction. I do however join with Baber and Bartlett in arguing that 'communicative contexts can be designed and developed to supply incentives for a significantly better approximation to communicative rationality than is usual in policy deliberations'.[64] Not to experiment would, in any event, run counter to the central tenet of deliberative

[60] Tewdwr-Jones and Allmendinger, 'Deconstructing Communicative Rationality', 1988.

[61] Ibid.; Baber and Bartlett, 'Deliberative Environmental Politics', p. 142; Dobson, 'Democratising Green Theory', pp. 140–1.

[62] Dobson, 'Democratising Green Theory', p. 141. [63] Ibid.

[64] Baber and Bartlett, 'Deliberative Environmental Politics', p. 228. Smith also concludes from his studies of democratic innovations (see Smith, 'Democratic Innovations', p. 162) that 'many of the challenges laid down by sceptics and critics of citizen participation',

theory: that discursive democracies are transformative of the real world.[65] The only certainty is that a failure to challenge the status quo would leave in place a system that is wholly incapable of supporting an ecological transition.

6.3.1 *Unpredictability: problem or opportunity?*

An issue that is frequently raised with claims made over deliberation's potential to alter public attitudes towards the environment is that the process will not necessarily result in environmentally beneficial outcomes.[66] It cannot be guaranteed that citizens will set aside their self-interested preferences or become 'motivated by a concern for the ecological common good'.[67] It would not be fair to describe this as a problem that is peculiar to deliberation. No political system, save perhaps for one that employs extreme coercion, can ensure that people subject to it will adopt desired behavioural patterns. In any event, deliberation is to be preferred to other mechanisms for participation because it at least creates the potential that those involved will come to appreciate the value of a healthy environment and start acting responsibly towards it in the choices they make. Deliberation, as Smith notes, 'opens up the political space' for environmental values to be articulated and considered alongside other matters.[68] If the case for improved ecological protection is compelling, as I contend it is in this book, the hope is that, through debate and the internalisation of ecological considerations, it will be recognised as such.[69] The nature of deliberation also mitigates the concern, although it cannot be eradicated, that participants will simply adhere to the same preferences and prejudices with which they entered the process or that these, even if their proponents convey no interest in shared concerns, will win the day. Deliberation within political decision-making, because it is a public process, requires

including those levelled at deliberative democracy, 'can be met if careful attention is given to institutional design'.

65 Dobson, 'Democratising Green Theory', p. 141.

66 Lundqvist, 'Ecological Governance', p. 200; Barry, 'Rethinking Green Politics', p. 232; Barton, 'Underlying Concepts', p. 107; Smith, 'Deliberative Democracy', pp. 66–7; Bäckstrand et al., 'New Modes of Environmental Governance', p. 17; Lövbrand and Khan, 'The Deliberative Turn', pp. 52–4.

67 Barry, 'Rethinking Green Politics', p. 232.

68 Smith, 'Deliberative Democracy', p. 72.

69 Dobson, 'Democratising Green Theory', pp. 139–40.

that arguments be put in terms of the public good.[70] Participants may, as Meadowcroft notes, insist on their perspectives being 'admitted to the deliberative exchange'.[71] However, if their arguments are to convince others, they will need to persuade them that their preferred outcome 'is in the wider public interest, or can be justified in terms of general principles which can also apply to others'.[72]

A second aspect of the 'no guarantee' problem is that communicative rationality envisages a complete absence of external influence or direction as a precondition for genuine deliberation. The simple response to this is that our aim here is not to create ideal situations for rational communicative dialogue, but to find the means that would be most likely to advance ecological ends whilst adhering to democratic principles. Public participation in ecological governance would be concerned not with distilling an ideal position from the pool of possibilities, but with problem-solving under a statutory framework that is purposefully designed to guide decisions towards ecologically desirable outcomes. A directional approach, whilst it may not chime with the deliberative ideal, is not viewed as objectionable by proponents of discursive democracy.[73] Barry sees no reason to suppose that pure communicative rationality should be regarded as the only procedural standard.[74] Jacobs also suggests that deliberation is more likely to be effective if it is guided by some initial sense of what is good or better (whilst allowing scope for this to be challenged), and that it would be legitimate to provide this by asking participants to attempt to reach conclusions that advance a positive end value or that respect negative end values including, in this context, that preferences for ecologically destructive actions would be beyond the pale.[75] In this regard, both commentators recognise that deliberation does not take place in a theoretical bubble, but that it forms part of, and operates within, the structures and institutions of representative government.[76] Deliberative processes will be used not because of their theoretical credibility, but because they are thought likely to serve an end

70 Barry, 'Rethinking Green Politics', p. 217; Meadowcroft, 'Deliberative Democracy', p. 185; Jacobs, 'Environmental Valuation', pp. 219–21; Smith, 'Deliberative Democracy', p. 63.

71 Meadowcroft, 'Deliberative Democracy', p. 185.

72 Jacobs, 'Environmental Valuation', p. 220.

73 Lövbrand and Khan, 'The Deliberative Turn', pp. 52–4.

74 Barry, 'Rethinking Green Politics', pp. 216–17.

75 Jacobs, 'Environmental Valuation', pp. 227–8.

76 Barry, 'Sustainability', p. 122; Jacobs, 'Environmental Valuation', pp. 222–3. See also Smith, 'Democratic Innovations', p. 11.

whether that be improving the quality of democracy or, in this case, increasing the likelihood that policies for ecological governance will enjoy public support.

6.3.2 *Levelling the playing field*

A further criticism of the theory of deliberation is that it anticipates a neutral space for debate in which participants cast off their 'everyday' identities and interests and take on a citizen persona 'simply by virtue of coming into some deliberative forum'.[77] The contention is that deliberation, when it is conducted in the real world, is more likely to reflect and replicate existing power relationships between different strata of society, the private and public sectors, and those motivated by economic or environmental matters, than to transform them.[78] This concern over power relations has two aspects. The first is that deliberative processes may favour those possessing the education, knowledge and experience to participate effectively, the feared effect being that outcomes will inevitably correspond with their desires.[79] In contrast, those who are less well-blessed with the capacities to engage in debate, and the basic requirements of time and financial ability to take part, may be marginalised in the process or effectively excluded from it. Deliberation's potentially beneficial effects would be severely restricted if, in practice, participatory processes simply hold 'a mirror up to the pattern of power in the community; if the rich and well-organized are heard, while the poor and minorities are weakly represented'.[80]

The second is that economically and socially powerful actors may not approach deliberation with a willingness to listen to others and to be persuaded, but may instead see it as an opportunity to manipulate public opinion.[81] Tewdwr-Jones and Allmendinger are pessimistic about the possibilities for actualising the deliberative ideal when it is likely that

[77] Owens, 'Engaging the Public', 1146.

[78] Barton, 'Underlying Concepts', p. 109; Tewdwr-Jones and Allmendinger, 'Deconstructing Communicative Rationality', 1981, 1985; Baber and Bartlett, 'Deliberative Environmental Politics', p. 167.

[79] Tewdwr-Jones and Allmendinger, 'Deconstructing Communicative Rationality', 1986; Baber and Bartlett, 'Deliberative Environmental Politics', pp. 167–71.

[80] Barton, 'Underlying Concepts', p. 109.

[81] Tewdwr-Jones and Allmendinger, 'Deconstructing Communicative Rationality', 1981, 1985; Baber and Bartlett, 'Deliberative Environmental Politics', p. 179; Stokes, 'Pathologies of Deliberation', p. 123. See also Smith, 'Liberal Democracy', p. 148 on the influence of disproportionate funding and media campaigns on the outcomes of referenda.

some, if not all, participants will enter the process with no intention of reviewing their interests, but with every intention of advancing them if the opportunity arises.[82] They argue that self-interest is likely to remain the default setting in participation rather than some abstract notion of citizenship, and, consequently, that 'power and political action will remain dominant determinants' of society's course.[83]

As with the general lack of certainty over outcomes, the possibility that existing power imbalances would skew deliberative processes cannot be dispelled. Despite this, the discursive nature of deliberation is, for the reasons I consider below, more likely to challenge and overcome the negative influences of vested interests over decision-making in the long-term than other mechanisms for public participation. The first consideration is, again, the transformative potential of deliberation.[84] Whilst initial reluctance to abandon personal preferences is to be expected, prolonged involvement with a new style of politics and exposure to an ecological orientation in political decision-making may result in the evolution of different attitudes. The hope is that people and commercial entities alike will begin to appreciate both their shared interests in maintaining a healthy environment and to see themselves as politically responsible for advancing the common well-being in their behaviours and choices.

Deliberation under a system of ecological governance would form a key part of the experimental approach I refer to in Chapter 4, the purpose of which is to explore whether an ecological transition in which all sectors of society are willing participants is possible.[85] If the experiment in governance reveals that people are inherently venal and unmoved by appeals to values other than their own, the inescapable conclusion may be that a more directional mode of government is needed if ecological goals are to be advanced. The evidence I refer to concerning peoples' readiness to reconsider what is in their own and others' interests gives some grounds for confidence that this will not prove to be the case.

The second is that deliberative institutions can be designed to overcome inequalities in wealth and power to the extent that these would be inimical to open debate in which a wide range of interests are

[82] Tewdwr-Jones and Allmendinger, 'Deconstructing Communicative Rationality', 1981.

[83] Ibid., 1981, 1985.

[84] See Chapter 6, Section 6.2.3, and Dobson, 'Democratising Green Theory', p. 141.

[85] Chapter 4, Section 4.1.

represented. The former imbalance could be addressed by the provision of public funding and assistance to enable those who would otherwise be excluded to take part in decision-making.[86] With regard to the latter, the informality of deliberation provides scope for the use of procedural innovations to ensure that participants, whatever their position in society, are given an equivalent opportunity to exercise their democratic rights.[87] Baber and Bartlett suggest the use of voting rights and allocating set times for participants to speak as means by which the effect of social differentials can be lessened in deliberative fora.[88] Jacobs also notes the important role of a moderator in deliberation as a non-participant whose responsibility is to oversee the fairness of the process in general, and, as part of this, to make certain that all participants are able to communicate their views and to prevent those who would seek to dominate the process from doing so.[89] Similarly, Smith suggests that effective facilitation or moderation in participatory processes can be used to ensure 'that marginalised voices are heard', and, in the case of deliberative mini-publics, that 'proceedings are not dominated by the politically skilled and charismatic'.[90]

Third, the extent to which variance in deliberative capabilities and attempts by participants to coordinate the process are problematic will depend on whether outcomes reached are determinative of the issue under consideration. If the role of deliberation is to feed information about public opinion, views and values into political decision-making processes, rather than to reach final decisions on what should be done, then positions promoted by vested interests will not bind decision-makers.[91] They may of course have an effect on the views that they form, but there are practical means available of reducing the risk that subsequent decisions will be influenced by the preferences of articulate or forceful citizens where these are manifestly self-advancing. Jacobs suggests that transcripts could be taken from which attempts to dominate, manipulate and coerce proceedings should be evident to those basing judgements on them.[92]

The overarching point is that concerns over imbalances in power should not prevent deliberative fora from being used. It is through

[86] Baber and Bartlett, 'Deliberative Environmental Politics', p. 180.
[87] Smith, 'Democratic Innovations', pp. 21–2.
[88] Baber and Bartlett, 'Deliberative Environmental Politics', p. 180.
[89] Jacobs, 'Environmental Valuation', p. 230.
[90] Smith, 'Democratic Innovations', pp. 168–9, 197–8.
[91] Chapter 6, Section 6.3.3.
[92] Jacobs, 'Environmental Valuation', p. 230.

trialling different techniques that a body of empirical evidence can be developed and brought to bear upon important issues for the effective conduct of deliberation, including how power is deployed within relevant processes and how this bears upon the identities and values that participation in them produces.[93] It is inevitable that there will be a wide variance in knowledge and deliberative skills in any process that aims to be inclusive, and particularly one whose purpose is to explore with individuals from disparate backgrounds whether there is a 'public good' outcome on which, notwithstanding their different social and economic statuses, they would be able to converge.[94] When viewed in this light, a divergence in capabilities is a necessary feature rather than a problematic aspect of deliberation. However, to the extent that difficulties do arise, the indication is that it may be possible to deal with them through the use of mechanisms that are intended to promote procedural fairness.

6.3.3 Deliberation's reach

Doubt has been cast on the claim that deliberative democracy would promote the adoption of ecological values and a renewed confidence in government on a sufficient scale to secure the acceptance of ecological governance and decisions made under it. A perceived difficulty is that deliberative participation is most likely to be effective when the size of deliberating groups is restricted.[95] Whilst this is seen as necessary because mass participation would not be conducive to the profound reflection on issues that may lead to a transformation of preferences, the trade off between the quality of deliberation and the numbers of participants will inevitably constrain deliberation's capacity to influence public attitudes directly. The fact that deliberative procedures usually involve relatively small groups and that participants are chosen or attend freely also raises questions about the representativeness of conclusions reached through them.[96] It is generally accepted that, in practice, it would not be appropriate for consensus positions formed in deliberation

[93] Owens, 'Engaging the Public', 1146.
[94] Baber and Bartlett, 'Deliberative Environmental Politics', pp. 170–1.
[95] Meadowcroft, 'Deliberative Democracy', p. 198; Smith, 'Liberal Democracy', p. 147.
[96] Meadowcroft, 'Deliberative Democracy', pp. 198, 201–2; Smith, 'Deliberative Democracy', p. 91; Lövbrand and Khan, 'The Deliberative Turn', pp. 48, 55; Smith, 'Democratic Innovations', p. 187.

to bind wider constituencies.[97] The danger is, however, that deliberation, if it has no formal influence on decision-making, would amount to nothing more than a talking shop.[98]

The need to control the size of participating groups clearly does place a practical limit on the potential for peoples' views to be altered through involvement with deliberative processes. Even so, the reach of deliberation can be maximised by providing a variety of opportunities for citizens to participate in discursive democracy.[99] A range of procedures are used for deliberation. Some of these such as citizens' juries and consensus conferences that involve problem-solving and debate between participants are suited to smaller groups (typically 12 to 25 persons).[100] Others, such as deliberative opinion polls in which members of the public listen to and question cases presented for different policy options and vote for their preferred alternative, combine some deliberative content with participation by larger groups (typically 200 to 500 persons).[101] Evidence from Fishkin's case study of polls held in Texas over the introduction of renewable energy suggests that this process, although it is more concerned with testing governmental positions than the independent development of solutions, can have a significant effect on participants' outlooks 'because the public is arriving at a considered judgment where previous responses would have represented 'top of the head' views'.[102]

Whatever combination of procedures is employed, what counts if the aim is to improve democracy's public image is the quality of the overall process of decision-making.[103] The imaginative design of new institutional structures for ecological governance could promote this end by requiring that the public be engaged through deliberative fora at different stages of decision-making with a view to raising 'the deliberative democratic content' of the political system as a whole.[104]

[97] Meadowcroft, 'Deliberative Democracy', pp. 201–2; Smith, 'Deliberative Democracy', pp. 73, 93.

[98] Tewdwr-Jones and Allmendinger, 'Deconstructing Communicative Rationality', 1983.

[99] Meadowcroft, 'Deliberative Democracy', p. 199; Smith, 'Democratic Innovations', pp. 188–9, 197.

[100] Smith, 'Liberal Democracy', p. 147. [101] Ibid. [102] Ibid. p. 149.

[103] Meadowcroft, 'Deliberative Democracy', p. 199. See also the examination of complementarities between innovations for public participation when used at separate stages and sometimes also simultaneously under democratic political systems at Smith, 'Democratic Innovations', pp. 188–93.

[104] Meadowcroft, 'Deliberative Democracy', p. 200.

An alternative possibility is that smaller-scale deliberative procedures could be combined with less-intensive but more-inclusive participatory mechanisms, such as consultation or referenda.[105] The recorded conclusions of participants in deliberation could be used in these processes to provide a catalyst for wider debate in civil society.[106] I argue in the following section that reliance on remote consultation over governmental proposals alone would be unlikely to create public support for an ecological transition. However, I agree with Petts that using consultation to augment deliberative participation would provide a means of dispelling 'complaints from outsider groups that the process is elitist or biased in the decision authority's favour', and thereby of increasing the likelihood that decisions which deliberation has informed will be accepted by participants and non-participants alike.[107]

The obvious response to the suggestion that the outcomes of deliberation between unelected individuals cannot be treated as representative is to provide, in the design of institutional structures, for clear links between deliberative stages and formal decision-making processes.[108] This would address the concern that participants in deliberation are unaccountable by leaving decision-making authority with the representatives of elected administrations. It may also, by requiring that decisions reached should take into account the views and values expressed by participants in deliberative processes, have a salutary effect on public confidence in the political system. In this regard, discursive democracy is not seen by its proponents as a replacement for representative democracy, but as a supplementary mode of democratic practice that would enhance the authenticity of representative government as a whole and raise the quality of decision-making by making governmental authorities aware of public attitudes and perspectives on matters under

[105] See the discussion of using referenda as a vehicle for widespread debate of political issues at Smith, 'Liberal Democracy', p. 148 and Smith, 'Democratic Innovations', p. 197.

[106] Smith, 'Deliberative Democracy', p. 147. The importance of publicising conclusions reached through deliberative processes if they are to enhance the perceived legitimacy of the political system amongst non-participants is also emphasised in Smith, 'Democratic Innovations', pp. 25–6, 177.

[107] Petts, 'Evaluating the Effectiveness of Deliberative Processes', 215.

[108] Meadowcroft, 'Deliberative Democracy', p. 197; Baber and Bartlett, 'Deliberative Environmental Politics', p. 234; A. Klinke, 'Inclusive Risk Governance through Discourse, Deliberation and Participation' in M. Everson and E. Vos (eds) *Uncertain Risks Regulated* (Abingdon: Routledge, 2009), p. 411; Smith, 'Democratic Innovations', p. 11.

consideration.[109] The chain of governance that I propose in Chapter 4 is intended, by building strategies from the bottom up and by providing continuity between layers of governance, to promote the influence of views expressed in and the outcomes of deliberative participation at all levels of decision-making.[110]

A final consideration is whether it is right to equate representativeness solely with the numbers of people involved, whether directly or indirectly, with making a decision. To do so is to misunderstand the reasons for supplementing representative democracy with deliberative institutions. The introduction of deliberative democracy is called for because there is a perceived need to replace democratic practices that simply aggregate preferences with ones that use the best means available of identifying what courses of action would be in the interests of society as a whole. The essence of deliberative participation is 'to dig deeper into people's values and beliefs than private surveys can do' in the hope that outcomes capturing what is genuinely valuable for participants, rather than those that would provide immediate satisfaction but at a long-term cost, will be revealed.[111] In view of this more extensive approach to exploring what would be beneficial for society at large, it could be argued that 'even though smaller numbers are involved, the people are actually being better represented'.[112] It is in the nature of the process and the opportunity it affords for participants to reflect upon a wide variety of experiences and perspectives, and consider where their true interests lie, that the legitimacy of deliberation and conclusions reached through it rests, rather than in the numbers of those involved with the process.[113]

6.3.4 *Consultation's inadequacy*

A concluding argument in favour of participation through deliberative institutions is that there are grounds for questioning the capacity for the consultation of citizens, when used as the sole means of obtaining popular input to political decision-making, to promote the transformation in preferences that may lead to broad public support for ecological

[109] Barry, 'Sustainability', pp. 121–2; Jacobs, 'Environmental Valuation', pp. 223–4; Smith, 'Deliberative Democracy', pp. 74–5; Meadowcroft, 'Deliberative Democracy', p. 208.

[110] Chapter 4, Sections 4.4, 4.5 and 4.6.

[111] Jacobs, 'Environmental Valuation', p. 223.

[112] Ibid. See also J. Dryzek, 'Legitimacy and Economy in Deliberative Democracy' (2001) 29 *Political Theory*, 651–69.

[113] Smith, 'Deliberative Democracy', p. 91.

governance.[114] Indeed, consultation is more likely to confirm individuals in their preferences and values (where these are in conflict with governmental proposals) than to encourage reflection on them.

The first is that, in consultation, the public is invited to comment on preformed proposals which reflect value judgments that have already been made, and the values of those previously involved with the decision-making process. This creates an adversarial situation in which respondents contest judgments by reference to values they already hold rather than examine their preferences in a process that would provide an opportunity for the government to explain why stronger ecological protection is thought to be necessary and to explore how outcomes promoting ecological objectives, whilst accommodating values of importance to citizens in localities and regions, might be identified.

The second and related reason is that consultation processes do not provide a space in which participants are able to reconsider and, perhaps, to revise their positions in light of other participants' views and values. As I note in Section 6.2.3., initial reaction to proposals may be modified through reflection on the perspectives of others in a process where equal participants have an opportunity to influence each other's views. However, consultation, which provides no scope for the clarification of initially held views through interaction, is more likely to entrench whatever potential there is for opposition to an ecological transition than to alleviate it. Third, consultation may not increase acceptance of following decisions significantly (unless it is clear that these have been influenced by responses) because the information provided feeds into another's reasoning.[115] It is involvement with the process of reasoning as part of a problem-solving approach which, as I argue in Section 6.2.4., is most likely to secure acceptance of ecological policies and decisions made for their implementation.

Consultation's obvious limitations for promoting change in attitudes provides a final and, in my view, conclusive reason for arguing that

[114] Consultation could be used to engender transformative perspectives when outputs of preceding deliberative processes and fully reasoned governmental responses to them are used as supporting materials for the exercise. See Chapter 6, Section 6.3.3, and Niemeyer, 'The Emancipatory Effect of Deliberation'. This section criticises approaches to consultation that present an authority's view on why a particular outcome would be desirable both without this having been subjected to prior scrutiny by deliberating groups, and without an explanation of the conclusions reached by deliberants and the authority's reasons for accepting or rejecting them being made available to consultees.

[115] Smith, 'Democratic Innovations', pp. 17–18.

public involvement in ecological governance should be conducted primarily through deliberative processes. It is clear that, even if it proves impossible to address the potential difficulties with introducing deliberative democracy that I have considered, this would still be more likely to provide effective support for an ecological transition than participatory procedures, which do not encourage members of the public to reflect on their values. The necessary recourse in the event that people remain reluctant to change their preferences and lifestyles, notwithstanding reforms to the political system, may be either to further increase public participation by devolving responsibility for decision-making or, as I note at Section 6.3.2., to adopt a more directional mode of government.

6.4 Deliberative participation under ecological governance

Public participation in ecological governance has three main purposes: to enhance the perceived legitimacy of the system, and therefore the acceptability of decisions produced under it; to encourage the spread of ecologically sustainable behaviours throughout society; and to improve the quality of environmental decisions by ensuring that knowledge of local impacts and views are available to decision-makers and taken into account by them.[116] In this concluding section, I consider how arrangements for deliberative participation in decision-making could be designed to advance these ends.

Opportunities would be provided under ecological governance for members of the public to participate in developing the raft of draft plans that local authorities are required to produce as the first stage in the bottom-up planning process. The starting point would be for small groups to examine issues connected with the reduction of consumption, the deployment of ecologically preferable policy options, and the withdrawal of those identified for 'sunsetting' in localities. Small-scale deliberations allow for focused debate and promote a depth of reflection that may lead participants to reappraise their values and preferences.[117] Empirical evidence from citizens' juries and planning cells, both of

[116] Chapter 4, Section 4.6.

[117] G. Smith and C. Wales, 'Citizens' Juries and Deliberative Democracy' (2000) 48 *Political Studies*, 51–65; Smith, 'Democratic Innovations', pp. 94–101; Goodin and Dryzek, 'Deliberative Impacts', 221–4.

which typically involve no more than 25 persons, indicates that they can have the transformative effect that deliberative theorists predict.[118] This may lead in turn to support for protection of the environment in the interests of communities over the personal advantages that its exploitation may afford, and to increased levels of civic engagement amongst participants.[119]

The small-group approach would be combined with measures that seek to enhance its credibility with the public at large, and thereby to bolster confidence in the system of governance as a whole. First, local authorities would be obliged under the legal framework for planning to organise the review by deliberating groups of citizens of issues raised by efforts to reduce environmental pressures. This would be done in connection with the periodic formation and review of local plans. The selection of participants would be random, the only qualifications being their eligibility to vote and that they live within areas under the local authority's jurisdiction. Outputs from regularly recurring decision-making processes in which anyone could be asked to participate are less likely to be regarded with distrust by persons who could themselves be called upon to deliberate over matters of local importance.[120] The prospect of being approached could also raise the profile of ecological concerns and of possible responses to them amongst the wider public.

Second, the careful selection of issues to be examined by deliberative fora is important for their effectiveness. The issues must be clear as deliberations are unlikely to produce valuable outcomes where participants are uncertain about what they are being asked to consider.[121] In view of this, I suggest that local planning authorities should choose issues to be considered following initial rounds of information gathering and consultation, and the preparation of outline proposals based on them. However, agenda-setting by local authorities at the outset could itself raise a concern that public freedom to contribute to plan formation is being limited from the outset.[122] If those who are the recipients of

118 Smith and Wales, 'Citizens' Juries'; Niemeyer, 'The Emancipatory Effect of Deliberation'; Smith, 'Democratic Innovations', pp. 94–5.

119 Niemeyer, 'The Emancipatory Effect of Deliberation'; Smith and Wales, 'Citizens' Juries', 60.

120 Smith and Wales, 'Citizens' Juries', 57.

121 Smith, 'Democratic Innovations', pp. 88–91.

122 Smith, 'Democratic Innovations', pp. 88–91; Smith and Wales, 'Citizens' Juries', 58.

outcomes from deliberations define their parameters, they could use this power to exclude areas from debate where it is feared that public views may not be consistent with political goals. To address this potential problem, the first round of citizens' juries would review proposals by planning authorities for the issues to be examined by deliberating groups. Participants in the following processes should also be able to add issues to those that they have been charged to consider once they have become sufficiently acquainted with the subject matter to identify further matters for review by them.

Third, requirements for groups to explain why conclusions have been reached and for decision-makers to state their reasons for accepting or rejecting the group's views can be used to lay bare the sometimes obscure reasoning underlying political decisions. Niemeyer suggests that brief statements of key reasons for the conclusions drawn by citizens' juries could extend the transformative effect of deliberation by encouraging reflection by non-participants on the defensibility of their compatriots' views.[123] The opening up to critical scrutiny of their proposals by a wider audience also places pressure on politicians to use coherent reasons to explain why they believe an approach to be beneficial for society, and particularly where they depart from a group's recommendations.[124] Deliberation's reach could be extended by using statements of reasons made by deliberants and by decision-makers in response to them as supporting documents for larger participatory exercises.

Fourth, the preparation of draft local plans is the first stage in a process that feeds into the formation of regional proposals for stress reduction.[125] These proposals are subsequently reviewed at the national level.[126] Further opportunities to participate through deliberative fora in decision-making at these levels would be used to build on and scale up the initial benefits of engagement with local planning. Continuity in the personnel involved, if people are willing and able to give more of their time to democratic processes, would assist with creating links between local and national planning processes. Increasing opportunities for public involvement with decision-making in general and creating structures that enable views expressed in local participation to influence decisions made at higher governmental levels both provide means, as

[123] Niemeyer, 'The Emancipatory Effect of Deliberation', 125–8. [124] Ibid., 127–8.
[125] Chapter 4, Section 4.5. [126] Chapter 4, Sections 4.3, 4.4 and 4.5.

I suggest in Sections 6.2.4 and 6.3.3, by which public confidence in politics could be improved.

Representatives of local planning authorities would work together with a regional planning authority to meld local proposals into a plan that pools regional capacities for stress reduction to best effect.[127] One way of maintaining continuity between local and regional decision-making would be to invite those involved with local deliberations to take part in deliberative reviews of proposals made by the regional body. Invitations would be extended to all participants, with those who accept being randomly selected to take part in groups made up from representatives of different communities in the region. Particular issues arising from the regional process would be selected for debate (again following the review by citizens' juries of initial proposals for issues to be examined). Another way of promoting continuity would be to conduct a larger-scale exercise in which the original local groups examine draft regional plans with a focus on how they affect the draft plans for localities that were submitted for consideration under the regional planning process. They would be asked to consider whether the reasons provided by regional planners for departing from local proposals are valid. Equivalent approaches could be used for the review of plans at the national level with those involved in regional deliberations invited to participate in reviews of issues raised by national planning, and with local groups reviewing those aspects of national plans that further depart from their original proposals and the reasons given for this by central government.

Proposals for a major scaling-up of public participation in decision-making of the type I suggest have been criticised because of the expense involved with arranging participatory exercises.[128] Critics also argue that it is unrealistic to expect people to devote large amounts of time to public matters.[129] Both of these concerns are valid and would need to be taken into account in the design of opportunities for public participation in decision-making under ecological governance. However, neither of them prevents innovative democratic practices from being tested with a view to exploring how costs and demands made on peoples' time can be kept to a minimum, although the identification of means by which the projected benefits of deliberation can be realised should be the main

[127] Chapter 4, Section 4.5. [128] Smith, 'Democratic Innovations', pp. 105–7.
[129] Ibid., p. 26, 105–7.

goal of such trials. In addition, a general response can be made to concerns that a democracy with higher levels of popular involvement would be much more expensive to run than purely representative models with limited scope for participation outside of voting. This is that investment in the quality of democracy would be money well spent if it leads to a reduction in the substantial and growing risks of human harm presented by the global deterioration in ecological conditions.

7

Informing ecological governance

7.1 Introduction

My proposals for ecological governance move away from exclusive reliance on the accurate prediction of impacts of planned activities and proposed development for preventing harm to ecosystems. Growing appreciation of the complexity of ecosystems, of their innate dynamism, and of our ignorance of how cumulative stresses affect them or of whether they are exposed to the risk of structural breakdown have combined to erode historic confidence in science's ability to establish whether activities can be pursued without having negative effects. It would not, in any event, be appropriate under a system of governance that is founded on a prioritisation of ecological values to stake the health of ecosystems on the exactitude of conclusions reached through scientific research when, in practice, these will always be provisional. The failure of established regulatory practices that are based on scientific input to stem ecological degradation only serves to reinforce this point.

It is for these reasons that I have argued for an approach to governance that observes due caution and respect for ecological values in applying regulatory controls. That said, ecology does have a key supporting role to play in the reduction of stresses that socioeconomic systems place on the natural world. Concerted efforts to improve our understanding of resilience and of how systemic processes and the different components of ecosystems contribute to this may enhance our ability to determine the compatibility of proposed policies, plans and projects with the overarching goal of supporting their functionality. Even if they do not, heightened awareness of our ignorance would serve a purpose by reinforcing the need for normative precaution in governing human activities.

I do not presume to suggest what research should be conducted. Rather, the focus in this chapter is on exploring how law can be used to ensure that information is produced which may advance the objectives of ecological governance. I comment in the following section on the particular difficulties that would confront efforts to generate information for governing activities from an ecological perspective. I then go on, in Section 7.1.2, to explain the respects in which law can be used to meet these challenges.

7.1.1 Addressing the information deficit

Current levels of information concerning environmental conditions and legal mechanisms for generating this data are regarded as inadequate for effective environmental protection.[1] This general concern is echoed in the literature concerning the need for new legislative approaches as the objectives of environmental law move from addressing discrete problems and the protection of particular species and habitat types towards the management of the individual and cumulative effects of human activities on the functionality of ecosystems.[2] Indeed, the need for new approaches for generating information is emphasised in this context because of a common perception that our knowledge and understanding of ecosystems is at low levels,[3] and as the characteristics of natural systems present particular difficulties for those seeking to collect the information necessary to support a legal system for their protection.

The legal prescription that some commentators have advanced for responding to the complexity, variability and unpredictability of natural systems is to establish structures that allow for adaptive management of them.[4] The essence of an adaptive approach is that, through requiring the on-going monitoring and assessment of the effects of human activities, it

[1] D.C. Esty, 'Environmental Protection in the Information Age' (2004) 79 *New York University Law Review*, 115; D.A. Farber, 'Bringing Environmental Assessment into the Digital Age' in J. Holder and D. McGillivray (eds) *Taking Stock of Environmental Assessment: Law, Policy and Practice* (Abingdon: Routledge Cavendish, 2008), pp. 219–22; W.E. Wagner, 'Commons Ignorance: The Failure of Environmental Law to Produce Needed Information on Health and the Environment' (2004) 53 *Duke Law Journal*, 1619.

[2] Ruhl, 'Environmental Law as a Complex Adaptive System', 940, 954–8; H. Doremus, 'Adaptive Management, the Endangered Species Act, and the Institutional Challenges of "New Age" Environmental Protection' (2001) 41 *Washburn Law Journal*, 54.

[3] Tarlock, 'Ecosystems', p. 579; C.S. Holling (ed.) *Adaptive Environmental Assessment and Management* (London: John Wiley & Sons, 1978), p. 7.

[4] J.B. Ruhl, 'Regulation by Adaptive Management – Is it Possible?' (2005) 7 *Minnesota Journal of Law, Science and Technology*, 21; Doremus, 'Adaptive Management', 50; Karkkainen, 'Collaborative Ecosystem Governance', 189; A. Iles, 'Adaptive Management: Making Environmental Law and Policy more Dynamic, Experimentalist and Learning' (1996) 13 *Environmental and Planning Law Journal*, 288; W.T. Coleman, 'Legal Barriers to the Restoration of Aquatic Systems and the Utilization of Adaptive Management' (1998) 23 *Vermont Law Review*, 177.

may be possible to develop a deeper understanding of ecosystem dynamics through learning from experience, and to use knowledge secured to modify policies and decisions where it is apparent from new data that this is necessary. As understanding of ecosystem dynamics improves, confidence may also increase in pre-decision prediction of impacts whilst recognising that whatever advances in knowledge are made, the nature of ecosystems requires that on-going monitoring and assessment should be permanent features of a legal system for their protection. Karkkainen captures the aspirations of adaptive management for restoring confidence in prediction in advising that whilst attempts to protect ecosystems will always operate with incomplete knowledge, we can 'put ourselves on a trajectory to see continuous improvements in our understanding of the complex dynamics of the ecosystem' by making necessary investments in science and monitoring capacity.[5]

An ability to adapt would certainly be a necessary feature of ecological governance, but it is by no means sufficient for the protection of ecosystems. Proposals for adaptive management replicate the error of current environmental regulation to an extent in placing confidence in the utility of scientific research for identifying why particular effects have occurred. Whilst the long-term study of ecosystems may improve our ability to explain their behaviour, there is no reason for assuming that we will be any the wiser about the causes of their decline and failure after the event than beforehand. The adaptive approach also assumes that socioeconomic systems will be able to adjust quickly to new information about environmental harm, but that is unlikely to be possible for societies whose whole way of living has become locked in to the practices that are causing harm (as is the case with fossil fuel dependence).[6] In addition, the analysis of projects involving significant capital expenditure and construction must, for obvious reasons, precede rather than follow their authorisation. In view of this, the principal focus of the approaches I suggest for acquiring information is on providing support for the qualitative mechanisms for precautionary decision-making that were proposed in Chapters 3 and 5, and on improving our general knowledge and understanding of ecosystems in the hope that the efficacy of ecological regulation will be enhanced. Whilst a capacity to adjust is desirable, it is by getting it right in the first place that progressive reductions in ecological stresses are most likely to be achieved.

[5] Karkkainen, 'Collaborative Ecosystem Governance', 199.

[6] Chapter 2, Section 2.3.2.2.

7.1.2 Legal requirements for ecological information

Law, as I consider in this chapter, can be used in a variety of ways to require the provision of ecological information. There are, as explained in the following paragraphs and considered in detail in Sections 7.2–7.4, three important considerations in the design of legal and institutional structures if these are to provide support for decision-making processes under ecological governance. The first is that improving knowledge and understanding of ecosystem dynamics and of maintaining programmes of research which make that possible should be prioritised. This is a departure from prior approaches in which legal instruments have been used to generate environmental information only at the point where the adoption of plans or decision-making on particular projects is due to occur, and with that information being used to temper the pursuit of economic and social objectives. However, the focus under ecological governance is not on gathering information to determine the tolerability of particular disturbances. Instead, it is on learning more about ecosystems and about what makes them resilient so that we are better able to identify and reduce reliance on activities that could erode this property. Improved knowledge of how ecosystems function at landscape scales would also, as I contend in Chapter 5, be used to channel development towards areas in which it is judged to present low levels of risk for ecosystem integrity when the cumulative impacts of all other activities are taken into account.[7]

The second is that institutions for conducting research and for ensuring that flows of information are maintained should be legally embedded within, and given a central role in, the system's operation. This is to reflect the fact that the structures being put in place are to create a permanent capacity for increasing human understanding of ecosystem behaviour. The creation of an institutional capacity for learning and building on what has been learnt are also required if the core systemic objective of constant growth in levels of understanding and knowledge of ecosystems based on which our ability to forestall their further degradation might be enhanced is to be advanced. As argued in Section 7.2, the aim of creating a platform for better ecological regulation would not be furthered significantly by the ad hoc commissioning of research by decision-makers as environmental problems arise.

Third, legal mechanisms are required to maintain a flow of information about the health of ecosystems. Policies, plans and decisions on

[7] Chapter 5, Sections 5.3.2 and 5.3.4.

development consent are all based to a degree on assessment of the likely compatibility of activities and uses with ecosystem functionality. A capacity to revisit these assessments and revise decisions based on them is necessary in view of the impossibility of predicting reliably how ecosystems will react to human disturbance. Such a capacity is also needed to respond to changing ecological conditions that occur due both to their natural dynamism and the cumulative influences on them of externalities. Requirements for ongoing monitoring of ecosystems and the assessment and monitoring of the effect of the implementation of policies and of particular decisions are clearly important for this. However, these would not have a positive effect on ecological protection unless they are connected with corresponding legal provision for the review of policies, plans and decisions or with decision-making processes that, in emphasising the nature of the information required for decisions to be made, provide a stimulus for its generation. Sections 7.3 and 7.4 consider how law might be used to produce a steady stream of data to support the making and subsequent review of decisions, and to ensure that this is deployed if it reveals that new approaches are needed to achieve the system of governance's objectives.

7.2 Developing a capacity for institutional learning

The bodies that will take responsibility for the production and processing of information should be established during the introduction of a system of ecological governance. Doremus recognises this need in arguing that to be able to conserve nature over meaningful lengths of time, 'we must develop management institutions suited to the efficient and effective production, identification and integration of new scientific knowledge into our natural resource management decisions'.[8] The institutions for generating information in a system concerned with protecting ecosystems are of two types. A capacity for scientific advice is needed for the initial system to be established and subsequently revised as knowledge of ecosystems grows, for the direction and analysis of ongoing research into and monitoring of systemic conditions, and for advising on the conclusions to be drawn from information gathered for decision-making on how activities that may have negative effects should be conducted. A practical capacity for implementing and maintaining monitoring programmes, and for ensuring that the knowledge of those

[8] Doremus, 'Adaptive Management', 51.

who are local to or use ecosystems can feed into the bank of information that the system is designed to produce also needs to be developed. Both capacities must work together and be integrated with each other if institutions for producing and analysing information are to be capable of bearing the responsibilities to which Doremus refers.

The creation of institutional capacities that have allowed ecologists to collaborate with policymakers in determining legal responses to environmental problems has, as I discuss below, some precedents in international law and its implementation at national levels. However, the role of institutions in a legal system for the holistic protection of ecosystems is of a different order as they form part of a permanent regime for managing activities in order to prevent problems from arising, rather than one which comes into existence to address difficulties that are already extant. Accordingly, it is important that these institutions should be given a clear and central role in the legal framework for establishing the system so that they have a mandate for undertaking tasks that would support its operation. Legally embedded institutions would also be better placed to withstand the political pressure that they would be likely to encounter as ecological and economic objectives come into conflict.

7.2.1 Combining ecology and law: from problem-solving to permanence

The discoveries of ecological science have had a growing influence on the contents of policy and law since the environmental crises of the 1970s. In their study of the relationship between ecology and law, Brooks, Jones and Virginia argue that there has been a gradual convergence between the disciplines and particularly in the formation of policy and legal responses in the United States and internationally to the environmental problems of acid rain and the depletion of atmospheric ozone.[9] They describe the role of ecology in developing legal frameworks to tackle these problems as an 'experimental jurisprudence' in which systematic research preceded legislation and, in the case of international action on substances that affect the ozone layer under the Montreal Protocol, has an ongoing periodic involvement with the review of the controls that the Protocol puts in place.[10]

[9] Brooks, Jones and Virginia, 'Law and Ecology', p. 231.

[10] Ibid., pp. 242–3. United Nations: Protocol on Substances that Deplete the Ozone Layer, Montreal, 16 September 1987, in force 1 January 1989, 1522 UNTS 3, 26 ILM 1541 (1987).

They also refer to the influence of 'epistemic communities' of scientists that have formed where a group sharing a common perspective on the causes and possible solutions to an environmental problem has come together, and particularly in circumstances where policymakers confronted with that problem are uncertain about its implications and the costs and benefits of international cooperation for its resolution.[11] Haas' study of the role of scientists in the creation of the Mediterranean Action Plan provides an example of the empowerment, through shared concerns over the degradation of the Mediterranean, of a group of experts in a way which allowed them to contribute to the development of state policies on tackling marine pollution.[12] The work of the Intergovernmental Panel on Climate Change (IPCC) as a body that has formed a consensus on global climate change science which creates a platform for action to address its causes provides a more recent example of the influence that such a community can have where a political will to address an environmental problem is present.[13]

These examples of ecology having an influence on the formation of policy and law have some basic parallels with the role that a scientific advisory body would need to play in generating information and providing advice to support the ongoing management of anthropogenic impacts on ecosystems. Programmes of research were initiated by law and with the purpose of developing a sufficient understanding of the proposed subject matter of legislation for appropriate restrictions on harmful activities to be developed. The provision for the review of controls under the Montreal Protocol also bears some resemblance to an adaptive approach to regulation that allows the revision of laws as new information becomes available (although decision-making on what controls should be applied remains very much the preserve of the parties to the Protocol).[14] However, the need in each case for the stimulus of an environmental crisis before politicians were willing to involve ecologists in policy-making evidences an attitude of reluctance to relinquish authority to external advisers which would certainly not sustain support for a system that is intended to have a permanent role in advising on the control of human activities to prevent ecological problems from arising. Instead, if the relationship between ecology and law is to move on from occasional congruence once environmental damage or the possibility of an

[11] Brooks, Jones and Virginia, 'Law and Ecology', pp. 243–5.

[12] P. M. Haas, 'Do Regimes Matter? Epistemic Communities and Mediterranean Pollution Control' (1989) 43 *International Organization*, 377.

[13] Brooks, Jones and Virginia, 'Law and Ecology', pp. 252–3.

[14] United Nations: Protocol on Substances that Deplete the Ozone Layer, Article 6.

existential threat becomes apparent to a coexistence that seeks to avoid harm, the production of relevant scientific information needs to be driven by embedded legal processes and an entrenched institutional capacity for directing and analysing the results of monitoring and research.

Four arguments emerge from the literature on adaptive management of human impacts on ecosystems in support of building a legal system that will facilitate this approach around institutions for gathering and analysing information rather than relying on the commissioning of research by governments as and when it appears to them that support for intended action or reaction to problems is necessary.

First, the progressive improvement of ecological knowledge is necessary because of our poor understanding of ecosystems, and of the likely consequence of this that premises for action that may have seemed well-founded may subsequently prove to be erroneous as our knowledge of natural systems and the way that they react to stresses increases. Tarlock argues that the new understanding of ecosystems as dynamic entities requires, if we are to conserve them, a dynamic regulatory approach that 'incorporates a continuous process of acquiring and evaluating scientific information' with a view to producing what he calls 'a regulatory science'.[15] Karkkainen places emphasis on collaboration between governments and researchers that is aimed at generating the 'continuous stream of high-quality, policy-relevant, locally-situated ecosystem science' that will allow an adaptive approach to ecosystem management to be adopted.[16] It is clear from this emphasis on continuity that bodies need to be established with responsibility for ensuring that the flow of relevant information is maintained. The sporadic gathering of information will not, of itself, provide an adequate knowledge base for an enhanced understanding of how human activities affect ecosystem functionality.

The second is that an institutional capacity for learning from new information is essential if adaptive management is to amount to more than a means of responding to the unanticipated.[17] It is hoped that learning from new information will improve baseline knowledge about ecosystem behaviour, and that this, in turn, will better enable us to appreciate how controls might be applied to conserve natural systems. Brunnée and Toope describe a legal framework that would allow this progress towards effective regulation as one which would be 'facilitative

[15] Tarlock, 'Ecosystems', p. 581.

[16] Karkkainen, 'Collaborative Ecosystem Governance', 202.

[17] Iles, 'Adaptive Management', 292.

initially' but 'help to promote real normativity in the longer term'.[18] The learning process also requires an ability to assess whether the basis on which past policies were formed or decisions founded remains valid and to draw conclusions from the knowledge base and from new information as to how existing measures might be revised and better decisions made subsequently. Karkkainen argues that a critical part of the task for instituting adaptive management lies in putting into place 'the resources and institutional mechanisms to ensure that we are generating the new learning that must occur, and to see that subsequent rounds of policy adjustment are informed by that new learning'.[19]

The locus for this institutional learning must lie primarily with the bodies that are responsible for producing and assimilating information and advising on its implications. It is essential therefore that institutions with a mandate to learn from information as it is generated and to react to new learning should be established. The concern is that, if they are not, adaptive management will remain essentially reactive and decision-making reliant on assessments which are of limited value because they lack the contextual backdrop for firm conclusions about a system's condition and the effects of activities on it to be reached.

The third is that adaptive management requires an on-going investment in the research, monitoring and information management systems that allow decisions to be made and understanding advanced through new learning.[20] However, the open-ended nature of this commitment may leave it vulnerable to political and economic pressure, and particularly, as Iles suggests, at times when strategies appear to have failed.[21] It is also the case that willingness to support programmes of research and to allow conclusions drawn from them to influence policy may vary according to governmental perception of environmental problems and whether they pose a sufficient threat to be prioritised over other objectives. Haas notes this in contrasting the influence of ecologists in Germany when the Black Forest was seen to be under threat from acid rain with their lack of influence with the US Government for tackling the same problem when it was understood to present more of a problem for its neighbours than itself.[22] A means of maintaining this investment, although it is by no means a guarantee that it

[18] J. Brunnée and S.J. Toope, 'Environmental Security and Freshwater Resources: Ecosystem Regime Building' (1997) 91 *American Journal of International Law*, 41.

[19] Karkkainen, 'Collaborative Ecosystem Governance', 199.

[20] Iles, 'Adaptive Management', 291; Karkkainen, 'Collaborative Ecosystem Governance', 199.

[21] Iles, 'Adaptive Management', 292.

[22] Haas, 'Do Regimes Matter?', 402–3.

will be sustained, lies in legally embedding the institutional capacity within an overarching framework whose operation, in part, is predicated upon the work of bodies tasked with the generation and analysis of information. Conversely, it is clear from the examples provided by Brooks, Jones and Virginia, and that are cited in Haas' work, that scientific resources for producing information that are not entrenched are inherently vulnerable to governmental perception of the seriousness of environmental crises.

Finally, it is desirable, in view of this potential for political and economic pressure to compromise the pursuit of ecological objectives, that responsibility for collecting and interpreting information and for giving advice should be devolved to an independent body with statutorily founded authority for performing these tasks rather than being left with governmental agencies that are more likely to be diverted by extraneous considerations in undertaking them.[23] In this regard Brunnée and Toope suggest, in the context of international collaboration over environmental problems, that giving power to independent bodies to take on the collection and evaluation of data would help to depoliticise the identification of problems and the setting of priorities for responding to them.[24] Again, there is no guarantee that establishing an independent body will ensure its political insulation. However, this devolution of power is at least more likely to result in the continuous production of information than leaving responsibility for this with an agency whose will to improve understanding of ecosystems may be eroded over time by the need to consider other governmental objectives in performing its duties.

A legal system in which a scientific advisory body is embedded may have a capacity for directing the production of and interpreting ecological information, but thought should also be given to how and by whom that information will be generated. In practice, arrangements will vary according to the need for research to advance understanding of ecosystem behaviour and for monitoring systemic responses to particular disturbances. However, at a basic level, interaction is most likely to be between a central scientific advisory body and governmental authorities at local, regional and national levels. Collaboration between them would build 'a common set of understandings upon which to base future management efforts and further efforts to generate additional information'.[25] Bodies that are directly concerned with governance can, through coordinating monitoring and public

[23] Doremus, 'Adaptive Management', 81.
[24] Brunnée and Toope, 'Environmental Security', 43.
[25] Karkkainen, 'Collaborative Ecosystem Governance', 220.

involvement with their management, provide a stream of information on the condition of ecosystems and the array of economic and social drivers of anthropogenic stresses on them at regional and local levels.

I envisage that a centralised institution for data collection and analysis would process that information and use it to advise on whether policies and measures for their implementation should be modified in light of changes in systemic conditions. Such a body would have the advantage over regional and local units of being able to apply its expertise and wider experience with a variety of different systems 'to spot harms that individuals cannot see, recognize trends that might not be visible at a decentralized level, and make judgements about which interventions are most effective'.[26] A broader perspective than that which can be provided at local or regional levels is also important for assessing interaction between, and effects of, activities conducted in one ecosystem on others, and to keep under review natural processes that operate on a broader scale than individual management units.[27]

Karkkainen argues that, through working together, these different entities would be better placed to tackle the complexities of ecosystem management and 'to avoid the pitfalls of relying on an excessively narrow information base'.[28] The concept of democratic experimentalism that he and others advance as a means of improving environmental regulation through decentralising core responsibilities to local institutions is based on an ideal of localities working with a centralised agency for monitoring and assessing information. This would be done with a view to generating a rich and continuous flow of information passing 'from localities to the center and back again'.[29]

7.3 Using law to maintain the flow of information

There are two ways in which law might be used to stimulate the production of ecological information in addition to ensuring that the institutional structures for its generation are in place, and through the

[26] Esty, 'Environmental Protection in the Information Age', 144

[27] J. B. Ruhl, S. E. Kraft, and C. L. Lant, *The Law and Policy of Ecosystem Services* (Washington, DC: Island Press, 2007), p. 51.

[28] Karkkainen, 'Collaborative Ecosystem Governance', 224.

[29] B. C. Karkkainen, A. Fung and C. F. Sabel, 'After Backyard Environmentalism: Toward a Performance-Based Regime of Environmental Regulation' (2000) 44 *American Behavioral Scientist*, 693.

mandatory environmental assessment of proposed actions.[30] The first is by making the monitoring of activities and systemic conditions in general obligatory with a view to increasing knowledge and understanding of ecosystems, to enable adaptation to change in ecological conditions, and to allow responsiveness to unexpected systemic reactions. The second is to require both that research, monitoring and assessment be conducted for examination of whether measures for controlling activities are adequate and, if monitoring data indicates that they have failed to improve ecosystem health or, indeed, to halt ecological degradation, that consideration be given to adopting new and more exacting constraints.

The three grounds for requiring in law that monitoring be conducted and that action be taken in response to new data under a system of ecological governance are considered below. In doing so, I draw from provision made in existing legal systems for generating information with a view to conserving or improving the condition of ecosystems.

7.3.1 Increasing knowledge and understanding of ecosystems

Legal provision can be made to promote an ongoing improvement in our understanding of ecosystems by obliging the institutions responsible for directing the production of ecological information to draw up programmes of research and monitoring. Requirements that these programmes be maintained and revised as necessary can also be used to ensure that the responsible institutions keep under review whether measures taken for ecological protection can be improved upon in light of increased knowledge of how ecosystems function.

The importance of building a solid foundation of information for ecological governance is recognised in the EU's Marine Strategy Framework Directive. This requires that 'an analysis of the essential features and characteristics, and current environmental status' of European waters be conducted as a first step in devising a strategy for their protection.[31] However, the 2012 completion date for this, with updating to follow only at intervals of 6 years following its completion,

[30] Chapter 5, Sections 5.3.5 and 5.4.

[31] Council Directive 2008/56/EC of 17 June 2008 establishing a framework for community action in the field of marine environmental policy ('Marine Strategy Framework Directive'), [2008] OJ L 164/19, Article 8(1)(a).

represents an unrealistic level of expectation that a reliable basis for regulation can be created through research within a prescribed timeframe. It also disregards both our current level of understanding of marine ecosystems and their highly dynamic nature. Instead, a legal mandate for research is needed which recognises that efforts at improving ecological knowledge should be a permanent feature of a system of governance that seeks to preserve ecosystem functionality. These should be maintained, even if significant improvements in our knowledge of how human activities affect this are made, to reflect the fact that the objects of protection and what is important to their functionality and resilience are prone to change.

The Committee for Environmental Protection established for the Operation of the Protocol on Environmental Protection to the Antarctic Treaty has a permanent role in advising parties on the collection, archiving, exchange and evaluation of information related to environmental protection, the state of the Antarctic environment and the need for scientific research, including environmental monitoring, where this is required for effective implementation of the Protocol.[32] I envisage a similar role for a scientific advisory institution in a regime for ecological governance, although this would also have responsibility for determining what research should be undertaken and information gathered to service the system's objectives and to implement programmes for investigation and monitoring. This greater authority is necessary for the reasons explored in Section 7.2 of insulation from political pressures and a resulting freedom to focus on establishing a knowledge base for ecological protection.

7.3.2 *Enabling reaction to change*

Provision for monitoring that is capable of generating data concerning changing systemic conditions should be made to enable the modification of controls on activities as new information becomes available. Recognition of the need for a ready supply of such information is already apparent in legal regimes that are concerned with ecological protection. The Protocol on Environmental Protection to the Antarctic Treaty requires that regular and effective monitoring of the Antarctic environment and associated ecosystems should be conducted 'to allow

[32] Protocol on Environmental Protection to the Antarctic Treaty, Madrid, 3 October 1991, in force 14 January 1998, 30 ILM 1461 (1991), Article 12(1).

assessment of the impacts of ongoing activities' and 'to facilitate early detection of the possible unforeseen effects of activities carried on both within and outside the Antarctic Treaty area'.[33]

Article 11(1) of the Marine Strategy Framework Directive also requires Member States to 'establish and implement coordinated monitoring programmes for the ongoing assessment of the environmental status of their marine waters'. The programmes must be capable of achieving a variety of ends set out in Annex V to the Directive, including the provision of information from which the status of waters under review and its distance from or progress towards the Directive's objective of a 'good environmental status' for the marine environment can be identified. The establishment of capacities for monitoring would facilitate the adaptive management of activities affecting Europe's seas. However, the Directive does not build on this platform by requiring that management measures and other aspects of marine strategies (including the programmes for monitoring themselves) be reviewed in light of new information. This is surprising as the Water Framework Directive with which it shares many features does provide for targeted investigation, the review of prior decisions and monitoring programmes, and consideration of whether additional controls are needed where monitoring data indicates that its objectives for improving the environmental quality of terrestrial and coastal waters are unlikely to be achieved.[34]

Provisions that trigger focused research into how controls might be modified in light of systemic change are a necessary corollary to obligations to monitor. They provide a stimulus for the production and analysis of information with a view to tailoring regulation to changing conditions. Accordingly, I suggest that power should be conferred on a scientific advisory body under ecological governance to undertake the review of existing controls where monitoring data indicates that they are not achieving desired ends or that natural changes in systemic conditions require a new approach. The inclusion of provisions for the immediate review of the ecological effects of activities is, as discussed below, required in existing ecological regimes if these diverge from what was predicted. It is, in any event, clearly appropriate for a system whose main purpose is to prevent the

[33] Protocol on Environmental Protection to the Antarctic Treaty, Articles 3(2)(d) and 3(2)(e) respectively.

[34] Council Directive 2000/60/EC of 23 October 2000 establishing a framework for Community action in the field of water policy [2000] OJ L 327/1, Article 11(5).

cumulative effects of activities from undermining ecosystem health that equivalent provision should be made for reaction where the behaviour of the system at large diverges from what was expected.

7.3.3 Enabling responsiveness to systemic reactions

There are a number of difficulties with accurate prediction of the impacts that human interventions in ecosystems may give rise to. Even if our understanding of ecosystems and how activities affect them improves significantly, a residual core of uncertainty will remain as an inevitable consequence of their complexity and tendency to non-linear responses to disturbance. In light of this, there is a need for flexibility in legal structures for ecological protection that allows policies, proposals for their implementation and decisions on projects to be revisited in the event that they affect ecosystems in ways that were not anticipated.

This flexibility can be provided by imposing requirements for monitoring activities that have been permitted and for reconsidering how they should be controlled when it becomes apparent from monitoring data that this is necessary. Collectively, their application would create a platform for what Fabra and Gascon call the 'feedback management' of natural resources in which information concerning the effects of development and exploitation allows the adjustment of management measures before irreversible change occurs.[35] They refer to the use of such an approach under the 1980 Convention on the Conservation of Antarctic Marine Living Resources (CCAMLR) to modify controls on fishing for krill, an important component of Antarctic ecosystems.[36]

The primary means by which law might be used to ensure adaptation of controls over activities in a regime for protecting ecosystems is through strengthening provision for post-assessment monitoring. As is considered in the following section, procedures for decision-making might also be used to add force to this strengthened provision by requiring that an appropriate programme for monitoring should be in place, and that decision-makers should be satisfied as to the feasibility of its implementation before a proposed activity can proceed.

[35] A. Fabra and V. Gascon, 'The Convention on the Conservation of Antarctic Marine Living Resources (CCAMLR) and the Ecosystem Approach' (2008) 23 *The International Journal of Marine and Coastal Law*, 567–98.

[36] Convention on the Conservation of Antarctic Marine Living Resources, Canberra, 20 May 1980, in force 7 April 1982, 1329 UNTS 47, 19 ILM 841 (1980).

7.4 Using structures for decision-making to stimulate information flows

In addition to positive requirements for the generation of information, legal constraints that make decision-making contingent on the quality of available information could also be used to stimulate its production and to ensure that provisions for research and monitoring are adhered to. These, as discussed below, would incentivise or drive efforts to advance knowledge and understanding of ecosystems by: preventing decisions from being taken unless adequate supporting information can be provided; allowing activities to proceed on an exploratory basis until information is available to form a view on the full extent of what is proposed; and preventing activities from proceeding unless a capacity for monitoring their impacts can be shown to exist.

7.4.1 The adequacy of information for decision-making

Mechanisms for generating information would be strengthened by restricting the ability of decision-makers to authorise a proposed activity until efforts to obtain prescribed information have been made. As Doremus notes, prohibitions on uninformed actions can serve as powerful incentives for information disclosure.[37] They can also encourage the production of full information and the allocation of appropriate timescales for this by those responsible for gathering data in environmental assessment.

Provisions have been used in the legal regime for protecting Antarctic ecosystems to restrict the circumstances in which decisions on proposed activities might be taken and thereby to emphasise the centrality of information about the protected environment and the effects that anthropogenic stresses might have on it for the regime's operation. Article 3(2)(c) of the Protocol on Environmental Protection to the Antarctic Treaty requires that activities should 'be planned and conducted on the basis of information sufficient to allow prior assessments of, and informed judgments about, their possible impacts'.[38] However, there is no express prohibition of activities for which information is judged to be insufficient. Conversely, Article 4(1) of the 1988 Convention on the Regulation of Antarctic Mineral Resource Activities

[37] Doremus, 'Adaptive Management', 81–2.
[38] Protocol on Environmental Protection to the Antarctic Treaty, Article 3(2).

(CRAMRA) establishes a threshold of knowledge concerning a proposed activity and its anticipated effects 'which must be crossed before mineral activities may proceed'.[39] It requires that decisions should be based on 'information adequate to enable informed judgments to be made about their possible impacts', and makes clear that 'no such activities shall take place unless this information is available for decisions relevant to those activities'.[40] CRAMRA has not come into force (and is unlikely to do so) because of opposition from Australia and France to the high level of protection it affords to the Antarctic area.[41]

Whichever of these approaches to decision-making is to be preferred, they both give rise to common issues concerning the production of information in a system for ecological protection. The first is how the information necessary for adjudication on the adequacy of information is itself to be produced. One means of securing this would be to require that the environmental statements or reports produced in connection with environmental assessment should state clearly both the respects in which information is felt to be inadequate, and the extent to which that absence prevents reliable assessment of an activity's potential impacts as well as containing proposed programmes of research and monitoring either to reach a sufficiently informed basis for decision-making or to assess the impacts of an activity if it is authorised. The intention behind these requirements is to provide a platform for judgments to be made on whether sufficient knowledge is available on which to base a decision, and, if not, how this might be obtained.

The second is that, whilst it might be possible to generate information about ecosystems that an activity may affect, the question arises as to whether either 'sufficient' or 'adequate' information is likely to be available about an activity's potential impacts without some practical experience and monitoring of the effects of trial projects. In this regard, I consider in the following section the practice under the Antarctic regime of allowing activities to proceed on a staged basis whilst information is gathered on them.

[39] C. R. Redgwell, 'Environmental Protection in Antarctica: The 1991 Protocol' (1994) 43 *International and Comparative Law Quarterly*, 608. Convention on the Regulation of Antarctic Mineral Resource Activities, Wellington, 2 June 1988, not in force, 27 ILM 868 (1988).

[40] Convention on the Regulation of Antarctic Mineral Resource Activities, Articles 4(1) and 4(2).

[41] C. C. Joyner, 'Fragile Ecosystems: Preclusive Restoration in the Antarctic' (1994) 34 *Natural Resources Journal*, 889.

A capacity for monitoring the impacts of activities after they have been authorised is essential for adaptive management of the effects of activities on ecosystems. The importance of monitoring is recognised in decision-making structures used in instruments for the protection of Antarctic ecosystems. The Protocol on Environmental Protection requires that judgments on proposed activities should take account of 'whether there exists the capacity to monitor key environmental parameters and ecosystem components so as to identify and provide early warning of any adverse effects of the activity'.[42] CRAMRA is again more restrictive in stating that no mineral resource activity may take place 'until it is judged that . . . there exists the capacity' for monitoring its impacts.[43] A requirement that the ability to monitor the effects of an activity after a decision has been made and implemented should be proven would ensure, to the extent it is possible, that appropriate programmes for monitoring are developed and applied to support efforts for improving controls if it becomes apparent after authorisation that this is necessary.

7.4.2 Generating information through exploratory development

Decision-making structures that prevent actions from being authorised where information is not judged to be adequate may provide a high level of ecological protection, but will also present decision-makers with a dilemma. Situations may arise where reliable data is lacking and levels of uncertainty are high because of poor levels of knowledge and understanding of ecosystems. This is particularly likely to be the case where a completely new activity is proposed or an existing activity is to be extended to areas in which it has not been pursued previously. A strongly precautionary approach that places a high threshold on the ability to predict systemic reaction before a decision can be made may result in paralysis. However, the assessment of proposals for major developmental programmes that, once authorised and implemented, cannot easily be undone, is also essential if the effects of human activities on ecosystems are to be controlled effectively.

A possible solution to this dilemma is an approach to decision-making in which the approval either of proposals for policy implementation in full or a project in its entirety is deferred until sufficient evidence is

[42] Protocol on Environmental Protection to the Antarctic Treaty, Article 3(2)(c)(v).
[43] Convention on the Regulation of Antarctic Mineral Resource Activities 1988, Article 4(4).

gathered through trial phases that are specifically designed to allow research and the generation of new information for a decision to be made. Such an approach has been used in the control of fisheries under CCAMLR.[44] Where a fishery is proposed for which there is insufficient information for controls to be devised at the outset, it is registered as a 'new fishery' and a Data Collection Plan is prepared that identifies data needed and operational research actions necessary to obtain it based on which proposals for commercial fishing of the stock concerned might be assessed.[45] During this period, 'fishing effort' is directed towards and limited to the acquisition of data that would enable authorities under the Convention to evaluate the scope of the fishery and its potential ecological impacts. Once sufficient information is available for a fishery to expand, it remains an 'exploratory fishery' with operations again directed to meeting the requirements of a Data Collection Plan. The scale of the fishery is limited to 'a level not substantially above that necessary to obtain the information specified' in the plan until enough information is available for effective controls on a full commercial fishery to be devised.[46]

The techniques applied under CCAMLR could be adapted to allow adaptive management of development where monitoring of and research into the likely effects of a development type is required. Such an approach would support efforts at improving knowledge and understanding of ecosystems and the effects that disturbances have on them so that effective controls over activities can be established.

[44] n. 36 above.

[45] Conservation Measure 21–01 (2010) of the Commission for the Conservation of Antarctic Living Marine Resources, available at: http://www.ccamlr.org/en/measure-21-01-2010.

[46] Conservation Measure 21–02 (2013) of the Commission for the Conservation of Antarctic Living Marine Resources, para 4, available at: http://www.ccamlr.org/en/measure-21-02-2013.

BIBLIOGRAPHY

Adelle, C. and Weiland, S., 'Policy Assessment: The State of the Art' (2012) 30 *Impact Assessment and Project Appraisal*, 25–33

AEA Technology, 'Support to the identification of potential risks for the environment and human health arising from hydrocarbons operations involving hydraulic fracturing in Europe' (report produced for the European Commission, 2012), http://ec.europa.eu/environment/integration/energy/pdf/fracking%20study.pdf

Ahmed, K. and Sanchez-Triana, E., 'Strategic Environmental Assessment and Policy Formation' in Ahmed, K. and Sanchez-Triana, E. (eds) *Strategic Environmental Assessment for Policies: An Instrument for Good Governance* (Washington, DC: The World Bank, 2008), pp. 1–10

Alden, J., 'Scenarios for the Future of the British Planning System: The Need for a National Spatial Planning Framework' (1999) 70 *Town Planning Review*, 385–407

Alder, J. and Wilkinson, D., *Environmental Law and Ethics* (Basingstoke: Macmillan Press, 1999)

Allen, C. R., Gunderson, L. H. and Holling, C. S., 'Commentary on Part One Articles' in Gunderson, L. H., Allen, C. R. and Holling, C. S. (eds) *Foundations of Ecological Resilience* (Washington, DC: Island Press, 2010), pp. 3–18

Amezaga, J. M., Boyes, S. L. and Harrison, J. A., 'Biofuels Policy in the European Union', conference paper presented at the 7th International Biofuels Conference, February 2010, New Delhi, http://research.ncl.ac.uk/reimpact/Related%20Documents/Reports/Biofuels%20Policy%20in%20the%20European%20Union.pdf

Anderson, K. L., 'Reconciling the Electricity Industry with Sustainable Development: Backcasting – a Strategic Alternative' (2001) 33 *Futures*, 607–623

van Asselt, M. B. A. and Vos, E., 'The Precautionary Principle and the Uncertainty Paradox' (2006) 9 *Journal of Risk Research*, 313–336

Aven, T., *Misconceptions of Risk* (Chichester: John Wiley & Sons, 2010)

Averill, M., 'Introduction: Resilience, Law, and Natural Resource Management' (2008) 87 *Nebraska Law Review*, 821–832

Baakman, K., *Testing Times: The Effectiveness of Five International Biodiversity-related Conventions* (Nijmegen: Wolf Legal Publishers, 2011)

Baber, W. F. and Bartlett, R. V., *Deliberative Environmental Politics: Democracy and Ecological Rationality* (Cambridge, MA: MIT Press, 2005)

Bäckstrand, K. et al., 'The Promise of New Modes of Environmental Governance' in Bäckstrand, K., Khan, J., Kronsell, A. and Lövbrand, E. (eds) *Environmental Politics and Deliberative Democracy: Examining the Promise of New Modes of Governance* (Cheltenham: Edward Elgar, 2010), pp. 3–27

Bagheri, A. and Hjorth, P., 'Planning for Sustainable Development: A Paradigm Shift Towards a Process-based Approach' (2007) 15 *Sustainable Development*, 83–96

Bailey, J. and Renton, S., 'Environmental Assessment of Policies' in Porter, A. L. and Fittipaldi, J. J. (eds) *Environmental Methods Review: Retooling Impact Assessment for the New Century* (Fargo: The Press Club, 1998), pp. 107–112

Bailey, R. G., *Ecoregion-based Design for Sustainability* (Seacus, NJ: Springer, 2002)

Baker, M. and Wong, C., 'The Delusion of Strategic Spatial Planning: What's Left after the Labour Government's English Regional Experiment?' (2013) 28 *Planning Practice and Research*, 83–103

Barry, J., *Rethinking Green Politics* (London: Sage Publications, 1999)

Barry, J., 'Sustainability, Political Judgement and Citizenship: Connecting Green Politics and Democracy' in Doherty, B. and de Geus, M. (eds) *Democracy and Green Political Thought: Sustainability, Rights and Citizenship* (London: Routledge, 1996), pp. 113–130

Barton, B., 'Underlying Concepts and Theoretical Issues in Public Participation on Resources Development' in Zillman, D. N., Lucas, A. R. and Pring, G. (eds) *Human Rights in Natural Resource Development: Public Participation in Sustainable Development of Mining and Energy Resources* (Oxford: Oxford University Press, 2002), pp. 77–120

Bell, S. and McGillivray, D., *Environmental Law*, 7th edn (Oxford: Oxford University Press, 2008)

Bengtsson, J. et al., 'Reserves, Resilience and Dynamic Landscapes' (2003) 32 *Ambio*, 389–396

Benhabib, S., 'Toward a Deliberative Model of Democratic Legitimacy' in Benhabib, S. (ed.) *Democracy and Difference: Contesting the Boundaries of the Political* (Princeton, NJ: Princeton University Press, 1996), pp. 67–94

Benson, J. F., 'What Is the Alternative? Impact Assessment Tools and Sustainable Planning' (2003) 21 *Impact Assessment and Project Appraisal*, 261–280

Biggs, R., Carpenter, S. R. and Brock, W. A., 'Turning Back from the Brink: Detecting an Impending Regime Shift in Time to Avert It' (2009) 106 *Proceedings of the National Academy of Sciences of the United States of America*, 826–831

Biggs, R. et al., 'Toward Principles for Enhancing the Resilience of Ecosystem Services' (2012) 37 *Annual Review of Environment and Resources*, 421–448

Bina, O., 'A Critical Review of the Dominant Lines of Argumentation on the Need for Strategic Environmental Assessment' (2007) 27 *Environmental Impact Assessment Review*, 585–606

Birnie, P., Boyle, A. and Redgwell, C., *International Law and the Environment*, 3rd edn (Oxford: Oxford University Press, 2009)

Bishop, K., 'Planning to Save the Planet? Planning's Green Paradigm' in Tewdwr-Jones, M. (ed.) *British Planning Policy in Transition: Planning in the 1990s* (London: UCL Press, 1996), pp. 207–222

Blair, J. M., Collins, S. L. and Knapp, A. K., 'Ecosystems as Functional Units in Nature' (2000) 14 *Natural Resources and Environment*, 150–155.

Blowers, A., 'Society and Sustainability: The Context of Change for Planning' in Blowers, A. and Evans, B. (eds) *Town Planning into the 21st Century* (London: Routledge, 1997), pp. 153–168

Blowers, A., 'The Time for Change' in Blowers, A. (ed.) *Planning for a Sustainable Environment* (London: Earthscan, 1993), pp. 1–18

Boardman, R., *Governance of Earth Systems: Science and its Uses* (Basingstoke: Palgrave Macmillan, 2010)

Bocking, S., 'Visions of Nature and Society: A History of the Ecosystem Concept' (1994) 20(3) *Alternatives*, 12–18

Bond, A. J. and Morrison-Saunders, A., 'Sustainability Appraisal: Jack of All Trades, Master of None?' (2009) 27 *Impact Assessment and Project Appraisal*, 321–329

Boothroyd, P., 'Integrating Economy, Society and Environment through Policy Assessment' in Woollard, R. and Ostry, A. (eds) *Fatal Consumption: Rethinking Sustainable Development* (Vancouver: University of British Columbia Press, 2000), pp. 130–65

Boothroyd, P., 'Policy Assessment' in Vanclay, F. and Bronstein, D. A. (eds) *Environmental and Social Impact Assessment* (Chichester: John Wiley, 1995), pp. 83–126

Bosselmann, K., 'From Reductionist Environmental Law to Sustainability Law' in Burdon, P. (ed.) *Exploring Wild Law: The Philosophy of Earth Jurisprudence* (Kent Town: Wakefield Press, 2011), pp. 204–213

Brandenburg, A. M. and Carroll, M. S., 'Your Place or Mine?: The Effect of Place Creation on Environmental Values and Landscape Meanings' (1995) 8 *Society and Natural Resources*, 381–398

Brierley, A. S. and Kingsford, M. J., 'Impacts of Climate Change on Marine Organisms and Ecosystems' (2009) 19 *Current Biology*, R602-R614

Brooks, R. O., Jones, R. and Virginia, R. A., *Law and Ecology: The Rise of the Ecosystem Regime* (Aldershot: Ashgate, 2002)

Brown, A. and Nitz, T., 'Applying Strategic Environmental Assessment to Policy Making: The Policy Cycle Model and the Queensland Policy Handbook' in Marsden, S. and Dovers, S. (eds) *Strategic Environmental Assessment in Australasia* (Sydney: The Federation Press, 2002), pp. 84–98

Brown, T. C., 'The Concept of Value in Resource Allocation' (1984) 60 *Land Economics*, 231–246

Brunnee, J. and Toope, S. J., 'Environmental Security and Freshwater Resources: Ecosystem Regime Building' (1997) 91 *American Journal of International Law*, 26–59

Buckley, R., 'Strategic Environmental Assessment' in Porter, A. L. and Fittipaldi, J. J. (eds) *Environmental Methods Review: Retooling Impact Assessment for the New Century* (Fargo: The Press Club, 1998), pp. 77–86

Buckley, R., 'Strategic Environmental Assessment of Policies and Plans: Legislation and Implementation' (2000) 18 *Impact Assessment and Project Appraisal*, 209–215

Bulkeley, H., 'Planning and Governance of Climate Change' in Davoudi, S., Crawford, J. and Mehmood, A. (eds) *Planning for Climate Change: Strategies for Mitigation and Adaptation for Spatial Planners* (London: Earthscan, 2009), pp. 284–296

Bundesamt für Naturschutz, 'Landscape Planning: The basis of sustainable landscape development', German Federal Government: Federal Agency for Nature Conservation (2008), http://www.bfn.de/fileadmin/MDB/documents/themen/landschaftsplanung/landscape_planning_basis.pdf

de Burca, G. and Scott, J., 'Introduction: New Governance, Law and Constitutionalism' in de Burca, G. and Scott, J. (eds) *Law and New Governance in the EU and the US* (Oxford: Hart Publishing, 2006), pp. 1–12

Burdon, P., 'Eco-centric Paradigm' in Burdon, P. (ed.) *Exploring Wild Law: The Philosophy of Earth Jurisprudence* (Kent Town: Wakefield Press, 2011), pp. 85–96

Callicott, J. B., 'Aldo Leopold's Concept of Ecosystem Health' in Callicott, J. B. (ed.) *Beyond the Land Ethic: More Essays in Environmental Philosophy* (Albany: State University of New York Press, 1999), pp. 333–346

Callicott, J. B., 'The Value of Ecosystem Health' in Callicott, J. B. (ed.) *Beyond the Land Ethic: More Essays in Environmental Philosophy* (Albany: State University of New York Press, 1999), pp. 347–364

Carfaro, P., 'Thoreau, Leopold and Carson: Toward an Environmental Virtue Ethics' in Goldstein, R. J. (ed.) *Environmental Ethics and Law* (Aldershot: Ashgate, 2004), pp. 23–37

Carpenter, S. R., 'Ecological Futures: Building an Ecology of the Long Now' (2002) 83 *Ecology*, 2069–2083

Carpenter, S. R. et al., 'From Metaphor to Measurement: Resilience of What to What?' (2001) 4 *Ecosystems*, 765–781

Carpenter, S. R. and Folke, C., 'Ecology for Transformation' (2006) 21 *Trends in Ecology and Evolution*, 309–315

Carpenter, S. R. et al., 'General Resilience to Cope with Extreme Events' (2012) 4 *Sustainability*, 3248–3259

Chalmers, D., 'The Reconstitution of European Public Spheres' (2003) 9 *European Law Journal*, 127–189

Chapin III, F. S. et al., 'Consequences of changing biodiversity' (2000) 405 *Nature*, 234–242

Chapin III, F. S., Folke, C. and Kofinas, G. P., 'A framework for understanding change' in Chapin III, F. S., Folke, C., and Kofinas, G. P., *Principles of Ecosystem Stewardship: Resilience-based Natural Resource Management in a Changing World* (New York: Springer, 2009), pp. 3–28

Chapin III, F. S., Matson, P. A. and Vitousek, P. M., *Principles of Terrestrial Ecosystem Ecology*, 2nd edn (New York: Springer, 2011)

Christoff, P., 'Ecological Citizens and Ecologically Guided Democracy' in Doherty, B. and de Geus, M. (eds) *Democracy and Green Political Thought: Sustainability, Rights and Citizenship* (London: Routledge, 1996), pp. 149–166

Christoff, P., 'Green Governance and the Green State: Capacity Building as a Political Project' in Paehlke, R. and Torgerson, D. (eds) *Managing Leviathan: Environmental Politics and the Administrative State*, 2nd ed. (Peterborough, ON: Broadview Press, 2005)

Churchill, R. R. and Lowe, A. V., *The Law of the Sea*, 3rd ed. (Manchester: Manchester University Press, 1999)

Clarke, L., 'The nuclear option' in Lever-Tracy, C. (ed.) *Routledge Handbook of Climate Change and Society* (Abingdon: Routledge, 2010), pp. 308–316

Coenen, F., 'Conclusions' in Coenen, F. (ed.) *Public Participation and Better Environmental Decisions: The Promise and Limits of Participatory Processes for the Quality of Environmentally Related Decision-making* (Dordrecht: Springer, 2009), pp. 183–209

Coenen, F., 'Introduction' in Coenen, F. (ed.) *Public Participation and Better Environmental Decisions: The Promise and Limits of Participatory Processes for the Quality of Environmentally Related Decision-making* (Dordrecht: Springer, 2009), pp. 1–19

Coleman, W. T., 'Legal Barriers to the Restoration of Aquatic Systems and the Utilization of Adaptive Management' (1998) 23 *Vermont Law Review*, 177–199

Connor, R. and Dovers, S., 'Strategic Environmental Assessment: Policy Integration as Practice or Possibility?' in Connor, R. and Dovers, S. (eds) *Institutional Change for Sustainable Development* (Cheltenham: Edward Elgar, 2004), pp. 153–173

Connor, R. and Dovers, S., 'Sustainable Management of Natural and Physical Resources: The New Zealand Resource Management Act 1991' in Connor, R. and Dovers, S. (eds) *Institutional Change for Sustainable Development* (Cheltenham: Edward Elgar, 2004), pp. 87–131

Connor, R. and Dovers, S., 'Principles and Elements of Institutional Change for Sustainable Development' in Connor, R. and Dovers, S. (eds) *Institutional Change for Sustainable Development* (Cheltenham: Edward Elgar, 2004), pp. 203–228

Cooke, M., 'Five Arguments for Deliberative Democracy' (2000) 48 *Political Studies*, 947–969

The Council of Australian Governments, 'National Strategy for Ecologically Sustainable Development' (Australian Government, 1992), http://www.environment.gov.au/about/esd/publications/strategy/index.html

Cowell, R., 'Stretching the Limits: Environmental Compensation, Habitat Creation and Sustainable Development' (1997) 22 *Transactions of the Institute of British Geographers*, 292–306

Cowell, R., 'The Greenest Government Ever? Planning and Sustainability in England after the May 2010 Elections' (2013) 28 *Planning Practice and Research*, 27–44

Cowell, R. and Owens, S., 'Sustainability: The New Challenge' in Blowers, A. and Evans, B. (eds) *Town Planning into the 21st[t] Century* (London: Routledge, 1997), pp. 15–32

Cowell, R. and Owens, S., 'Governing Space: Planning Reform and the Politics of Sustainability' (2006) 24 *Environment and Planning C*, 403–421

Craig, R. K., '"Stationarity is Dead" – Long Live Transformation: Five Principles for Climate Change Adaptation Law' (2010) 34 *Harvard Environmental Law Review*, 9–73

Crowder, L. B. et al., 'Resolving Mismatches in US Ocean Governance' (2006) 313 *Science*, 617–618

Crowder, L. B. and Norse, E. A., 'Essential Ecological Insights for Marine Ecosystem-based Management and Marine Spatial Planning' (2008) 32 *Marine Policy*, 772–778

Cullingworth, B. and Nadin, V., *Town and Country Planning in the United Kingdom*, 14th ed. (London: Routledge, 2006)

Curry, P., *Ecological Ethics: An Introduction* (Cambridge: Polity Press, 2011)

Davenport, M. A. and Anderson, D. H., 'Getting from Sense of Place to Place-based Management: An Interpretative Investigation of Place Meanings and Perceptions of Landscape Change' (2005) 18 *Society and Natural Resources*, 625–641

Davoudi, S., 'Sustainability: A New Vision for the British Planning System' (2000) 15 *Planning Perspectives*, 123–137

Department for Communities and Local Government, 'National Planning Policy Framework' (HM Government, 2012), https://www.gov.uk/government/publications/national-planning-policy-framework--2

Department of Energy and Climate Change, 'Appraisal of Sustainability for the revised draft Overarching National Policy Statement for Energy (EN-1): Main Report' (HM Government, 2010), http://www.decc.gov.uk/assets/decc/11/meeting-energy-demand/consents-planning/nps2011/1930-aos-for-en1-main-report.pdf

Department of Energy and Climate Change, 'Overarching National Policy Statement for Energy (EN-1)' (HM Government, 2011), http://www.decc.gov.uk/assets/decc/11/meeting-energy-demand/consents-planning/nps2011/1938-overarching-nps-for-energy-en1.pdf

Department for Environment, Food and Rural Affairs, 'Safeguarding our Seas: A Strategy for the Conservation and Sustainable Development of our Marine

Environment' (HM Government, 2002), https://www.gov.uk/government/uploads/attachment_data/file/6931/p66187-marine-stewardship-020425.pdf

Department for Environment, Food and Rural Affairs, 'Securing the Future: The UK Government Sustainable Development Strategy' (HM Government, 2005), http://www.defra.gov.uk/publications/files/pb10589-securing-the-future-050307.pdf

Department for Environment, Food and Rural Affairs, 'A Sea Change: A Marine Bill White Paper' (HM Government, 2007), http://www.official-documents.gov.uk/document/cm70/7047/7047.pdf

Department for Environment, Food and Rural Affairs, 'Conserving Biodiversity: The UK Approach' (HM Government, 2007), http://archive.defra.gov.uk/environment/biodiversity/documents/conbiouk-102007.pdf

Department for Environment, Food and Rural Affairs, 'England Biodiversity Strategy: Climate Change Adaptation Principles' (HM Government, 2008), http://www.defra.gov.uk/publications/files/pb13168-ebs-ccap-081203.pdf

Department for Environment, Food and Rural Affairs, 'Marine and Coastal Access Bill – Policy Paper' (HM Government, October 2009), http://archive.defra.gov.uk/environment/marine/documents/legislation/mab-policy.pdf

Department for Environment, Food and Rural Affairs, 'Mainstreaming sustainable development: The Government's vision and what this means in practice' (HM Government, 2011), http://sd.defra.gov.uk/documents/mainstreaming-sustainable-development.pdf

Diamond, J., *Collapse: How Societies Choose to Fail or Survive*, 2nd ed. (London: Penguin Books, 2011)

Dietz, T. and Stern, P. C., *Public Participation in Environmental Assessment and Decision Making* (Washington, DC: National Academies Press, 2008)

Dimitriou, H. and Thompson, R., 'Introduction' in Dimitriou, H. and Thompson, R. (eds) *Strategic Planning for Regional Development in the UK: A Review of Principles and Practices* (Abingdon: Routledge, 2007), pp. 3–9

Dobson, A., 'Democratising Green Theory: Preconditions and Principles' in Doherty, B. and de Geus, M. (eds) *Democracy and Green Political Thought: Sustainability, Rights and Citizenship* (London: Routledge, 1996), pp. 132–148

Dobson, A., *Green Political Thought*, 4th ed. (London: Routledge, 2007)

Dobson, A., 'All I left behind: The mainstreaming of ecologism' in 'Trajectories of Green Political Theory' (2009) 8 *Contemporary Political Theory*, 319–328

Doremus, H., "Adaptive Management, the Endangered Species Act, and the Institutional Challenges of "New Age" Environmental Protection" (2001) 41 *Washburn Law Journal*, 50–89

Dorf, M. C. and Sabel, C. F., 'A Constitution of Democratic Experimentalism' (1998) 98 *Columbia Law Review*, 267–473

Douvere, F., 'The importance of marine spatial planning in advancing ecosystem-based sea use management' (2008) 32 *Marine Policy*, 762–771

Douvere, F. and Ehler, C. N., 'New perspectives on sea use management: Initial findings from European experience with marine spatial planning' (2009) 90 *Journal of Environmental Management*, 77–88

Dovers, S., *Environment and Sustainability Policy: Creation, Implementation, Evaluation* (Sydney: The Federation Press, 2001)

Dovers, S., 'Too Deep a SEA? Strategic Environmental Assessment in the Era of Sustainability' in Marsden, S. and Dovers, S. (eds) *Strategic Environmental Assessment in Australasia* (Sydney: The Federation Press, 2002), pp. 24–46

Dovers, S., 'Precautionary policy assessment for sustainability' in Fisher, E., Jones, J. and von Schomberg, R. (eds) *Implementing the Precautionary Principle: Perspectives and Projects* (Cheltenham: Edward Elgar, 2006), pp. 88–112

Dovers, S. and Handmer, J. W., 'Ignorance, the precautionary principle and sustainability' (1995) 24 *Ambio*, 92–97

Dovers, S. and Handmer, J. W., 'Ignorance, Sustainability, and the Precautionary Principle: Towards an Analytical Framework' in Harding, R. and Fisher, E. (eds) *Perspectives on the Precautionary Principle* (Sydney: The Federation Press, 1999), pp. 167–189

Dreborg, K. H., 'Essence of Backcasting' (1996) 28 *Futures*, 813–828

Dryzek, J., *Deliberative Democracy and Beyond: Liberals, Critics, Contestations* (Oxford: Oxford University Press, 2000)

Dryzek, J., 'Legitimacy and Economy in Deliberative Democracy' (2001) 29 *Political Theory*, 651–669

Duit, A., 'Adaptive capacity and the ecostate' in Boyd, E. and Folke, C. (eds) *Adapting Institutions: Governance, Complexity and Social-Ecological Resilience* (Cambridge: Cambridge University Press, 2012), pp. 127–147

Eckersley, R., *The Green State: Rethinking Democracy and Sovereignty* (Cambridge, MA: MIT Press, 2004)

Elster, J., 'Introduction' in Elster, J. (ed.) *Deliberative Democracy* (Cambridge: Cambridge University Press, 1998), pp. 1–18

Esbjörn-Hargens, S. and Zimmerman, M. E., *Integral Ecology: Uniting Multiple Perspectives on the Natural World* (Boston, MA: Integral Books, 2009)

Esty, D. C., 'Environmental Protection in the Information Age' (2004) 79 *New York University Law Review*, 115–211

European Commission, 'Adapting to climate change: Towards a European framework for action', COM (2009) 147 final

European Commission, 'Proposal for a Directive of the European Parliament and the Council amending Directive 98/70/EC relating to the quality of petrol and diesel fuels and amending Directive 2009/28/EC on the promotion of the use of energy from renewable sources', COM (2012) 595 final

Evans, B., 'From Town Planning to Environmental Planning' in Blowers, A. and Evans, B. (eds) *Town Planning into the 21st Century* (London: Routledge, 1997), pp. 1–14

Fabra, A. and Gascon, V., 'The Convention on the Conservation of Antarctic Marine Living Resources (CCAMLR) and the Ecosystem Approach' (2008) 23 *The International Journal of Marine and Coastal Law*, 567–598

Farber, D. A., 'Bringing Environmental Assessment into the Digital Age' in Holder, J. and McGillivray, D. (eds) *Taking Stock of Environmental Assessment: Law, Policy and Practice* (Abingdon: Routledge Cavendish, 2008), pp. 219–258

Farber, D. A., 'Sustainable Consumption, Energy Policy, and Individual Well-Being' (2012) 65 *Vanderbilt Law Review*, 1479–1525

Fisher, E., Jones, J. and von Schomberg, R., 'Implementing the Precautionary Principle: Perspectives and Prospects' in Fisher, E., Jones, J. and von Schomberg, R. (eds) *Implementing the Precautionary Principle: Perspectives and Prospects* (Cheltenham: Edward Elgar, 2006), pp. 1–18

Flournoy, A. C., 'Protecting a Natural Resource Legacy While Promoting Resilience: Can it be Done?' (2009) 87 *Nebraska Law Review*, 1008–1035

Flynn, B., 'Planning Cells and Citizen Juries in Environmental Policy: Deliberation and its Limits' in Coenen, F. (ed.) *Public Participation and Better Environmental Decisions: The Promise and Limits of Participatory Processes for the Quality of Environmentally Related Decision-making* (Dordrecht: Springer, 2009), pp. 57–71

Foley, M. M. et al., 'Guiding ecological principles for marine spatial planning' (2010) 34 *Marine Policy*, 955–966

Folke, C., 'Resilience: The Emergence of a Perspective for Social-ecological Systems Analyses' (2006) 16 *Global Environmental Change*, 253–267

Folke, C., Holling, C. S. and Perrings, C., et al., 'Biological Diversity, Ecosystems, and the Human Scale' (1996) 6 *Ecological Applications*, 1018–1024

Folke, C. et al., 'Regime Shifts, Resilience and Biodiversity in Ecosystem Management' (2004) 35 *Annual Review of Ecology, Evolution and Systematics*, 557–581

Folke, C. et al., 'Resilience Thinking: Integrating Resilience, Adaptability, and Transformability' (2010) 15(4):20 *Ecology and Society*

Freeman, J., 'Private Parties, Public Functions, and the New Administrative Law' (2000) 52 *Administrative Law Review*, 813–858

Gaichas, S. K., 'A Context for Ecosystem-based Fishery Management: Developing Concepts of Ecosystems and Sustainability' (2008) 32 *Marine Policy*, 393–401

Galaz, V. et al., 'The Problem of Fit among Biophysical Systems, Environmental and Resource Regimes, and Broader Governance Systems: Insight and Emerging Challenges' in Young, O. R., King, L. A. and Schroeder, H. (eds) *Institutions and Environmental Change: Principal Findings, Applications and Research Frontiers* (Cambridge, MA: MIT Press, 2008), pp. 147–186

Garver, G., 'Introducing the rule of ecological law' in Westra, L., Soskolne, C. L. and Spady, D. W. (eds) *Human Health and Ecological Integrity: Ethics, Law and Human Rights* (Abingdon: Routledge, 2012), pp. 322–334

Gerstenberg, O. and Sabel, C. F., 'Directly-Deliberative Polyarchy: An Institutional Ideal for Europe?' in Joerges, C. and Dehousse, R. (eds) *Good Governance in Europe's Integrated Market* (Oxford: Oxford University Press, 2002), pp. 289–342

Geurs, K. and van Wee, B., 'Backcasting as a Tool for Sustainable Transport Policy Making: The Environmentally Sustainable Transport Study in the Netherlands' (2004) 4 *European Journal of Transport and Infrastructure Research*, 47–69

de Geus, M., 'The environment versus individual freedom and convenience' in Wissenburg, M. and Levy, Y. (eds) *Liberal Democracy and Environmentalism: The End of Environmentalism?* (London: Routledge, 2004), pp. 87–99

Gibson, R. et al., *Sustainability Assessment: Criteria and Processes* (London: Earthscan, 2005)

Giddens, A., *The Politics of Climate Change*, 2nd ed. (Cambridge: Polity Press, 2011)

Gillespie, A., 'The Precautionary Principle in the Twenty-First Century: A Case Study of Noise Pollution in the Ocean' (2007) 22 *The International Journal of Marine and Coastal Law*, 61–87

Glasson, J., 'Regional Planning and Sustainability Assessment' in Dimitriou, H. and Thompson, R. (eds) *Strategic Planning for Regional Development in the UK: A Review of Principles and Practices* (Abingdon: Routledge, 2007), pp. 220–248

Godard, O., 'The Precautionary Principle and Catastrophism on Tenterhooks: Lessons from a constitutional reform in France' in Fisher, E., Jones, J. and von Schomberg, R. (eds) *Implementing the Precautionary Principle: Perspectives and Prospects* (Cheltenham: Edward Elgar, 2006), pp. 63–87

Godard, O., 'Managing Global Risks through "Proportionate" Precaution: The Interplay between States, Civil Society, and International Regulation' in Brousseau, E., Dedeurwaerdere, T. and Siebenhüner, B. (eds) *Reflexive Governance for Global Public Goods* (Cambridge, MA: MIT Press, 2012), pp. 123–144

Goldblatt, D. L., *Sustainable Energy Consumption and Society: Personal, Technological, or Social Change?* (Dordrecht: Springer, 2005)

Goodin, R. E. and Dryzek, J. S., 'Deliberative Impacts: The Macro-political Uptake of Mini-publics' (2006) 34 *Politics and Society*, 219–244

Goodland, R., 'Strategic Environmental Assessment' in Porter, A. L. and Fittipaldi, J. J. (eds) *Environmental Methods Review: Retooling Impact Assessment for the New Century* (Fargo: The Press Club, 1998), pp. 87–94

Gross, C., 'Community Perspectives of Wind Energy in Australia: The Application of a Justice and Community Fairness Framework to Increase Social Acceptance' (2007) 35 *Energy Policy*, 2727–2736

Gunder, M., 'Sustainability: Planning's Saving Grace or Road to Perdition?' (2006) 26 *Journal of Planning Education and Research*, 208–221

Gunderson, L. H., 'Ecological Resilience – In Theory and Application' (2000) 31 *Annual Review of Ecology and Systematics*, 425–39

Gunningham, N., 'The New Collaborative Environmental Governance: The Localization of Regulation' (2009) 36 *Journal of Law and Society*, 145–166

Haas, P. M., 'Do Regimes Matter? Epistemic Communities and Mediterranean Pollution Control' (1989) 43 *International Organization*, 377–403

Haggett, C., 'Public Engagement in Planning for Renewable Energy' in Davoudi, S., Crawford, J. and Mehmood, A. (eds) *Planning for Climate Change: Strategies for Mitigation and Adaptation for Spatial Planners* (London: Earthscan, 2009), pp. 297–307

Halpern, B. S. et al., 'Managing for Cumulative Impacts in Ecosystem-based Management through Ocean Zoning' (2008) 51 *Ocean and Coastal Management*, 203–211

Harremoes, P. et al., 'Twelve Late Lessons' in Harremoes, P., Gee, D., MacGarvin, M., Stirling, A., Keys, J., Wynne, B. and Guedes Vaz, S. (eds) *The Precautionary Principle in the 20th Century: Late Lessons from Early Warnings* (London: Earthscan, 2002), pp. 185–215

Harris, G., *Seeking Sustainability in an Age of Complexity* (Cambridge: Cambridge University Press, 2007)

Harrison, C., Burgess, J. and Clark, J., 'Capturing Values for Nature: Economic, Ecological and Cultural Perspectives' in Holder, J. and McGillivray, D. (eds) *Locality and Identity: Environmental Issues in Law and Society* (Aldershot: Ashgate, 1999), pp. 85–110

Haughton, G. and Counsell, D., *Regions, Spatial Strategies and Sustainable Development* (London: Routledge, 2004)

Haughton, G., Allmendinger, P, Counsell, D. and Vigar, G., et al., *The New Spatial Planning: Territorial Management with Soft Spaces and Fuzzy Boundaries* (Abingdon: Routledge, 2010)

Hertin, J., Jacob, K. and Volkery, A., 'Policy Appraisal' in Jordan, A. and Lenschow, A. (eds) *Innovation in Environmental Policy? Integrating the Environment for Sustainability* (Cheltenham: Edward Elgar, 2008), pp. 114–133

Hilson, C., *Regulating Pollution: A UK and EC Perspective* (Oxford: Hart Publishing, 2000)

Hirst, P., 'Democracy and Governance' in Pierre, J. (ed.) *Debating Governance: Authority, Steering and Democracy* (Oxford: Oxford University Press, 2000), pp. 13–35

HM Government, 'UK Marine Policy Statement' (2011), http://www.defra.gov.uk/publications/files/pb3654-marine-policy-statement-110316.pdf

Holder, J., 'Building Spatial Europe: An Environmental Justice Perspective' in Scott, J. (ed.) *Environmental Protection: European Law and Governance* (Oxford: Oxford University Press, 2009), pp. 92–126

Holder, J. and Lee, M., *Environmental Protection, Law and Policy*, 2nd ed. (Cambridge: Cambridge University Press, 2007)

Holling, C. S. (ed.) *Adaptive Environmental Assessment and Management* (London: John Wiley & Sons, 1978)

Holling, C. S., 'Resilience and Stability of Ecological Systems' (1973) 4 *Annual Review of Ecology and Systematics*, 1–23

Holling, C. S., 'The Resilience of Terrestrial Ecosystems: Local Surprise and Global Change' in W. C. Clark and R. E. Munn (eds) *Sustainable Development of the Biosphere* (Cambridge: Cambridge University Press, 1986), pp. 292–317

Holling, C. S., 'Understanding the Complexity of Economic, Ecological and Social Systems' (2001) 4 *Ecosystems*, 390–405

Holling, C. S. and Gunderson, L. H., 'Resilience and Adaptive Cycles' in Gunderson, L. H. and Holling, C. S. (eds) *Panarchy: Understanding Transformations in Human and Natural Systems* (Washington, DC: Island Press, 2002), pp. 25–62

Hooper, D. U. et al., 'Effects of Biodiversity on Ecosystem Functioning: A Consensus of Current Knowledge' (2005) 75 *Ecological Monographs*, 3–35

Hoppe, R., 'Institutional Constraints and Practical Problems in Deliberative and Participatory Policy Making' (2011) 39 *Policy and Politics*, 163–186

Howarth, W., 'Substance and Procedure under the Strategic Environmental Assessment Directive and the Water Framework Directive' in Holder, J. and McGillivray, D. (eds) *Taking Stock of Environmental Assessment: Law, Policy and Practice* (Abingdon: Routledge, 2008), pp. 149–190

Iles, A., 'Adaptive Management: Making Environmental Law and Policy more Dynamic, Experimentalist and Learning' (1996) 13 *Environmental and Planning Law Journal*, 288–308

Intergovernmental Panel on Climate Change, *Climate Change 2007: Synthesis Report – Contribution of Working Groups I, II, and III to the Fourth Assessment Report of the Intergovernmental Panel on Climate Change*, Core writing team, Pachauri, A. K. and Reisinger, A (eds) (Geneva: IPCC, 2008)

Jackson, A. L. R., 'Renewable energy vs. biodiversity: Policy conflicts and the future of nature conservation' (2011) 21 *Global Environmental Change*, 1195–1208

Jackson, T., *Prosperity without Growth: Economics for a Finite Planet* (London: Earthscan, 2009)

Jackson, T. et al., 'Beyond Insatiability: Needs Theory, Consumption and Sustainability' in L. A. Reisch and I. Røpke (eds) *The Ecological Economics of Consumption* (Cheltenham: Edward Elgar, 2004), pp. 79–110

Jacob, K. et al., 'Improving the practice of impact assessment', EVIA (Evaluating Integrated Impact Assessments) Policy Briefing, Project No. 028889, European Commission, 6th Framework Programme (2008), http://userpage.fu-berlin.de/ffu/evia

Jacobs, M., 'Environmental Valuation, Deliberative Democracy and Public Decision-making Institutions' in Foster, J. (ed.) *Valuing Nature? Ethics, Economics and the Environment* (London: Routledge, 1997), pp. 211–231

Jax, K., 'Function and "Functioning" in Ecology: What does it Mean?' (2005) 111 *Oikos*, 641–648

Jay, S. A., *At the Margins of Planning: Offshore Wind Farms in the UK* (Aldershot: Ashgate, 2008)

Jay, S. A., 'Built at Sea: Marine Management and the Construction of Marine Spatial Planning' (2010) 81 *Town Planning Review*, 173–191

Joao, E., 'Key Principles of Strategic Environmental Assessment' in Schmidt, M., Joao, E. and Albrecht, E. (eds) *Implementing Strategic Environmental Assessment* (Berlin: Springer, 2005), pp. 3–14

Jones, C. et al., 'Environmental Assessment: Dominant or Dormant?' in Holder, J. and McGillivray, D. (eds) *Taking Stock of Environmental Assessment: Law, Policy and Practice* (Abingdon: Routledge, 2008), pp. 17–44

Jones, J. S. and Ganey, S., 'Building the Legal and Institutional Framework' in McLeod, K. and Leslie, H. M. (eds) *Ecosystem-based Management for the Oceans* (Washington, DC: Island Press, 2009), pp. 162–179

Jordan, A. and Lenschow, A., 'Environmental Policy Integration: A State of the Art Review' (2010) 20 *Environmental Policy and Governance*, 147–158

Joyner, C. C., 'Fragile Ecosystems: Preclusive Restoration in the Antarctic' (1994) 34 *Natural Resources Journal*, 879–904

Karkkainen, B. C., 'Collaborative Ecosystem Governance: Scale, Complexity, and Dynamism' (2002) 21 *Virginia Environmental Law Journal*, 189–243

Karkkainen, B. C., 'Toward Ecologically Sustainable Democracy?' in Fung, A. and Wright, E. O. (eds) *Deepening Democracy: Institutional Innovations in Empowered Participatory Governance* (London: Verso, 2003), pp. 208–224

Karkkainen, B. C., 'Information-forcing Regulation and Environmental Governance' in de Burca, G. and Scott, J. (eds) *Law and New Governance in the EU and the US* (Oxford: Hart Publishing, 2006), pp. 293–322

Karkkainen, B. C., Fung, A. and Sabel, C. F., 'After Backyard Environmentalism: Toward a Performance-based Regime of Environmental Regulation' (2000) 44 *American Behavioral Scientist*, 692–711

Karlsson, M., 'The Precautionary Principle, Swedish Chemicals Policy and Sustainable Development' (2006) 9 *Journal of Risk Research*, 337–360

Kenny, M. and Meadowcroft, J., 'Introduction' in Kenny, M. and Meadowcroft, J. (eds) *Planning Sustainability* (London: Routledge, 1999), pp. 1–11

Kinzig, A. and Starrett, D., 'Coping with Uncertainty: A Call for a New Science-Policy Forum' (2003) 32 *Ambio*, 330–335

Klein, U., 'Integrated Resource Management in New Zealand: A Juridical Analysis of Policy, Plan and Rule Making under the RMA' (2001) 5 *New Zealand Journal of Environmental Law*, 1–54

Klinke, A., 'Inclusive Risk Governance through Discourse, Deliberation and Participation' in Everson, M. and Vos, E. (eds) *Uncertain Risks Regulated* (Abingdon: Routledge, 2009), pp. 399–414

Klinke, A. and Renn, O., 'A New Approach to Risk Evaluation and Management: Risk-based, Precaution-based and Discourse-based Strategies' (2002) 22 *Risk Analysis*, 1071–1094

Klinke, A. and Renn, O., 'Adaptive and Integrative Governance on Risk and Uncertainty' (2012) 15 *Journal of Risk Research*, 273–292

Kramer, L., 'The European Commission's Opinions under Article 6(4) of the Habitats Directive' (2009) 21 *Journal of Environmental Law*, 59–85

Kronsell, A., 'Legitimacy for Climate Policies: Politics and Participation in the Green City of Freiburg' (2013) 18 *Local Environment*, 965–982

Lang, R., 'Achieving Integration in Resource Planning' in Lang, R. (ed.) *Integrated Approaches to Resource Planning and Management* (Calgary: University of Calgary Press, 1986), pp. 27–50

Lawton, J. H. et al., *Making Space for Nature: A Review of England's Wildlife Sites and Ecological Network* (Report to HM Government, 2010), http://archive.defra.gov.uk/environment/biodiversity/documents/201009space-for-nature.pdf

van der Leeuw, S. E., 'Climate and Society: Lessons from the Past 10000 Years' (2008) 37 *Ambio*, 476–482

Leslie, H. M. and Kinzig, A. P., 'Resilience Science' in McLeod, K. and Leslie, H. M. (eds) *Ecosystem-based Management for the Oceans* (Washington, DC: Island Press, 2009), pp. 55–73

Levin, S. A., 'Ecosystems and the Biosphere as Complex Adaptive Systems' (1998) 1 *Ecosystems*, 431–436

Levin, S. A., *Fragile Dominion: Complexity and the Commons* (Cambridge, MA: Helix Books, 1999)

Levin, S. A. and Lubchenco, J., 'Resilience, Robustness, and Marine Ecosystem-based Management' (2008) 58 *Bioscience*, 27–32

Lipschutz, R. D., 'Bioregionalism, Civil Society and Global Environmental Governance' in McGinnis, M. V. (ed.) *Bioregionalism* (London: Routledge, 1999), pp. 101–120

Lord, A. and Tewdwr-Jones, M., "Is Planning 'under attack'? Chronicling the Deregulation of Urban and Environmental Planning in England" (2014) 22 *European Planning Studies*, 345–61

Lövbrand, E. and Khan, J., 'The deliberative turn in green political theory' in Bäckstrand, K., Khan, J., Kronsell, A. and Lövbrand, E. (eds) *Environmental Politics and Deliberative Democracy: Examining the Promise of New Modes of Governance* (Cheltenham: Edward Elgar, 2010), pp. 47–64

Ludwig, D., Hilborn, R. and Walters, C., 'Uncertainty, Resource Exploitation, and Conservation: Lessons from History' (1993) 260 *Science*, 17 and 36

Lundqvist, L. J., 'A Green Fist in a Velvet Glove: The Ecological State and Sustainable Development' (2001) 10 *Environmental Values*, 455–472

Lundqvist, L. J., *Sweden and Ecological Governance* (Manchester: Manchester University Press, 2004)

Lyhne, I., 'Between Policy-making and Planning: SEA and Strategic Decision-making in the Danish Energy Sector' (2011) 13 *Journal of Environmental Assessment, Policy and Management*, 319–341

Mander, S. L. et al., 'The Tyndall Decarbonisation Scenarios – Part I: Development of a Backcasting Methodology with Stakeholder Participation' (2008) 36 *Energy Policy*, 3754–3763

Marocco, J., 'Climate Change and the Limits of Knowledge' in Vitek, B. and Jackson, W. (eds) *The Virtues of Ignorance: Complexity, Sustainability and the Limits of Knowledge* (Lexington: University Press of Kentucky, 2008), pp. 307–322

McGillivray, D. and Holder, J., 'Taking Stock' in Holder, J. and McGillivray, D. (eds) *Taking Stock of Environmental Assessment: Law, Policy and Practice* (Abingdon: Routledge, 2008), pp. 1–16

McGinnis, M. V., 'A Rehearsal to Bioregionalism' in McGinnis, M. V. (ed.) *Bioregionalism* (London: Routledge, 1999), pp. 1–9

McHarg, A., 'Climate Change Constitutionalism? Lessons from the United Kingdom' (2011) 2 *Climate Law*, 469–484

McLeod, K. and Leslie, H. M., 'Ways Forward' in McLeod, K. and Leslie, H. M. (eds) *Ecosystem-based Management for the Oceans* (Washington, DC: Island Press, 2009), pp. 341–351

McLeod, K. and Leslie, H. M., 'Why Ecosystem-based Management?' in McLeod, K. and Leslie, H. M. (eds) *Ecosystem-based Management for the Ocean* (Washington, DC: Island Press, 2009), pp. 3–12

Meadowcroft, J., 'Planning, Democracy and the Challenge of Sustainable Development' (1997) 18 *International Political Science Review*, 167–189

Meadowcroft, J., 'Planning for Sustainable Development: Insights from the Literatures of Political Science' (1997) 31 *European Journal of Political Research* 427–454

Meadowcroft, J., 'Deliberative Democracy' in Durant, R. F., Fiorino, J. and O'Leary, R. (eds) *Environmental Governance Reconsidered* (Cambridge, MA: MIT Press, 2004), pp. 183–217

Meadowcroft, J., 'Greening the State' in Steinberg, P. F. and VanDeveer, S. D. (eds) *Comparative Environmental Politics: Theory, Practice and Prospects* (Cambridge, MA: The MIT Press, 2012), pp. 63–87

Mertens, K, Cliquet, A. and Vanheusden, B., 'Ecosystem Services: What's in it for a Lawyer?' (2012) 21 *European Energy and Environmental Law Review*, 31–40

Millennium Ecosystem Assessment, *Ecosystems and Human Well-being: Synthesis* (Washington, DC: Island Press, 2005), http://www.maweb.org/documents/document.356.aspx.pdf

Miller, F. et al., 'Resilience and Vulnerability: Complementary or Conflicting Concepts?' (2010) 15(3):11 *Ecology and Society*

Mitchell, B., 'The Evolution of Integrated Resource Management' in Lang, R. (ed.) *Integrated Approaches to Resource Planning and Management* (Calgary: University of Calgary Press, 1986), pp. 13–26

Mont, O., 'The Swedish Product Choice Principle' (2001) 10 *European Environmental Law Review*, 351–363

Morgan, R. K., 'Environmental Impact Assessment: The State of the Art' (2012) 30 *Impact Assessment and Project Appraisal*, 5–14

Munthe, C., *The Price of Precaution and the Ethics of Risk* (Dordrecht: Springer, 2011)

Myers, N., 'Biodiversity and the Precautionary Principle' (1993) 22 *Ambio*, 74–9

Nadin, V., 'The emergence of the spatial planning approach in England' (2007) 22 *Planning, Practice and Research*, 43–62

Niemeyer, S., 'The Emancipatory Effect of Deliberation: Empirical Lessons from Mini-Publics' (2011) 39 *Politics and Society*, 103–140

Nilsson, A., 'The Precautionary Principle in Swedish Chemicals Law and Policy' in de Sadeleer, N. (ed.) *Implementing the Precautionary Principle: Approaches from the Nordic Countries, the EU and USA* (London: Earthscan, 2007), pp. 295–312

Nilsson, M. and Persson, A., 'Can Earth System Interactions be Governed? Governance Functions for Linking Climate Change Mitigation with Land Use, Freshwater and Biodiversity Protection' (2012) 75 *Ecological Economics*, 61–71

Noble, B. F., 'Strategic Environmental Assessment: What is it and What Makes it Strategic?' (2000) 2 *Journal of Environmental Assessment, Policy and Management*, 203–224

Noble, B. F., 'The Canadian Experience with SEA and Sustainability' (2002) 22 *Environmental Impact Assessment Review*, 3–16

Noble, B. F. and Christmas, L. M., 'Strategic Environmental Assessment of Greenhouse Gas Mitigation Options in the Canadian Agricultural Sector' (2008) 41 *Environmental Management*, 64–78

Norse, E. A., 'Ending the Range Wars on the Last Frontier: Zoning the Sea' in Norse, E. A. and Crowder, L. B. (eds) *Marine Conservation Biology: The Science of Maintaining the Sea's Biodiversity* (Washington, DC: Island Press, 2005), pp. 422–443

Norton, B. G., 'Biodiversity and Environmental Values: In Search of a Universal Earth Ethic' (2000) 9 *Biodiversity and Conservation*, 1029–1044

Norton, B. G., 'Marine Environmental Ethics: Where We Might Start' in Dallmeyer, D. G. (ed.) *Values at Sea: Ethics for the Marine Environment* (Athens, GA: The University of Georgia Press, 2003), pp. 33–49

Norton, B. G., *Sustainability: A Philosophy of Adaptive Ecosystem Management* (Chicago, IL: University of Chicago Press, 2005)

Norton, B. G. and Hannon, B., 'Democracy and Sense of Place Values in Environmental Policy' in Light, A. and Smith, J. M. (eds) *Philosophy and Geography III: Philosophies of Place* (Lanham: Rowman and Littlefield Publishers, 1998), pp. 119–145

O'Brien, M., 'Alternatives Assessment: Part of Operationalizing and Institutionalizing the Precautionary Principle' in Raffensperger, C. and

Tickner, J. A. (eds) *Protecting Public Health and the Environment: Implementing the Precautionary Principle* (Washington, DC: Island Press, 1999), pp. 207–219

O'Brien, M., 'Science in the Service of Good: The Precautionary Principle and Positive Goals' in Tickner, J. A. (ed.) *Precaution, Environmental Science and Preventative Public Policy* (Washington, DC: Island Press, 2003), pp. 279–295

Office of the Deputy Prime Minister, 'A Practical Guide to the Strategic Environmental Assessment Directive' (HM Government, 2005), http://www.communities.gov.uk/documents/planningandbuilding/pdf/practicalguidesea.pdf

Owens, S., 'Land, Limits and Sustainability: A Conceptual Framework and Some Dilemmas for the Planning System' (1994) 19 *Transactions of the Institute of British Geographers*, 439–456

Owens, S., 'Negotiated Environments: Needs, Demands and Values in the Age of Sustainability' (1997) 29 *Environment and Planning A*, 571–580

Owens, S., "Engaging the Public': Information and Deliberation in Environmental Policy' (2000) 32 *Environment and Planning A*, 1141–1148

Owens, S. and Cowell, R., *Land and Limits: Interpreting Sustainability in the Planning Process*, 1st ed. (London: Routledge, 2002)

Owens, S. and Cowell, R., *Land and Limits: Interpreting Sustainability in the Planning Process*, 2nd ed. (Abingdon: Routledge, 2011)

Peter, F., 'Political Legitimacy' in Zalta, E. N. (ed.) *The Stanford Encyclopedia of Philosophy* (2013), http://plato.stanford.edu/entries/legitimacy

Petts, J., 'Evaluating the Effectiveness of Deliberative Processes: Waste Management Case-studies' (2001) 44 *Journal of Environmental Planning and Management*, 207–226

Pring, G., Haas, A. S. and Drinkwine, B. T., 'The Impact of Energy on Health, Environment and Sustainable Development: The TANSTAAFL Problem' in Zillman, D. N., Redgwell, C. R., Omorogbe, Y. O. and Barrera-Hernández, L. K. (eds) *Beyond the Carbon Economy* (Oxford: Oxford University Press, 2008), pp. 13–37

Purvis, A. and Hector, A., 'Getting the Measure of Biodiversity' (2000) 405 *Nature*, 212–9

Quist, J. and Vergragt, P., 'Past and Future of Backcasting: The Shift to Stakeholder Participation and a Proposal for a Methodological Framework' (2006) 38 *Futures*, 1027–1045

Redgwell, C. R., 'Environmental Protection in Antarctica: The 1991 Protocol' (1994) 43 *International and Comparative Law Quarterly*, 599–634

Rees, W., 'Scale, Complexity and the Conundrum of Sustainability' in Kenny, M. and Meadowcroft, J. (eds) *Planning Sustainability* (London: Routledge, 1999), pp. 101–127

Renn, O., *Risk Governance: Coping with Uncertainty in a Complex World* (London: Earthscan, 2008)

Renn, O., 'Precaution and the Governance of Risk' in Adger, W. N. and Jordan, A. (eds) *Governing Sustainability* (Cambridge: Cambridge University Press, 2009), pp. 226–258

Rietig, K., 'Sustainable Climate Policy Integration in the European Union' (2013) 23 *Environmental Policy and Governance*, 297–310

Robinson, J., 'Energy Backcasting: A Proposed Method of Policy Analysis' (1982) 10 *Energy Policy*, 337–344

Robinson, J., 'Futures under Glass: A recipe for People who Hate to Predict' (1990) 22 *Futures*, 820–842

Robinson, J., 'Future Subjunctive: Backcasting as Social Learning' (2003) 35 *Futures*, 839–856

Rockström, J. et al., 'A Safe Operating Space for Humanity' (2009) 461 *Nature*, 472–5

Rockström, J. et al., Planetary Boundaries: Exploring the Safe Operating Space for Humanity' (2009) 14(2):32 *Ecology and Society*

Rodgers, C. P., *The Law of Nature Conservation: Property, Environment, and the Limits of Law* (Oxford: Oxford University Press, 2013)

Røpke, I., 'Ecological Economics: Consumption Drivers and Impacts' in Lever-Tracy, C. (ed.) *Routledge Handbook of Climate Change and Society* (Abingdon: Routledge, 2010), pp. 121–130

Rosenberg, A. A. and Sandifer, P. A., 'What do Managers Need?' in McLeod, K. and Leslie, H. M. (eds) *Ecosystem-based Management for the Oceans* (Washington, DC: Island Press, 2009), pp. 13–30

Rosenberg, A. A., et al., 'Lessons from National Level Implementation Across the World' in McLeod, K. and Leslie, H. M. (eds) *Ecosystem-based Management for the Oceans* (Washington, DC: Island Press, 2009), pp. 294–313

Ross, A., 'Modern Interpretations of Sustainable Development' (2009) 36 *Journal of Law and Society*, 32–54

Ross, A., *Sustainable Development Law in the UK: From Rhetoric to Reality?* (Abingdon: Earthscan, 2012)

Royal Commission on Environmental Pollution, 'Environmental Planning' (23rd Report CM 5459 2002), http://webarchive.nationalarchives.gov.uk/20080726220734/http://www.rcep.org.uk/epreport.htm

Ruhl, J. B., 'Thinking of Environmental Law as a Complex Adaptive System: How to Clean up the Environment by Making a Mess of Environmental Law' (1997) 34 *Houston Law Review*, 933–1002

Ruhl, J. B., 'Regulation by Adaptive Management – Is it Possible?' (2005) 7 *Minnesota Journal of Law, Science and Technology*, 21–57

Ruhl, J. B., Kraft, S. E. and Lant, C. L., *The Law and Policy of Ecosystem Services* (Washington, DC: Island Press, 2007)

Russel, D. and Turnpenny, J., 'The Politics of Sustainable Development in UK Government: What Role for Integrated Policy Appraisal?' (2009) 27 *Environment and Planning C: Government and Policy*, 340–354

Rydin, Y., 'Land Use Planning and Environmental Capacity: Reassessing the Use of Regulatory Policy Tools to Achieve Sustainable Development' (1998) 41 *Journal of Environmental Planning and Management*, 749–765

de Sadeleer, N., *Environmental Principles: From Political Slogans to Legal Rules* (Oxford: Oxford University Press, 2002)

Sadler, B., 'Strategic Environmental Assessment at the Policy Level: Recent Progress, Current Status and Future Prospects' (United Nations Economic Commission for Europe, 2005), http://www.unece.org/fileadmin/DAM/env/eia/documents/PolicySEA/SEA_of_Policies_volume.pdf

Sagoff, M., 'Values and Preferences' (1986) 96 *Ethics*, 301–316

Schaab, G. C., 'Beyond Dominion and Stewardship' in Burdon, P. (ed.) *Exploring Wild Law: The Philosophy of Earth Jurisprudence* (Kent Town: Wakefield Press, 2011), pp. 107–115

Scheffer, M. et al., 'Catastrophic Shifts in Ecosystems' (2001) 413 *Nature*, 591–6

von Schomberg, R., 'The Precautionary Principle and its Normative Challenges' in Fisher, E., Jones, J. and von Schomberg, R. (eds) *Implementing the Precautionary Principle: Perspectives and Prospects* (Cheltenham: Edward Elgar, 2006), pp. 19–41

Scott, K. N., 'Tilting at Offshore Windmills: Regulating Wind Farm Development within the Renewable Energy Zone' (2006) 18 *Journal of Environmental Law*, 89–118

Secretary of State for Communities and Local Government, 'Revoking Regional Strategies' (UK Government, July 2010) http://www.communities.gov.uk/statements/newsroom/regionalstrategies

Sheate, W. R. et al., 'Integrating the Environment into Strategic Decision-making: Conceptualizing Policy SEA' (2003) 13 *European Environment*, 1–18

Sivas, D. A. and Caldwell, M. R., 'A New Vision for California Ocean Governance: Comprehensive Ecosystem-based Marine Zoning' (2008) 27 *Stanford Environmental Law Journal*, 209–270

van der Sluijs, J. and Turkenburg, W., 'Climate Change and the Precautionary Principle' in Fisher, E., Jones, J. and von Schomberg, R. (eds) *Implementing the Precautionary Principle: Perspectives and Prospects* (Cheltenham: Edward Elgar, 2006), pp. 245–269

Smith, G., *Deliberative Democracy and the Environment* (London: Routledge, 2003)

Smith, G., 'Liberal Democracy and the Shaping of Environmentally Enlightened Citizens' in Wissenburg, M. and Levy, Y. (eds) *Liberal Democracy and Environmentalism: The End of Environmentalism?* (London: Routledge, 2004), pp. 139–151

Smith, G., *Democratic Innovations: Designing Institutions for Citizen Participation* (Cambridge: Cambridge University Press, 2009)

Smith, G. and Wales, C., 'Citizens' Juries and Deliberative Democracy' (2000) 48 *Political Studies*, 51–65

Speth, J. G., *The Bridge at the Edge of the World: Capitalism, the Environment and Crossing from Crisis to Sustainability* (New Haven, CT: Yale University Press, 2008)

Stallworthy, M., *Sustainability, Land Use and Environment* (London: Cavendish Publishing, 2002)

Stallworthy, M., 'Legislating Against Climate Change: A UK Perspective on a Sisyphean Challenge' (2009) 72 *The Modern Law Review*, 412–436

Stead, D. and Nadin, V., 'Environmental Resources and Energy in the United Kingdom: The Potential Role of a National Spatial Planning Framework' (1999) 70 *Town Planning Review*, 339–362

Steele, J., 'Participation and Deliberation in Environmental Law: Exploring a Problem-solving Approach' (2001) 21 *Oxford Journal of Legal Studies*, 415–442

Steffen, W. et al., *Global Change and the Earth System: A Planet under Pressure* (Berlin: Springer-Verlag, 2004)

Steffen, W. et al., 'The Anthropocene: Are Humans Now Overwhelming the Great Forces of Nature?' (2007) 36 *Ambio*, 614–22

Sterba, J. P., 'Reconciling Anthropocentric and Nonanthropocentric Environmental Ethics' (1994) 3 *Environmental Values*, 229–244

Steurer, R., 'Sustainable development as governance reform agenda: An aggregation of distinguished challenges for policy-making', Discussion Paper 1-2009, Institute of Forest, Environmental and Natural Resource Policy, Universität für Bodenkultur Wien (2009), http://www.wiso.boku.ac.at/fileadmin/data/H03000/H73000/H73200/InFER_Discussion_Papers/InFER_DP_09_1_SD_as_governance_reform_agenda_final_01.pdf

Stirling, A., 'Participation, Precaution and Reflexive Governance for Sustainable Development' in Adger, W. N. and Jordan, A. (eds) *Governing Sustainability* (Cambridge: Cambridge University Press, 2009), pp. 193–225

Stirling, A., Renn, O. and van Zwanenburg, P., 'A Framework for the Precautionary Governance of Food Safety: Integrating Science and Participation in the Social Appraisal of Risk' in Fisher, E., Jones, J. and von Schomberg, R. (eds) *Implementing the Precautionary Principle: Perspectives and Prospects* (Cheltenham: Edward Elgar, 2006), pp. 284–315

Stokes, S. C., 'Pathologies of Deliberation' in Elster, J. (ed.) *Deliberative Democracy* (Cambridge: Cambridge University Press, 1998), pp. 123–139

Suwa, A., 'Soft Energy Paths in Japan: A Backcasting Approach to Energy Planning' (2009) 9 *Climate Policy*, 185–2006

Tarlock, D., 'Ecosystems' in Bodansky, D., Brunnee, J. and Hey, E. (eds) *The Oxford Handbook of International Environmental Law* (Oxford: Oxford University Press, 2007), pp. 574–595

Tetlow, M. F. and Hanusch, M., 'Strategic Environmental Assessment: The State of the Art' (2012) 30 *Impact Assessment and Project Appraisal*, 15–24

Tewdwr-Jones, M. and Allmendinger, P., 'Deconstructing Communicative Rationality: A Critique of Habermasian collaborative planning' (1998) 30 *Environment and Planning A*, 1975–1989

Tewdwr-Jones, M. and Allmendinger, P., 'Regional Institutions, governance and the planning system' in Dimitriou, H. and Thompson, R. (eds) *Strategic Planning for Regional Development in the UK: A Review of Principles and Practices* (Abingdon: Routledge, 2007), pp. 28–39

Tewdwr-Jones, M., Gallent, N. and Morphet, J., 'An Anatomy of Spatial Planning: Coming to Terms with the Spatial Element in UK Planning' (2010) 18 *European Planning Studies*, 239–257

Tickell, A., John, P. and Musson, S., 'The North East Region Referendum Campaign of 2004: Issues and Turning Points' (2005) 76 *The Political Quarterly*, 488–496

Tickner, J. A., 'A Map Toward Precautionary Decision Making' in Raffensperger, C. and Tickner, J. A. (eds) *Protecting Public Health and the Environment: Implementing the Precautionary Principle* (Washington, DC: Island Press, 1999), pp. 162–186

Tickner, J. A. and Geiser, K., 'The Precautionary Principle Stimulus for Solutions – and Alternatives-based Environmental Policy' (2004) 24 *Environmental Impact Assessment Review*, 801–824

Tickner, J. A. et al., 'Alternatives Assessment in Regulatory Policy: History and Future Directions' in Hester, R. E. and Harrison, R. M. (eds) *Chemical Alternatives Assessment* (Cambridge: The Royal Society of Chemistry, 2013), pp. 256–295

Trouwborst, A., 'The Precautionary Principle in General International Law: Combating the Babylonian Confusion' (2007) 16 *Review of European Community and International Environmental Law*, 185–195

Trouwborst, A., 'The Precautionary Principle and the Ecosystem Approach in International Law: Differences, Similarities and Linkages' (2009) 18 *Review of European Community and International Environmental Law*, 26–37

UK National Ecosystem Assessment, 'The UK National Ecosystem Assessment: Synthesis of Key Findings', UNEP-WCMC, Cambridge (2011), http://uknea.unep-wcmc.org/Resources/tabid/82/Default.aspx

Vergragt, P. and Quist, J., 'Backcasting for Sustainability: Introduction to the Special issue' (2011) 78 *Technological Forecasting and Social Change*, 747–755

Vitek, B. and Jackson, W., 'Introduction: Taking Ignorance Seriously' in Vitek, B. and Jackson, W. (eds) *The Virtues of Ignorance: Complexity, Sustainability and the Limits of Knowledge* (Lexington: University Press of Kentucky, 2008), pp. 1–17

Wagner, W. E., 'Commons Ignorance: The Failure of Environmental Law to Produce Needed Information on Health and the Environment' (2004) 53 *Duke Law Journal*, 1619–1745

Wahlstrom, B., 'The Precautionary Approach to Chemicals Management: A Swedish Perspective' in Raffensperger, C. and Tickner, J. (eds) *Protecting*

Public Health and the Environment: Implementing the Precautionary Principle (Washington, DC: Island Press, 1999), pp. 51–69

Walker, B. and Salt, D., *Resilience Practice: Building Capacity to Absorb Disturbance and Maintain Function* (Washington, DC: Island Press, 2012)

Walker, B. and Salt, D., *Resilience Thinking: Sustaining Ecosystems and People in a Changing World* (Washington, DC: Island Press, 2006)

Walker, B. et al., 'Resilience, Adaptability and Transformability in the Goulburn-Broken Catchment, Australia' (2009) 14(1):12 *Ecology and Society*

Walker, B. and Westley, F., 'Perspectives on Resilience to Disasters across Sectors and Cultures' (2011) 16(2):4 *Ecology and Society*

Wallace, K., 'Classification of Ecosystem Services: Problems and Solutions' (2007) 139 *Biological Conservation*, 235–246

Welp, M., Kasemir, B. and Jaeger, C., 'Citizens' Voices in Environmental Policy: The Contribution of Integrated Assessment Focus Groups to Accountable Decision-making' in Coenen, F. (ed.) *Public Participation and Better Environmental Decisions: The Promise and Limits of Participatory Processes for the Quality of Environmentally Related Decision-making* (Dordrecht: Springer, 2009), pp. 21–34

Weston, B. H. and Bollier, D., *Green Governance: Ecological Survival, Human Rights and the Law of the Commons* (New York: Cambridge University Press, 2013).

Wheeler, S. M., *Planning for Sustainability: Creating Liveable, Equitable, and Ecological Communities* (London: Routledge, 2004)

Wheeler, S. M., 'Regions, Megaregions and Sustainability' (2009) 43 *Regional Studies*, 863–876

While, A., Jonas, A. E. G. and Gibbs, D. et al., 'From Sustainable Development to Carbon Control: Eco-state Restructuring and the Politics of Urban and Regional Development' (2010) 35 *Transactions of the Institute of British Geographers*, 76–93

White Jr. L., 'The Historical Roots of Our Ecologic Crisis' (1967) 155 *Science*, 1203–1207

White, L. and Noble, B. F., 'Strategic Environmental Assessment for Sustainability: A Review of a Decade of Academic Research' (2013) 42 *Environmental Impact Assessment Review*, 60–66.

Wiener, J., 'Precaution' in Bodansky, D., Brunnee, J. and Hey, E. (eds) *The Oxford Handbook of International Environmental Law* (Oxford: Oxford University Press, 2007), pp. 597–612

Wilding, S. and Raemaekers, J., 'Environmental Compensation for Greenfield Development: Is the Devil in the Detail?' (2000) 15 *Planning Practice and Research*, 211–231

Wilkinson, D., 'Using Environmental Ethics to Create Ecological Law' in Holder, J. and McGillivray, D. (eds) *Locality and Identity: Environmental Issues in Law and Society* (Aldershot: Ashgate, 1999), pp. 17–50

Williams, I., 'The Resource Management Act 1991: Well Meant But Hardly Done' (2000) 9 *Otago Law Review*, 673–695

Wilson, E. and Piper, J., *Spatial Planning and Climate Change* (Abingdon: Routledge, 2010)

Wong, C., 'Is There a Need for a Fully Integrated Spatial Planning Framework for the United Kingdom?' (2002) 3 *Planning Theory and Practice*, 277–300

Wong, C. et al., 'Uniting Britain: The Evidence Base – Spatial Structures and Key Drivers' (London: The Town Planning Institute, 2006), http://www.rtpi.org.uk/media/6003/Uniting-Britain.pdf

Wong, C. et al., 'A Map for England: Spatial Expression of Government Policies and Programmes' (London: The Town Planning Institute, 2012), http://www.rtpi.org.uk/knowledge/publications

Woolley, O. A., 'Trouble on the Horizon? Addressing Place-based Values in Planning for Offshore Wind Energy' (2010) 22 *Journal of Environmental Law*, 223–250

World Wildlife Fund, 'Living Planet Report 2012: Biodiversity, biocapacity and better choices' (Biennial Report, 2012), http://www.wwf.org.uk/what_we_do/about_us/living_planet_report_2012

Worster, D., 'The Ecology of Order and Chaos' in C. Pierce and D. VanDeVeer (eds), *People, Penguins, and Plastic Trees: Basic Issues in Environmental Ethics* (Belmont, CA: Wadsworth Publishing Company, 1995), pp. 280–288

Wynne, B., 'Uncertainty and Environmental Learning: Reconceiving Science and Policy in the Preventative Paradigm' (1992) 2 *Global Environmental Change*, 111–127

Young, O. R. et al., 'Solving the Crisis in Ocean Governance: Place-based Management of Marine Ecosystems' (2007) 49 *Environment*, 20–32

Young, R. A., *Uncertainty and the Environment: Implications for Decision-making and Environmental Policy* (Cheltenham: Edward Elgar, 2001)

Zander, J., *The Application of the Precautionary Principle in Practice: Comparative Dimensions* (Cambridge: Cambridge University Press, 2010)

INDEX

adaptive governance, 12–13
Complex Adaptive System Theory, 43
Adelle, C, 69
Allmendinger, P., 202–203

Baber, W. F., 195, 199, 204
backcasting, 86–88, 89
Bartlett, R. V., 195, 199, 204
Barlow Report,1940, 167
Barry, John, 111, 123, 191, 194, 201
Barton, B., 193–194, 197
behavioral change promotion, ecological governance, 136–137
Biodiversity Convention, 4
bioregionalists, ecological governance, 108
Boardman, R., 24–25
Boothroyd, P., 69, 95
Brierley, A. S., 31
Brooks, R. O., 220–221, 224
Brown, T. C., 190
Brundtland Report, 98
Brunnee, J., 222–223, 224
Buckley, R., 97
Burgess, J., 194

Callicott, J. B., 45
CCAMLR. *See* Convention on the Conservation of Antarctic Marine Living Resources
Christoff, P., 107, 120
Clark, J., 194
Climate Change Act 2008, United Kingdom, 102
collaborative ecological governance, 10–12
communicative state, 120
commutesheds, 128
complexity, regime shifts, environmental decision-making, 25–27
Convention on the Conservation of Antarctic Marine Living Resources (CCAMLR), 229, 233
Convention on the Regulation of Antarctic Mineral Resource Activities (CRAMRA), 230–232
coordinating state, ecological governance, 121–123
Counsell, David, 153, 173
Cowell, R., 112–113, 122, 178, 180, 185
CRAMRA. *See* Convention on the Conservation of Antarctic Marine Living Resources
Crowder, L. B., 157, 170
Cullingworth, B., 162, 166
Curry, Patrick, 41–42

Davoudi, S., 150
de Sadeleer, Nicholas, 62–63
devolution limitations, ecological governance, 107–115
deliberation procedures, 206
deliberative democracy and, 188–198
Diamond, Jared, 1–2
Dobson, Andrew, 112, 199
Doremus, H., 219–220, 230
Dorf, Michael, 124–125
Dovers, S. R., 62–63, 64
Dreborg, K. H., 59
Drury, William, 20
Dryzek, J. S., 90, 195

Earth System, 16, 23–25, 37, 156
ecological governance. *See* governance
  decision-making, 59–61
  duties and principles, 47–52
  epistemic challenges, 6–8
  normative precaution, 65–67
  precaution under ecological paradigm, 61–64
  precautionary action, 64–65
ecological planning. *See* planning
ecological regime shifts, 22–23
ecology of chaos, 20
ecosystems
  as complex adaptive systems, 20–23
  biotic, abiotic components, 21, 32
  Earth System interaction, 23–25, 37, 156
  ecological degradation, 2–6
  external challenges to, 50–51
  nonlinearity of, 21, 161
  stable states of, 21–22
Elster, J., 190
environmental assessment, 38, 57, 68–69, 73, 183–186
Environmental Impact Assessment Directive, EU, 178
environmental limits, governance and, 153–164
  limits-based regulation limitations, 158–159
  utility of limits and, 152, 155–156
ethical foundations, 40–42
  anthropocentric perspective, 46–47
  dominion perspective of nature, 42–44
  ethic of humility, 18
  ethical difficulties, ecological planning, 159–162
  geographical approach, 46
  revaluing nature, 44–47
European Spatial Development Perspective, 168
European Union (EU)
  Marine Framework Strategy Directive, 39, 226–227, 228
  Renewable Energy Directive of 2009, 80–82, 84
  Strategic Environmental Assessment Directive, 178, 185–186

Fabra, A., 229
Fishkin, James, 206
Flynn, B., 91
Foley, M. M., 157

Gascon, V., 229
Goodin, R. E., 90
governance. *See* ecological governance
  adaptive, 12–13
  behavioral change promotion and, 136–137
  bioregionalists and, 108
  collaborative, 10–12
  communicative state, 120
  coordinating state, 121–123
  devolution limitations, 107–115
  ecological sustainability and, 133–136
  economic constraints, wealth accumulation and, 105
  guiding state, 118–120
  legitimacy, 132–133
  local government and, 131–139
  maritime governance, planning, 139–144, 156–158, 170
  public participation in, 134–135
  regional government and, 126–130
  state's role in, 115–126
  sustainable places, constructing a sense of, 137–139
green political theory, 115–116
guiding state, ecological governance, 118–120
Gunderson, L. H., 21, 31

Haas, P. M., 221, 223–224
Habitats Directive, Article 6(4), 183
Haggett, C., 135
Handmer, J. W., 62–63, 64
Harremoes, Poul, 79
Harrison, C., 194
Haughton, Graham, 129, 153, 173
high-income states, 3–4
Holling, C. S., 31
Hoppe, Robert, 90

Iles, A., 223
information flows, ecological information
decision-making structures and, 230–233
establishing permanent institutions and, 220–225
exploratory development and, 232–233
information adequacy for decision-making and, 230–232
information deficit, 216–217
institutional learning and, 219–225
knowledge, understanding of ecosystems and, 226–227
legal requirements for, 218–219
reaction to change and, 227–229
responsiveness to system reactions and, 229–230
use of law, 225–229
Intergovernmental Panel on Climate Change (IPCC), 221

Jacobs, M., 191, 193, 194, 201, 204
Jones, R., 220–221, 224

Karkkainen, B. C., 109, 124, 217, 222–223, 225
Kiev Protocol, 94
Klein, U., 169
Klinke, A., 79
Kramer, Ludwig, 183

land use planning reform, 150–153
Lang, R., 148
legitimacy, 132–133
Leopold, Aldo, 18, 47–48
Levin, S. A., 21, 48
Lipschutz, R. D., 111, 138
local government, 131–139. *See also* state's role
Lundqvist, Lennart, 111, 133

Marine Framework Strategy Directive (EU), 39, 226–227, 228
Marine Management Organisation (MMO), United Kingdom, 142
maritime governance, planning, 139–144, 156–158, 170
McHarg, Aileen, 102
Meadowcroft, J., 201
Mediterranean Action Plan, 221
Millennium Ecosystem Assessment, 3
MMO. *See* Marine Management Organisation
modularity, 176
Montreal Protocol, 220–221

Nadin, V., 162, 166
National Planning Policy Framework, United Kingdom, 173
need concept, 49, 51
New Zealand, Resource Management Act, 58, 71
Niemeyer, S., 212
Nisbet, Ian, 20
Noble, Bram, 78
normative precaution, 8–10, 65–67, 178–179
Norse, E. A., 22–23, 157, 170
Norton, B. G, 41, 45–46
nuclear energy, 83–84

O'Brien, M., 77–78
Odum, Eugene, 19
Owens, S., 112–113, 122, 178, 180, 185

Petts, J., 207
planning
analytical planning, 169–172
comprehensive planning, 165–169
comprehensive structures for, 147–148
decision rules, 177–183
ecological land use planning, 175–177
environmental assessment, 183–186
environmental capacities identification, 154–158
European Spatial Development Perspective, 168
in England, Wales, 149, 167
incrementalism and, 148
land use planning reform, 150–153
maritime ecosystems, 139–144, 156–158, 170

planning (cont.)
  national framework for, 164–183
  planning mechanisms, 162–164
  state-led, 148–149
  strategic planning, 172–175
  top-line approach, 146–147
Planning Act 2008, United Kingdom, 135
policy-making
  alternatives assessment stage of, 9–10
  ecosystem functionality preservation and, 56
  environmental assessment and, 38, 57, 68–69, 73
  forward-looking strategies, 56–57
  political will and, 58–59
  whole of government approach, 56, 72, 98
policy-making, legal framework
  alternative policy options assessment, 77–85
  backcasting, 86–88, 89
  consumption reduction, 71–73
  current practices, 67–70
  development obviation, 73–74
  ecological protection, 37–40, 70–71
  independent review of policy proposals, 101–103
  policy impact assessment, 88–89
  principles, 71–77
  process reforms, 93–103
  promoting change in governmental decision-making culture, 98–103
  public participation, 89–93
  rolling review of policy, 99–101
  strategic visions of desired futures formation, 85–89
  substitution, 74–76
  sunsetting, 76–77, 170–171
  sustainability and, 71
precautionary principle, 8–10, 54–55, 178–179
  definitions of, 62
  precaution under an ecological paradigm, 61–64
  proportionality and, 65
Protocol on Environmental Protection to the Antarctic Treaty, 227–228, 230, 232
provisioning services, 2
public participation, 89–93, 134–135
  citizenship and, 192–193
  communicative rationality and, 198
  consultation's inadequacy and, 208–210
  deliberation's reach, size of deliberation group and, 205–208
  deliberative participation under ecological governance and, 210–214
  ecological governance acceptability and, 195–198
  environmental considerations internalisation, 191–192
  environmental policy acceptance and, 187–188
  expense, time concerns, 213–214
  giving reasons for political decisions, 212
  issue selection and, 211–212
  levelling playing field and, 202–205
  personnel continuity and, 212–213
  power relations and, 202–205
  preferences transformation and, 190–191
  purposes of, 210
  size of participating groups, 205–208
  small group approach and, 210–211
  unpredictability of outcomes, problem *vs.* 200–202
  value formation and, 193–195

redundancy, 35
regional government and, 126–130
regulating services, 2
Renewable Energy Directive of 2009, European Union (EU), 80–82, 84
Renn, O., 79, 81
resilience, 6–8, 16–17, 26–28, 45–46, 49, 55, 160–161
  biodiversity and, 34–36
  modularity and, 176
  redundancy and, 35
  response diversity and, 35
  socio-ecological perspective, 32–34
  specified, general, 28–32
  tightness of feedbacks and, 36–37

Resource Management Act, New Zealand, 58, 71, 169
resource under-utilisation, 50, 57
response diversity, 35
Rockström, Johan, 24, 37, 156
rolling review of policy, 99–101
Ross, A., 156
Royal Commission on Environmental Pollution, United Kingdom, 127, 150–151, 169–170, 173, 174–175, 185
Ruhl, J. B., 20
Rydin, Y., 178

Sabel, Charles, 124–125
Salt, David, 22, 29, 31–32, 34, 36
scientific foundations, ecological law
  complexity, regime shifts, environmental decision-making, 25–27
  ecosystems and Earth System interaction, 23–25, 37
  ecosystems as complex adaptive systems, 20–23
  stability to complexity, 18–20
Smith, G., 194–195, 196, 200, 204
societal collapse, avoiding, 1–2
Stallworthy, M., 150, 163
state's role, 115–130
  communicative state, 120
  coordinating state, 121–123
  guiding state, 118–120
  high income states, 3–4
  in ecological planning, 148–149
  state, non-governmental actors, collaborative governance, 10–12
Steele, J., 193
Steffen, W., 23
Stirling, O., 79
Strategic Environmental Assessment Directive (EU), 178, 185–186
sunsetting, 76–77, 170–171
supporting services, 2
sustainability, 71, 133–136, 137–139
Swedish Environmental Code, 75–76

Tansley, Arthur, 19
Tarlock, D., 222
technological solutions, control, 43–44
Tewdwr-Jones, M., 202–203
Thoreau, Henry David, 49
Tickner, J. A., 77–78
tightness of feedbacks, 36–37
Toope, S. J., 222–223, 224
Trouwborst, Arie, 62, 65
Turkenburg, W., 63

uncertainty, 54–56, 59–61
United Kingdom
  Barlow Report, 1940, 167
  Climate Change Act 2008, 102
  government guide of 2005 on strategic environmental assessment, 73–74
  Marine Management Organisation, 142
  National Planning Policy Framework, 173
  national policy planning statement on energy infrastructure, 82–83
  Planning Act 2008, 135
  regional ecological governance in, 126–130
  Royal Commission on Environmental Pollution, 127, 150–151, 169–170, 173, 174–175, 185

van der Sluijis, J., 63
Virginia, R. A., 220–221, 224

Walker, Brian, 22, 29, 31–32, 34, 36
Weiland, Sabine, 69
Wheeler, Stephen, 113, 128
White, Lynn Jr., 42
whole of government approach, 56, 72, 98
Wong, C., 168–169
World Wildlife Fund, 3
Worster, Donald, 20